The Long Road to The Sixth ROK

The Bloody History of South Korea:

The Struggle for a True Democracy

Young Ran Kim, Ph.D.

I will be eternally grateful.

Dedicated to my parents who survived the horrors of war and

to all the national leaders and the innocent civilians

who perished in the violent storm

And

To General Douglas MacArthur and all the

countries and their brave men who fought and

died in the Korean War to prevent the

communist expansion in Asia.

Table of Contents

Prologue

I grew up in South Korea during the politically chaotic period after World War II. I have chilling childhood memories of events that almost killed my parents which would have left me, a young girl, to take care of my five younger siblings. I left Korea many decades ago, alone, as a young woman, searching for a place where government lawfully protects innocent civilians and prevents the kind of crimes my family and my people endured. While I was concentrating on my academic pursuits in America, receiving three advanced degrees in science and dealing with a ferociously competitive corporate career, I never forgot what had happened to my family back in Korea. For decades I thought about writing a book revealing the techniques and the secret organizations that allowed criminal events to take place. I felt a moral duty to my father and to all those who had perished at the hands of unidentified evil forces to expose what really happened. I spent many years after my retirement pursuing information about the responsible parties and the details previously well hidden behind the convoluted political system and under the cover of secret intelligence gathering and the building of a new democratic nation.

South Korea is known today as "Miracle on The Han River," a description of a transformation from a developing country to an industrialized modern country. What is still tragically obscured is its bloody history— thousands of lives maimed, lost, and displaced during South Korea's struggle to become a truly democratic civilian government, the Sixth Republic of Korea, THE SIXTH ROK. This personal memoir of my family's survival during those dark and violent times seeks to recover the long-silenced lives, buried in the ashes of the Cold War between the US and the USSR following WWII. The story navigates the labyrinth of a corrupt political system by exposing secrets well hidden for over a half century; the secrets that allowed for not only rampant criminal activities and undisclosed assassinations of beloved national leaders, but also the shocking massacre of thousands of innocent civilians. From the political to the personal, THE LONG ROAD journeys through decades of violence and corruption to the ultimate emergence of a democratic nation, a story told through the eyes of my father and our family.

THE LONG ROAD reveals in historical prose, the realities of what happened to my father including the effects of the US Army Military Government in Korea (USAMGIK) that succeeded Imperial Japanese occupation, the First Republic of Korea and the Korean War. An intellectual and a conscientious educator, my father was deceptively accused of being a communist and survived life-threatening torture, starvation, and homelessness with six children when a powerful and sadistic security head for the president of the nation confiscated our beautiful home. At the time we were unaware of this man's identity and his powerful connections. This is a memoir woven through bloody eyewitness history and life-threatening trials. Through it all my father maintained his integrity, inspiring his children to become well-educated, good citizens of the society. This story is a ceaseless struggle of the people of South Korea for over half a century for a truly democratic civilian government for what ultimately became The Sixth Republic of Korea.

Much of this may sound like fiction - a tale of the lives of people living in an Orwellian, fabricated underground society or in the past century's fascist society. My intense research about the past half-century in South Korea kept turning up new data previously unavailable because of changing times and governments, and thus the material supported a much broader overview of the hidden criminal history of South Korea. Many decades later, and after countless hours of research, I identified many of the forces previously hidden behind the secret organizations. It's a shocking and seemingly implausible story – but it's an account of events that should never be repeated in any compassionate society.

Why tell this story now? The facts unravel the geopolitical games played by the two world powers, the United States and the former Soviet Union, that divided the Korean peninsula and preset the fate of the Korean people, both north and South, after World War II. The book also describes how the US military, after liberating Korea from imperial Japan and being welcomed by Koreans enthusiastically as their heroes, blundered and created anti-American sentiment among Korean populace. In 2009, newly elected American president Barrack Obama stated that the mistakes the American government has often made in foreign policy with disastrous results were made because the American government has a tendency to dictate, instead of listening and trying to understand a situation first before taking any action. Much of that can be seen in this history.

The goal of this book is not to criticize the political leaders of the United States of the previous century but to reveal the historical consequences of miscalculated and short-sighted actions. Accurate historical facts are good reference points for present and future world leaders, especially the leaders of the United States, to develop better judgments and implement wiser long-term sustainable policies to resolve complicated geopolitical problems. All of us who live on this planet need a more peaceful world -indeed a new paradigm - where we can coexist, without slaughtering each other, pursuing our dreams and hopes of a God-given life, free of the constant threat of war and the nuclear destruction of civilization itself.

Chapter 1: Born on the Cusp of the Violent 20th Century (1907)

My father came into this world in 1907, three years before the annexation of Korea by imperial Japan. He spent his infancy in South Chungcheong Province, during the tumultuous last days of the Joseon dynasty. When the inept government failed to negotiate with the leaders of the Donghak Peasant Revolt—a protest movement against corrupt government, social injustice, and economic exploitation of the poor by the rich landlords—and brought in foreign forces to put down the movement, the protest turned into a rebellion. This movement was fiercer in the southern provinces, Chungcheong and Cholla Provinces, where the majority of farms were located. The rebels confiscated farm lands and properties from Yangban class families and distributed to poor farmers. Many Yangban class families had to relocate to avoid being killed by the mob. This was a very difficult time for Yangban class families such as my father's family.

It was an unfavorable time and place for any baby to be born. The early 20th century was a violent period, especially in East Asia surrounding the Korean Peninsula. Not long before the turn of the 20th century, October 8, 1895, Queen Min of the Joseon dynasty was murdered and burned by assassins who entered Kyongbok Palace under orders from Miura Goro, the Japanese minister to Korea. Then, from 1904 until 1905, a conflict grew out of the rival imperialist ambitions of the Russian and Japanese empires over Manchuria and Korea: the Russo-Japanese War. Since the end of the First Sino-Japanese War in 1895, negotiations between Russia and Japan had continually broken down. Japan chose war to protect its exclusive dominance in Korea. Japanese victory over Russia dramatically transformed the balance of power in East Asia, reassessment of Japan's place on the world stage. An embarrassing string of defeats increased the Russian peoples' dissatisfaction with their corrupt Tsarist government. Some historians believe that this was a major cause of the Russian Revolution, which began in St. Petersburg on "Bloody Sunday," January 22, 1905.

It turned out Japan's territorial ambition in East Asia was partly responsible for communist revolutions in both Russia and China. Continuing wars against imperial Japan drained large portion of those two countries' national budgets and resources, hampering their ability to properly manage their own internal affairs. The Treaty of Portsmouth formally ended the 1904–1905 Russo-Japanese War. It was signed on September 5, 1905, after negotiations at the Portsmouth Naval Shipyard near Portsmouth, New Hampshire, in the United States. Negotiations for the treaty were made under the mediation of Theodore Roosevelt, the US president, for which he won the 1906 Nobel Peace Prize. Prior to the beginning of negotiations, the Japanese had signed the Taft-Katsura Agreement with the United States in July 1905, agreeing to Japanese control in Korea in return for American dominance in the Philippines. The U.S. influence over Korea goes back pretty far.

It is ironic what America gained by the shortsighted Taft-Katsura Agreement. The United States made a deal with imperial Japan whereby Japan annexed Korea; in exchange, the United States dominance in the Philippine Islands. This agreement violated the Korean-American Treaty of Amity and Commerce, drafted in 1882 and signed in 1884 between the two governments. After the annexation of Korea, the imperial Japan continued its territorial expansion and attacked Pearl Harbor on December 7, 1941; the next day Japan invaded the Philippines, without formal declaration of war, and took the Philippines away from the United States. There followed the atrocities of the Bataan Death March and three and a half years of harsh treatment of Allied survivors in miserable Japanese prison camps, resulting in an enormous human suffering. The Taft-Katsura Agreement only helped imperial Japan begin its first move toward an ambitious territorial expansion by annexing Korea, which was the major threshold for its territorial expansion to other Asian countries.

Of course, the Taft-Katsura Agreement was not the main source of the fall of the Joseon dynasty. There were many other factors, such as the notorious factional fighting toward the dynasty's close; the isolation of the country by Daewongun, the stubborn regent of Joseon; and a long list of Japanese invasions of the Korean

Peninsula dating back as far as the 13th century. Eventually, the long war with Japan reduced the productive capacity of farmlands and used up a large portion of the national budget to defend the country. All those factors gradually weakened the nation. The facts about cruelty during Hideyoshi's invasions of Korea (1592–1598) are not very well known in the world. The most hideous historical evidence remains even today in the Hyideyoshi's Great Buddha, called the "Mound of Ears," which contains many thousands of ears of Korean prisoners they captured, killed, and cut off their ears during their invasions of Korea. The Japanese had practically been warmongers who attacked peaceful neighboring countries throughout history until the end of World War II. It was General Douglas MacArthur of the United States who taught those warmongers to become civilized citizens of the world and to live in peace, respecting the rights of their neighbors, after their unconditional surrender at the end of World War II. Thus the United States did resolve one of the major problems Korea had suffered for a long time.

My father was born in this troubled nation, one of thirteen children; of the thirteen, only three sons survived. He was the last of those three. There were considerable age gaps among the brothers due to the high rate of infant death during that period. Where proper medical intervention to treat sick children was unavailable, only the healthiest babies survived. By 1910, the number of Japanese settlers in Korea reached over 170,000, creating the largest overseas Japanese community in the world at the time. Many Japanese settlers were interested in acquiring fertile agricultural land in Korea. Japanese Governor-General Terauchi Masatake facilitated settlement through land reform. A huge amount of Korean land was seized by the government and sold at subsidized costs to Japanese willing to settle in Korea as part of a larger colonization effort. This situation created a bitter and hostile environment. Koreans in their own land suffered from famine due to over taxation by the imperial government of Japan. Only the willing Japanese collaborators were able to hold on to large portions of their land.

My father grew up deprived of the privileges any child in a Yangban class household might have considered normal. It seemed that there was also an additional misfortune in the family. When my father was a young boy, his father was not even living in the same home. The story was that Grandfather had a business as a leading rice supplier to Seoul from his town. At some point, the distributor in Seoul decided to take all the money from the sale of the rice and disappear, totally wiping out our family business. Grandfather was distraught and outraged and determined to find the thief. He began what ultimately became an endless chase. This is a sad story because my father had to grow up in a family environment, poverty stricken by then, without the head of the household.

Despite the depressing conditions in which Father grew up he didn't seem to have been a miserable and unhappy little boy. Once when I asked him to tell me his childhood stories, he enthusiastically described the funny monkey tricks he saw in the market where his mother sent him to buy a bag of rice. He was so absorbed in watching the show he forgot about guarding the bag of rice he just bought. By the time the monkey show was over the rice was gone. When we were very young Father took me and John to visit our grandparents during a summer vacation. On our way we passed a creek where I saw many ladies in their fifties and sixties doing laundry. As we passed by the ladies whispered, "that mischievous boy has now grown up and it looks like he did well". Apparently Father was a very active, healthy and mischievous boy giving hard times to all those ladies.

My grandfather was back home by the time my parents were married. When my father took me and my brother John to meet with our grandparents, Grandfather was living in a nice wing of the home of his first son, my father's eldest brother, who became a doctor of Chinese medicine. There were many books in his room. He showed us how to use a calligraphy brush to write our names in Chinese characters on a piece of rice paper. He wore all-white Korean men's costume and a tall hat when he went out to visit friends in town. He treated my brother and me equally well without any discrimination, indicating that he was not a male chauvinist as many old men were in those days. I heard that the family was a wealthy landowner for many generations until my father's generation. The Donghak Peasant Revolt of 1894 was certainly one cause, and the annexation of Korea by imperial Japan was another. But Grandfather's mishandling of the remaining family fortune trusting the con man was the real end point.

My father never blamed his father and never brought it up to explain any details to us about his family situation when he was growing up. It was not his character to look back on the hard times he lived through and complain. So I was always curious and wanted to ask my grandfather directly where he was when Father was growing up. But, being shy, I asked him about Kim family history instead, hoping his story would lead to the topic I was most interested in. He told us that our original ancestor (Gimhae Kim, not related to Kim Il-sung's family clan) is the legendary founder and king of the state of Geumgwan Gaya, King Suro. His wife was an Indian princess and his tomb was in Gimhae in Gyeongsang Province. An Indian princess? It's hard to believe. To confirm his story, I researched Korean history and found the following interesting narrative.

According to the founding legend of Geumgwan Gaya in the 13th century texts of the chronicle *Garakguk-gi* of *Samguk Yusa*, King Suro was one of six princes born from eggs that descended from the sky in a golden bowl wrapped in red cloth. Suro was the first-born among them and led the others in setting up six states while asserting the leadership of the Gaya confederacy. King Suro's queen, Heo Hwang-ok, was a princess from the Indian country of Ayuta. She is said to have arrived in Gaya by boat. They had ten sons and two daughters in all. Ayuta is today often identified with Ayuta in India. A tomb attributed to King Suro is still maintained today in Gimhae, and many people, including my brother Soo, have visited his tomb. The great general Kim Yusin (595–673), in the seventh-century kingdom of Silla, who led the unification of the Korean Peninsula under the reign of King Muyeol and then King Munmu of Silla, is said to have been the great-grandson of King Guhae of Geumgwan Gaya, the last ruler of the Geumgwan Gaya. The history of Silla discloses that Kim Yusin was faithful to both of his kings all his life despite of his enormous power, never attempting a coup d'état. The tomb of General Kim Yusin, as splendid as any king's, is in Gyeongju, and many people still visit his tomb and pay respect even today.

Chapter 2: Desire for Learning
(1914–1932)

Until my father was nine years old his two elder brothers didn't even bother to register him at school to begin his elementary education. My grandfather still had not returned home from his endless pursuit throughout the peninsula of the missing thief who wiped out the family fortune. One day my father suddenly realized that he ought to be at school because all his playmates of the same age in his neighborhood were already enrolled, so he went by himself to register for school to begin his education. When he was in the fifth grade he thought that he had to make up for lost time so he went to Seoul, again by himself, and took a qualifying exam to enter a junior high school, Choongdong. After three years in junior high he took another qualifying exam to enter the very prestigious Kyungsung Imperial University. My father passed the entrance exam getting the top grade among all the applicants. I saw a copy of the university newspaper clipping Mother pasted on one of the family albums that she was able to save during the Korean War. The title of the article and a photograph clearly identified my father - Kim Choong Sun - as a country boy who had passed the entrance examination at the top. The article also listed 20 other Koreans who passed the entrance exam along with my father (class of 1930). I recognized some of those listed names such as Goh Hyung-gon, the father of Goh Kun, a former prime minister of South Korea, and father's longtime friend Dr. Cho Gyuichan. All the others who entered the university were Japanese who lived in Korea at the time. My father's class was the fourth and there were only 160 students in the entire graduating class.

During his college days in Seoul my father supported himself as a private tutor to the children of a wealthy family. I was always curious to see how he managed to escape his difficult situation, how he went to Seoul with no help from his family and managed to graduate from the nation's highest educational institution. One day, I asked my father many questions including the reason why he ended up majoring in English literature instead of math or engineering or physics. I knew he excelled in math and physics as he helped us with our home work when we were in high school and college. Because of our family situation during the Korean War when our family became homeless I missed many semesters of school work and I had to catch up later with Father's help in trigonometry, logarithms, and even calculus sometime later. He said that the university did not have any engineering department at the time—the Japanese were very careful to keep science and technology to themselves—and he didn't have to choose his major during his freshman year.

During the summer vacation, after completing his freshman year, he read many books written in English including history, short stories, philosophy, and religion. He became fascinated with Western culture that was completely foreign to him and he wanted to know more about the West. He felt that he was receiving a very restricted education under Japanese control and wanted to find out more about the outside world. He also attended weekly Bible classes taught by American missionaries—not only to learn English but also to understand Christian religion and its God in more detail. He was a voracious reader, very inquisitive, always trying to learn more information on every subject. This is how he became knowledgeable in many areas, not just in English literature, but also world history, philosophy, and religion.

With all my advanced education in the area of life science such as developmental biology, nutrition, biochemistry, anatomy, and cell biology, it's still not clear to me how my father managed to do so well academically considering the conditions under which he had grown up. This is my greatest admiration for my father. How did he do it? I know growing children must be well nourished to develop their brains, and they must be in an environment that stimulates intelligence. But his family didn't help him in any of those areas. Although the first stages of brain development are strongly affected by genetic factors genes do not design the brain completely. When and where genes are dominant is fine-tuned according to the input they receive from the environment. The only explanation I can think of for my father's expertise in many fields is that he ate many soy products which contain the best-quality plant protein with all essential amino acids such as lysine and methionine. He loved soybean soup, tofu, soybean sprouts. He also loved fresh lettuce, cabbage, and barley—sources of vitamins A, B, and C, minerals, and omega-3 fatty acids—the kinds of food that were available to him when he was growing up. I have also heard that he drank his mother's milk until he was seven years old which might have helped him to develop his health and brain.

He told me a story that he once solved a very difficult math problem in a dream when he dozed off at his desk after trying all night to solve a problem. He woke up and quickly wrote down an answer he had just worked out in his dream and there it was, the correct answer to the problem he was unable to solve all evening. Many years later, I heard a similar story about August Kekulé who said in his 1890 German Chemical Society speech that he saw a snake seizing its own tail when he dozed off during a trip on a horse carriage, which gave him the idea of the ring structure of benzene. Like my father Kekulé struggled for a long time to figure out how an equal number of six molecules of carbon and hydrogen could form a stable compound. (The carbon atom has four radicals, while the hydrogen atom has only one. Benzene has three double bonds to form a stable ring structure.). I suppose there is a certain class of people like my father and Kekulé who have the ability to concentrate in such intensity that they can resolve difficult problems even in their dreams. I think my father was a person of exceptional intelligence who could have achieved something far more significant in his life if he were born at the right time and in the right place.

My father was selected as the valedictorian of his college graduating class and he missed no opportunity to express his strong feelings about the injustice of the Japanese occupation of the Korean Peninsula. Of course his speech attracted the attention of Japanese secret police who were combing the campus gathering intelligence. The continuous monitoring of his daily activities by the Japanese secret police made it difficult for father to stay in Seoul.

京城帝國大學

金忠善이 文B서 수석合格··· 級長

朝鮮人은 李崇寧 方鍾鉉 高亨坤 申基碩 李鎭淑 金泰昊 申淳彥 曺圭璟 洪鳳珍

李國柱 趙平載 金聖煥 文仁柱 崔正憲 金承鉉 文榮會 李重業 朴廷徽 金在河

疾風怒濤같은 술주정··· 「스톰」즐겨

Photo 1. The Newpapaer Clipping Mother saved in one of the albums we were able to rescue when we lost our home during the Korean War. It clearly shows Father's name as the applicant who received the top score at the entrance examination. The clip also shows twenty other names of Koreans who passed the entrance exam along with Father (Class of 1930)

Chapter 3: Marriage and Life in Pyongyang
(1933–1938)

My parents were married by arrangement, a typical marriage of their time, in 1933. My mother was born in 1914 in South Jeolla Province and was brought up in a faithful Christian family. Her tall, handsome, and very bright mother, my maternal grandmother, taught Korean language to American missionaries while at the same time learning English from them. Her whole family became Christian. Since she was taller than the average woman in Korea, people would make fun of her tall and slender figure, so she tried to shrink her height by bending her posture. She did this for so long that her back became permanently bent. It was a great shame; she had a perfect figure for a fashion model of today.

My grandmother was very proud of the Yangban class status of both her and her husband's families. When I was young I was always very inquisitive about everything and naturally I asked my grandmother many questions about the family history. She was a very good storyteller. She told me how the family of my grandfather, a wealthy landowner, had to escape Suncheon in a hurry during the Donghak Peasant Revolt in 1894. My maternal grandparents settled in Gwangju to avoid being killed by the revolutionary mob. She also told me very proudly about her family history and how many male members of her family fought during the Hideyoshi invasion as leaders of the civilian militia. From the beginning of many Hideyoshi invasions, Koreans organized militias that they called "righteous armies" to resist the Japanese invasion. During the first invasion Jeolla Province remained the only untouched area on the Korean Peninsula because of the very strong local militia. In addition to the successful patrols of the sea by Admiral Yi Sun-sin's navy, the activities of volunteer forces pressured the Japanese troops to avoid the province in favor of other priorities.

My Grandmother talked a great deal about Admiral Yi Sun-sin as if he was a local hero because his navy successfully protected the province by patrolling the sea. Yi assumed his new post at Yeosu in

Jeolla Province in 1591. From there, he was able to undertake a buildup of the regional navy which was later used to confront the Japanese invasion force. He subsequently began to strengthen the province's navy with a series of reforms including the construction of the turtle ship. Yi Sun-sin was a famous Korean naval commander, a brilliant strategist, famed for his victories against the Japanese navy during the Hideyoshi invasions of Korea. He is well respected not only by Koreans but also by Japanese admirals for his impeccable character on and off the battlefield. Military historians have placed Admiral Yi Sun-sin unquestionably on par with Admiral Horatio Nelson as the greatest naval commander in history for his undefeated record against seemingly insurmountable odds. Although Hideyoshi's army had been very successful on land his navy was always defeated during their four campaigns against the Joseon navy under Admiral Yi Sun-sin.

My maternal grandfather then became a businessman to support his family. He was quite successful, but he had to close down his business after a series of armed robberies which frightened him. He opened a pawnshop with the money he made from the sale of his business. His pawnshop was almost like a local community bank lending money to small businesses since Koreans didn't trust banks under Japanese control at the time. At the time, if you lost your inherited wealth as a landowner other job opportunities as we have today did not exist. He also kept himself busy as a high-ranking official of his church. My maternal grandfather was an old-fashioned man who did not believe in educating his daughters but Grandmother insisted on sending all of her daughters to school. They had six daughters and just one son; my mother was the second born. Their only son, my uncle, studied music and voice at Seoul National University. He hoped to become an opera singer. He had a wonderful tenor voice but after an abdominal hernia operation he found it difficult to bring out the necessary volume of voice to sing as an opera singer, so he became a music teacher.

My mother was a student at Gwangju Girl's High School when the Gwangju Student Independence Movement against Japanese rule took place in October and November 1929. It is considered the second-most important Korean independence movement during the Japanese occupation, with the March 1st, 1919 Movement the most important. The Gwangju Student Independence Movement spread out throughout the Korean Peninsula. In response, Japanese police invaded the school campuses to arrest and beat students mercilessly and the Japanese authorities decided to impose suspension of all students who participated in the movement. This encouraged more people to join the movement. This movement became nationwide struggle for independence. Although their protests resulted in the severe repression by the Japanese government, the students' efforts not only encouraged the national independence movement but became the predecessor of later student movements.

After the liberation, the National Assembly of South Korea announced in 1953 the establishment of Student Day to celebrate students' efforts every November 3. In 2006, the name was changed to Student Independence Movement Day. But strangely enough, mother didn't mention much about that rebellion until the last days of her life when she was under the influence of morphine treatment. She kept yelling and screaming, saying that the Japanese police were coming to arrest everybody on the campus. She looked frightened. It must have been a very painful memory she tried to completely forget or suppress, but obviously the memory was still buried in her brain until the last days of her life.

Although the Japanese police brutally suppressed the student rebellion, my mother seemed to have been on good terms with her Japanese physical education teacher. My mother longed to become a prima ballerina as recommended by her Japanese physical education teacher. My mother was a pretty woman with an oval face, large eyes, a perfect-sized nose and full lips. Her teacher told her that she had the body and talent to become a famous ballerina and that she could get her a scholarship to go to Japan to study ballet. However, my strict grandmother adamantly rejected the idea and tried to marry her off instead. My father was introduced to my maternal grandmother by one of her cousins, who happened to be my father's classmate at Kyungsung University. My grandmother, who considered higher education of the utmost importance in judging a character, thought that it would be a great honor to marry off one of her daughters to a Kyungsung University graduate. But my mother was not so impressed by my father at first sight and was reluctant to go through with it. However, my father insisted on getting engaged before he returned to his work after he met my mother. Before my mother realized, their engagement was facilitated by my grandmother and my father in a hurry, so they became engaged before my father returned to his job in Pyongyang. Some months later, their wedding took place in my father's hometown.

My mother could never erase the memory of what happened on her wedding day; she told us the story so many times. They had to have their wedding in my father's village, as was customary. After the wedding ceremony, she had to walk along the wet country road surrounded by rice paddies to reach the house where she was going to meet all her husband's family members. At the far end of the road, she could see a small farmhouse with a grass roof. She wondered "Could that be the house where I have come so far to meet his family members and spend my first night with my husband?" She could not believe it, confused and shocked. She went into the house and had to go through a ceremony bowing to all the family elders: his father, his mother, his two elder brothers, and their wives. Finally she was allowed to enter a tiny room to spend the first night with her husband. The room had a door facing the backyard and this door was made of bamboo with a rice paper screen similar to Japanese Shoji screens. As an old custom in Korea, neighborhood women poked peepholes on the rice paper on the door to look into the room to see what was going on all night. She didn't tell us what happened next. This was how they spent their first night. Of course, this custom is no longer in practice in Korean society today.

Following my father's valedictory speech at his graduation ceremony at Kyungsung University, in which he eloquently expressed his strong feelings against the unjust Japanese occupation of Korea, the Japanese secret police monitored his activities and made it difficult for him to stay in Seoul. This was of course a time when there were no computers, GPS systems, or cell phones to monitor the movement of fugitives, so he decided to slip out of Seoul and move far away to Pyongyang, the city that became the capital of North Korea after 1948. He secured a teaching job at the Soong-shil Middle School. Father learned that many people who graduated from this school became Korean independence fighters against imperial Japan.

When my mother arrived in Pyongyang after their marriage, she found that my father was living in a boarding house and there was no furniture except a desk and his books in his room. My mother found that Father was sending money from his salary to his eldest brother as requested by his family to support the education of his brother's eldest son, my father's nephew, the most important member of the third generation, who was supposed to inherit the family jokbo, the clan lineage genealogy. These records show lineage structure and cite achievements of family members. They show male descendants in linked patrilineal sequence from founding ancestors, indicating generational order and the creation of branches. Typical entries include generational order, surnames, and usually multiple given names of males and their death dates or burial dates and places. Usually there is little information about wives and daughters. More recent genealogies provide the given names of women and sometimes marriage dates. Entries may include titles and honors for the more noteworthy individuals. Korea used to be a very chauvinistic society.

Mother thought his family's request for money was not fair to Father since his family never did anything to help his education. Such an unfair request from family elders would not be honored nowadays even in Korea, but my father followed the family request without any protest. Mother was very anxious to buy a home as soon as possible to start a family, so she got a job as a grammar school teacher and saved up enough money to buy a small charming house at the foothill of the beautiful Moran-bong. That's where I was born. One day, when my mother came home from school, she discovered that the live-in maid had left me, a baby, all alone on the Korean-style hot floor—the room's heat source during the winter—with a letter explaining that she was taking the salary mother paid her the day before and eloping with her boyfriend. The bottom of my right foot's little toe had a burn from the hot floor and I still have the scar from that incident. Mother was very upset with the maid because she could have told my parents of her plan in advance and another maid could have been arranged.

I have no memory of this house or Pyongyang but I would love to visit the place if Korea ever becomes united in my lifetime. It seems that my mother, who was very personable and diplomatic, quickly made many new friends with faculty members and played Ping-Pong with them after work. She began to enjoy her life in that new environment. Unfortunately, her bossy mother-in-law visited them occasionally and stayed extended periods of time, carrying on unreasonable criticism over every little family affair, interrupting her busy routine. This was how mother-in-laws used to behave toward their daughters-in-law in old days in Korea, repeating what they went through themselves when they were young brides.

There was another very strange episode when my parents were living in Pyongyang. Mother was holding me in her arms when I was just an infant, standing at a street corner waiting for my father one day. A woman passerby stopped, looked me over carefully, and said, "Well, when this baby grows up, she will be going to a faraway place. She will be very independent and successful. But she is missing one very important piece of luck in her life: finding a rich husband." The passerby was probably a fortune-teller or a shaman. Shamans are intermediaries between the human and spirit worlds to those who believe in shamanism, as ancient Koreans did. Some Koreans even in the present day still go to fortune-tellers to ask for predictions. My mother was a devout Christian and was not very pleased to hear this kind of comment coming from a shaman, whether the prediction was good or bad. But when I was about to leave Korea to come to study in the United States, she remembered this incident and said, "How did she know such a long time ago that this was going to happen? In those days, women didn't go abroad to study. If she was right, you will never find a rich husband." I said, "Don't worry mother, I am pretty confident that I can make my own living very well and I am not looking for a rich husband anyway." Finding a husband, rich or poor, was the last thing on my mind. In any case, I found the shaman's comment very puzzling. How did she come up with that kind of story?

How was my father doing in his teaching job? He apparently enjoyed teaching and got along well with both faculty members and students at the school. In later years, he enjoyed talking about life in Pyongyang when his old friends, the faculty members from the school where he taught, came to visit him. His very proud and the most unforgettable experience during his stay in Pyongyang was the story of his school basketball team's triumphant success. First, he noticed that the performance of the student basketball team at his school was outstanding. Thus, he suggested to the school principal that he send the team to compete in a basketball tournament that was to take place in Tokyo. His request was rejected not just because of the travel expenses but also because the Japanese would not like to see any Korean sports team beating any Japanese sports team in any sport.

What did my father do next? He had so much confidence in this team and he was so delighted to have an opportunity to show that a Korean team could beat all the Japanese teams that he could not miss such a chance. He was so determined to go through his plan no matter what happened to his own job at the school. Thus he decided to cover the expenses with his own salary and contributions from other people who had the same idea and took the team to Tokyo, competed, and beat all the Japanese teams and won the championship trophy. This was an impressive victory for a Korean sport's team and they were all exuberant. That's my father's character; he pursued what he believed in to see the end results. But, of course, the school principal was not pleased, so there was tension in the atmosphere when they returned.

Chapter 4: Manchuria, the Lawless Place
(1938–1942)

After a couple of years in Pyongyang, Father was approached by the Korean Community in Shengyang to inform him that there was no Korean language school to teach Korean children in Shenyang, Manchuria. The Korean community in Shenyang was searching for someone who could come and help them to build a new school to educate their children. Shenyang, formerly known as Mukden, is the capital of Liaoning Province. Historically, many Koreans used to live in this area of Manchuria because the Liadong Peninsula, where the famous Port Arthur is located, was under the rule of an ancient Korean kingdom of Gojoseon, from 1281 BC (an unverified but traditionally accepted date) until the late fourth century BC when the Chinese state of Yan invaded and conquered this region. Later, other Korean kingdoms like Buyur, Goguryeo, and Balhae also ruled this region, which includes Jilin and Vladivostok, until Balhae was finally defeated by the Khitans in AD 926, and most of its northern territories were absorbed into the Liao dynasty. Afterward the region became the focus of an international territorial battle between Russia and Japan, especially because of Port Arthur. The Yanbian Korean autonomous prefecture still exists in northeastern Jilin Province of the People's Republic of China. The prefecture has an important archaeological site of Balhae: the Ancient Tombs at Longtou Mountain which includes the Mausoleum of Princess Jeonghyo. Jilin is located about 200 miles north of Shengyang.

Therefore this region has not always been foreign to Korean people. After the annexation of Korea by Japan in 1910, Manchuria and Siberia became the main stages of Korean independence activities. Lyuh Woon-hyung, the well-known Korean nationalist, wanted to get connected with fellow Korean nationalists in these regions and traveled from Shanghai where he was living at the time, in January 1919 to visit Jilin and Vladivostok, the main hubs of Korean nationalists. He met and organized various nationalist factions and directed them to declare Korea's independence on February 15, 1919, at Nicholsk, Siberia. The Nicholsk conference established a provisional government of Korea months ahead of the Provisional Government of the Republic of Korea (PGRK) founded in Shanghai on April 13, 1919.

Shenyang has more than its share of violent and complicated history. A brief summary of how imperial Japan was able to occupy Manchuria is as follows: Following the Russo-Japanese War, Japan obtained the Kwantung Leased Territory and the areas adjacent to the South Manchurian Railway. The Kwantung Garrison was established in 1906 to defend this territory. In 1919, the Kwangtung Garrison was renamed the Kwantung Army. Kwangtung Army officers carried out the assassination of Manchurian warlord Chang Tsolin in 1928, and its leadership engineered the Mukden (Shengyang's old name) Incident and the subsequent invasion of Manchuria in 1931. With the foundation of Manchukuo in 1932, the Kwangtung Army was the controlling power in the new state political administration. At this time the Kwantung Army commander was the sole authority to approve or disapprove any command of the puppet emperor Puyi of Manchukuo. This army was heavily augmented over the next few years up to 700,000 troops by 1941, and its headquarters was re-located to the new Manchukuo capital of Hsinking. The Kwantung Army also fought in the opening phase of the Second Sino-Japanese War and various actions in Inner Mongolia to extend Japanese domination over portions of northern China and Inner Mongolia.

In 1934, Japan officially crowned Puyi the last emperor of the Qing dynasty after he was deposed from the Forbidden City in Beijing in 1924 by the warlord Feng Yuxiang as the emperor of Manchukuo. As part of Japanese colonialism in Manchukuo, Puyi was living in the Wei Huang Gong in Jilin Province during this time. His brother Pujie, whose marriage was arranged with Hiro Saga, a distant cousin of the Japanese emperor Hirohito, was to produce an heir to the throne, another well-planned, systematic manipulation by the Japanese Empire to take over Manchuria as it had Korea. Bernardo Bertolucci's movie *The Last Emperor*, released in 1987, which received nine (9) Academy Awards, includes a dramatized version of how the Japanese government tried to prevent the empress from having an heir, killing her baby shortly after it was born, and making her an opium addict. The movie is not far removed from the historical facts.

By the time my parents arrived in Manchuria the Kwantung Army was the most feared force in Manchuria but they had more important things to do for their territorial expansion than harassing Koreans living in Manchuria. On many occasions my father witnessed Kwantung Army officers and their soldiers kicking and beating Chinese residents almost to death. Father wholeheartedly hated that kind of subhuman behavior no matter what the reasons were. They were so brutal and lack of any human feelings toward fellow human beings. Even in such an environment my father still thought that providing a good education to Korean children was a very important task to ensure the welfare of Korea's future. Thus he was more than happy at the prospect of building a new school for those children and he decided to take the difficult task.

My mother was dead set against the idea of moving to an unfamiliar place like Manchuria only a few years after she barely established a stable family life in Pyongyang. She preferred staying behind in Pyongyang. However in most Korean families particularly at that time, the husband is always the boss and makes all the big decisions. Besides he didn't want to leave his pretty young wife alone behind without his protection. He sold the home so mother had no choice but to follow him to Manchuria with me. I don't approve of what my father did without his wife's agreement but it turned out well in the end.

My father was a very capable administrator and a good organizer so he succeeded in building the new school. He named it Dong-gwang (meaning Eastern Light) Middle School. He persuaded many of his colleagues and acquaintances to come to Manchuria to participate in this endeavor and organized a qualified teaching staff. One of the people he brought there was his fellow university alumnus, Che Gui-tek, the man who introduced him to my grandmother to arrange the marriage with my mother. The school project was very successful and it appears that there was very close cooperation among the teachers, the students, and their parents. I know this because some of his former students from that school used to come to visit my father many years later when we were living in Seoul. This kind of lasting relationship rarely seems to exist between teachers and students in modern society.

My brother John, who is three years younger than I, was born in Shenyang so I must have been about three years old when we lived there. I have very hazy memories of a large front yard and a huge, tightly locked front door that opened to reveal a large lake in front of the house (I thought it was an ocean but Mother said its a lake). I remember it was terribly cold and windy and I had frostbite on my fingers from playing outside in the yard. I also remember an incident when I was on a horse-driven carriage with mother going somewhere (Mother said we were going to a hospital). A man approached us on horseback very close to our carriage and snatched away Mother's handbag that I was holding. I remember being very frightened and that I cried.

Manchuria was a scary and lawless place to live in those days. My parents told me that the gap between rich and poor was huge in China then. A few very rich men had as many as a dozen wives as their property and when they gambled and lost at mah-jongg they might give away their wives, the last acquired first. Because rich men had so many wives, poor manual laborers, called coolies, could not even find women to marry. Thus those coolies used to live together in dormitory-like facilities, eating steamed buns and scallions, playing mah-jongg after a hard day's work to entertain themselves. There were also many opium traders as well as opium addicts and many dangerous armed robbers. Chinese people used to hide valuables such as jewelry in their walls and seal them off for emergency needs. My father thought that a revolution was inevitable in such a society. For better or worse people living in such unfair circumstances will revolt against their own government since it supports the rich upper class and has no policy to help poor people. They will revolt because they have no alternative.

My parents had witnessed many horrifying opium-related crimes. My father blamed the British for introducing opium to China during the Qing Dynasty. Britain began exporting opium to China from British India in the 18th century to counter its trade deficit. When the Qing Dynasty sought to restrict British opium trafficking, the first Opium War began in 1839 and lasted until 1842; the Second Opium War was waged from 1856 to 1860. Vladivostok had been part of many nations in the past, starting with the ancient kingdoms of Korea and later Mongol Empire and then the Qing Dynasty, before Russia acquired the entire maritime province, including Sakhalin Island through the Treaty of Adigun (1858). Because the Qing Dynasty was so weakened by the Opium War, it was unable to defend Vladivostok. Then Manchuria became a haven for opium dealers. When my parents were traveling on a train to visit Seoul, Korea from Manchuria they saw a woman carrying a child on her back completely covered except for the child's legs which dangled below. A Japanese policeman at the Seoul train station became suspicious and searched the child; he found that it was a dead child's body filled with opium.

Besides the political situation Manchurian weather patterns are not ideal for human life. Shenyang has a monsoon-influenced moist continental climate characterized by hot, humid summers and dry, cold winters and the Siberian anticyclone. Nearly half of the annual rainfall occurs in July and August. Average monthly temperatures range from 12.2°F in January to 76.46°F in July. The temperatures range from −27.58°F to 102.74°F. It's not an easy place to maintain human health, especially for fragile women and children.

After a few years in Shenyang my mother developed a serious health problem because of the bad weather and Siberian wind. Dangerous human conditions also contributed to her difficulty. My brother and I also became very ill. Only my father who was born with healthy DNA and survived through his infancy under awful conditions was unaffected. As Mother's condition worsened Father had no choice but to move all his family to Seoul to hospitalize Mother at Severance Medical Centre for surgery. But sometimes bad news eventually turns into good fortune. If my parents hadn't moved back to Seoul then, our family might have been trapped in Manchuria which ended up in Mao's communist China after World War II. If our family hadn't moved to Manchuria from Pyongyang, we would have been stuck under Kim Il-sung's dynasty in North Korea, perhaps even in one of its harsh labor camps. Life is unpredictable; we don't have a reliable crystal ball. Fortunately mother gradually and slowly recovered in Seoul.

Photo 2: The above photo was taken when we were living in Shenyang, Manchuria.

Chapter 5: Childhood Memories of The Liberation of Korea (1942–1945)

My early childhood memories begin when I was about four or five years old. We were living in Seoul, just north of Hyewha-dong. It was a clean middle-class neighborhood with decent and educated people. There were no Japanese families in our neighborhood. What's still in memory are the clear blue skies, fresh air, many butterflies with beautifully patterned wings, and dragonflies with crimson bodies and transparent wings. They were flying so low that we children were able to catch them easily with homemade insect nets. I also remember a bright full moon at night with the silhouette of a rabbit grinding some grain with a mortar and a pestle under the gesu tree - so we were told by grown-ups—and millions of twinkling stars in the night sky. Mars was a very bright reddish color and stood out in the night sky; we were told that Martians with frighteningly ugly features were going to attack our planet Earth someday. I drew a series of Martians with ugly features attacking Earth and made a cartoon of them which I distributed to the neighborhood children.

A folded mountain range with low hills and beautifully shaped pine trees surrounded the town where our home stood at the foot of a little hill. We could see from our home the man-made tunnels in those mountains that would be used as bunkers for protection from possible American air raids and we were in those long tunnels many times during air-raid drills. These bunkers were never used for actual air raids because American planes never dropped a bomb in Korea during World War II, except one empty gasoline drum dropped in the middle of the city, probably for fun by the fun-loving American airmen, to scare the hell out of people. A couple of times I clearly remember seeing a shiny but very tiny object very high in the blue sky. Father used to watch such objects with a happy smile on his face saying that they were American planes surveying and taking photos of the city. He seemed fascinated to see such advanced American technology that could surely beat the determined warmongers of imperial Japan. Father loved science and technology. It's unfortunate he never had a chance to pursue his real talent in those areas.

Father had a teaching job at Hee-moon High School at the time, but the Japanese government often sent school teachers and students to the countryside to perform field work. After a day's work they were given a sack of rice for compensation—a cheap wage. Father used to come home with many blisters on his back from working under the sweltering midsummer sun. To supply a large number of military personnel as well as the Japanese civilian population nutritious food such as fish or meat was very scarce to Koreans. This was especially a big problem for women like my mother who was pregnant with her fourth child at the time. My sister Oak was born three years earlier when the food supply was a little better. Unlike Father, Mother did not like soybean soup, which made it difficult for her to obtain enough high-quality protein for the proper brain development of a growing fetus. I still have a clear vision of two mackerels father saved for Mother's next protein source dangling from the roof of our house. Father was trying to prevent stray cats from snatching them away. No one we knew had a refrigerator to store food in those days.

People didn't even have enough water to drink, wash, or clean. Since our house was located at the low end of the hill we could be supplied water from the public water system. But all other homes on the same hill could not pump up water due to low water pressure. My parents were very kind and thoughtful people, always willing to help others. They allowed the whole neighborhood to come to our home to get water daily. I still remember the constant traffic of our neighbors in and out of the house or standing in a long line for water. Maybe my parents also paid high water bills because they never collected any money from the neighbors. Naturally our parents were very popular in the neighborhood and Mother was elected neighborhood captain. She organized the neighborhood to conduct occasional air-raid drills and managed the distribution of government rations of rice and other daily needs. I occasionally overheard Mother discussing with neighborhood ladies where to hide some of their metal-alloy vessels for rice and soup. Japanese officials were trying to confiscate anything made of metal, such as copper, tin, steel, or even aluminum to build more planes since they were rapidly losing their air force, shot down by American fighter planes in the Pacific theater.

Japanese officials also began drafting young Korean men to join the Japanese army in their fight against the allied forces. My cousin Young-gi was also drafted at the time. One of the worst crimes the Japanese imperialists committed in Korea during World War II was forcibly drafting many young girls from their parents' homes to serve Japanese military men, making them their sex slaves. Many of them were preteen innocent virgins. The drafted girls who were unwilling to serve those Japanese soldiers were beaten and punished. Many of those girls committed suicide instead of going through the unbearable task; some were returned barely alive after World War II as badly ruined women without any future in Korean society. One of the girls who developed unattractive pimples on her face was locked up in a closet and starved to death (this story came up during the testimony of the survivors who returned to Korea after the war).

My maternal grandmother was trying to marry off her teenaged daughter, my aunt, to prevent her from being drafted for this service. My aunt was living at our home at the time, attending Sookmyung Girl's Middle School in Seoul. My father arranged the marriage with one of the students at his school, so my aunt was able to avoid this awful fate. She was barely seventeen years old at the time. Many Korean families who had young teenage daughters during World War II tried to marry off their young daughters for the same reason. There was a constant fear in every family with young daughters in those days when someone came knocking on their door. I am a witness to this story.

In the evenings neighborhood adults often gathered around talking about how to escape the organized official recruitment of Koreans to work in mainland Japan, often involving intimidation and bullying. As the labor shortage increased by 1942 the Japanese authorities extended the provisions of the National Mobilization Law to include the involuntary recruitment of Korean workers for factories and mines on the Korean Peninsula, in Manchukuo, or in Japan as needed. Of the 5,400,000 Koreans drafted, about 670,000 were taken to mainland Japan, including Karafuto, present-day Sakhalin, which is now a part of Russia, for civilian labor. Those who were brought to Japan were often forced to work under appalling conditions. About

60,000 are estimated to have died between 1939 and 1945 from harsh treatment, inhumane working conditions, and as collateral casualties of Allied bombings. The total deaths of Korean forced laborers in Korea and Manchuria is estimated to be about half a million. The 43,000 ethnic Koreans in Karafuto, which had been occupied by the Soviet Union just prior to Japan's surrender, were refused repatriation by the Soviets either to mainland Japan or to the Korean Peninsula, and were thus trapped in Sakhalin, stateless. They became the ancestors of the Sakhalin Koreans. It's heartbreaking to learn about so much suffering of those poor souls traveling through this long and perilous 20th-century time tunnel because their own government was incapable of protecting its own citizens.

By 1939, ethnic Koreans were to surrender their Korean family names and adopt Japanese surnames. Although this was an officially voluntary measure, individuals who would not create a new Japanese-style surname were pressured and harassed. My family had to adopt a Japanese surname, changing from our Korean surname, Kim, to the Japanese surname Omodo. The Japanese name had to be displayed on the door for mailmen or others to see. Imperial Japan made sure any book written in the Korean language was burned and made sure only the Japanese alphabet was taught in schools during its rule. Libraries had to burn all Korean history books as if the Korean kingdoms never existed. All school textbooks were written in the Japanese alphabet. The Japanese were very thorough in their attempt to alter the history. They are the experts in rewriting history books to teach fake history to their own younger generation.

My father wrote the Korean alphabet (Hangul) on a piece of cardboard and tried to teach us, but he had to hide it behind the large dresser when it was not in use. Hangul is a phonemic alphabet organized into syllabic blocks comprising 14 consonants and 10 vowels. It was created in the mid-15th century under King Sejong with a group of bright scholars and is now the official script of both North Korea and South Korea, being co-official in the Yanbian Korean Autonomous Prefecture of China. This region in China used to belong to Balhae (AD 698–926), an ancient multiethnic Korean kingdom established after the fall of Goguryeo by a former Goguryeo general, Dae Jo-young, after Goguryeo's capital and it's southern territories fell to United Silla.

In 1943, I entered Heawha kindergarten in Seoul, run by American missionaries. Every morning my father left home with me and we walked to the kindergarten, which took about 30 minutes. Then he took the trolley to go to his school to teach. The kindergarten faculty was made up of all Korean teachers and the principal of the kindergarten was none other than Chang Myun, a devout Roman Catholic who had graduated from Manhattan College in the United States. This was when Father had a chance to meet with Chang Myun in person although he very seldom showed up at the kindergarten. I remember Father mentioned that Chang Myun was a good and decent man. After the liberation of Korea, Chang Myun served as the First Republic's ambassador to the United States and was elected to vice president from 1949 to 1951 and in 1959. After Syngman Rhee's government was ousted by the student-led prodemocracy uprising, he became prime minister of the Second Republic in 1960. Although there was a president, Chang Myun functioned as the head of the government. Chang Myun's government ended when Park Chung-hee led a successful coup d'état that ended the Second Republic.

At the kindergarten everyone including teachers spoke only Korean. We were taught how to sing, dance, draw, and color with crayons. In my very first class I drew a girl feeding grains to a hen with her chicks. When the teacher saw my drawing she was all smiles and told me I had done a very good job and I should take it home to show it to my parents. So I brought my drawing home and showed it to my mother proudly, but she just cracked up laughing. I had no idea what was so funny. So I asked her, "What's so funny, Mother?" Then she asked me to take a look at the drawing more carefully and go to the yard and take another look at a hen and her chicks and count their legs. Finally it dawned on me that the hen and all those chicks had only two legs, not four as I had drawn them. This was a good lesson for me at an early age to pay attention to details very carefully before presenting my scientific observations later in life. As the American saying goes, "The devil is in the details."

The most vivid memory of my childhood happened on August 15, 1945. This is one of few memories I still remember in detail as if I were watching a film of what happened on that day. First my father was sitting on a chair at his desk listening to a radio broadcast of Japanese emperor Hirohito's unconditional surrender to the Allied forces. The war had taken many millions of human lives, not only the fighting force but also so many civilians, in occupied territories as well as in Japan proper, not to mention the number of the Allied soldiers killed during the Pacific War. This was the first time anyone heard this supposedly divine voice of Japanese emperor Hirohito who finally confessed that he was just a man, not of divine origin. I had not seen such a high exuberance on my father's face before that day. I also remember all the neighborhood children pouring out onto the street shortly after Hirohito's broadcast with small Korean flags in their hands shouting excitedly, "Long Live Korea!" Father took out the cardboard hidden behind the dresser with the Korean alphabet (Hangul) he had written on it and began to teach us openly how to read it.

Thus after the atomic bombings of Hiroshima and Nagasaki and a declaration of war by the Soviet Union, the Empire of Japan finally surrendered ending World War II. Many people—including Alexander Solzhenitsyn, a former Soviet army officer who published the book *Gulag Archipelago* describing his experience in a Soviet Gulag and knew all about Joseph Stalin's manipulative tactics— thought involving Soviets at the end of World War II to obtain the Japanese surrender was a big mistake by the US president Franklin D. Roosevelt and was unnecessary because the power of atomic bombs. During the Pacific War millions of people died in the fighting, from starvation and disease, and, as survivors generally describe it, the sheer cruelty of the Japanese. Some people criticize the United States for dropping atomic bombs in Hiroshima and Nagasaki. It was indeed a tragedy that so many innocent Japanese citizens had to be sacrificed to end the war. Ordinary Japanese citizens were not responsible for starting the war or for their nation's empire building. This would not have happened if their leaders, imperial Japanese samurais, had not been so ambitious and cruel in their empire building.

If the Japanese Empire had won the Pacific War instead of the Allied forces, the world today would be a much different place. No doubt, Japanese empire-building activity would have continued to expand the nation's authority by territorial conquest, establishing economic and political powers in Asia and other territories or nations, forever maintaining its autocratic imperialistic attitude of extreme superiority, subordination, and dominion over foreign people. This trend had to be terminated once and for all! For this I am forever grateful for all those American and Allied soldiers who fought and died in the Pacific War to terminate the territorial ambition of Japan. They saved us from further cruelty by Japanese Imperialism.

Imperial Japanese leaders brainwashed their citizens to fight in the war, sacrificing their lives for their divine emperor. Suicide tactics were not invented by Al-Qaeda or ISIS but by the imperial Japan. Kamikaze was the most common and best-known form of Japanese suicide attack during World War II. The Japanese military used or made plans for various types of suicide attacks including the use of submarines, human torpedoes, speedboats, and divers. The tradition of committing suicide instead of accepting defeat and perceived shame was deeply entrenched in the Japanese military culture; it was one of the main traditions of the samurai life and the Bushido code. It's a difficult task to fight against such an army without causing considerable casualties to your own.

The Japanese attack on Pearl Harbor on December 7, 1941, was not the only Japanese attack on America. In fact Japan was the only country that directly attacked North America although attacks on North America during World War II by the Axis power were rare, mainly due to the continent's geographical separation from the central theaters of conflict in Europe and Asia. I am surprised to find that not many Americans are aware of the Japanese attack on Alaska in 1942. On June 3, the Aleutian Islands, running southwest from mainland Alaska were invaded by Japanese forces. American forces engaged the Japanese on Attu Island and regained control by the end of May 1943, after taking significant casualties in difficult terrain in which hundreds died. In short, imperial Japanese aggression had to be ended to save the world from further tyranny.

Changing times and lives also changed Japanese ideology, and the present-day Japanese population no longer exhibits a desire for territorial expansion as did their samurai forefathers. However, it's disheartening to see the current nationalist prime minister, Shinzo Abe, of Japan fail to properly apologize for his country's aggression in the past. He denies the clear history of drafting and using innocent Korean preteens and teenagers as sex slaves in Japanese military brothels. Further, a trio of Japanese cabinet ministers visited the controversial Yasukuni shrine to remember the 70th anniversary of the end of World War II. This shrine is seen by neighboring countries like Korea, China, and the Philippines as a symbol of Tokyo's militarist past. Most Japanese people, however, just concentrate on building their industry to market their products in the global market and they have been very successful. After the liberation of Korea from Japanese rule, the "Name Restoration Order" was issued on October 23, 1946, by USAMGIK south of the 38th parallel, enabling Koreans to restore their Korean surnames.

Many Korean expatriates who had fought for Korean independence abroad for 35 long years were returning home one by one. They were met with enthusiastic welcome by freshly energized Koreans. This was a very exciting time for Koreans young and old, like my father, full of hopes and dreams. At the height of the independence movement, the PGRK was established in Shanghai as the de jure Korean government during the Japanese rule of Korea. The PGRK did its best to fulfill the international obligations of the Korean government. It declared war on imperial Japan and provided close cooperation with the Allied powers during World War II. For 27 years until its return home on November 23, 1945, the PGRK endeavored to represent the Korean people (it was dissolved in 1948 after the establishment of ROK). At the time of Korean liberation from Japan, Kim Gu was the president, and Kim Gyu-sik was the vice president of the PGRK. Besides Kim Gu and Kim Gyu-sik, there were many able and respected Korean leaders who had devoted their entire adult lives to Korean independence before the liberation. Were they finally able to achieve their dreams of building a unified Korea? That was the big question in the mind of many Koreans, including my father.

Chapter 6: Prelude to the Partition of the Korean Peninsula (1945–1946)

After the initial euphoria of liberation from Imperial Japanese occupation my father was beginning to worry about whether there would be a smooth transition toward building a peaceful and united Korea. The month of August in Korea was hot and humid, a common season for mosquito infestation. Right after the liberation, our friendly neighborhood adults frequently gathered in the evening in our home, burned some dry weeds in the front yard to repel mosquitoes, and sat around to chat about the future of Korea. I still remember listening to many interesting stories they shared. They talked a lot about Korean leaders abroad as well as in Korea who fought for the independence of Korea and what roles they should each play in building the new liberated Korea. My father — who was more familiar with world affairs than average Koreans in those days because he read reports published in English when they were available to him — explained what had happened at the Cairo and the Yalta conferences. Father was very pleased about one definite condition that Japan would not be allowed to retain Korea as an extension of Japan proper after its unconditional surrender to the Allied powers. During its occupation of Korea, Japan did everything possible to make the entire Korean Peninsula and its people their own, even by changing our surnames to Japanese surnames, burning all Korean history books and rewriting all the school texts in Japanese. But father didn't know any details of how the Allied powers planned to proceed in building the new Korea. Because of this uncertainty, Father was worried about some possible complications that might happen in the process to build the united and democratic Korea.

The Cairo Conference of November 22–26, 1943, held in Cairo, Egypt, addressed the Allied position against Japan during World War II and made decisions about postwar Asia as well as the Korean issue. The meeting was attended by President Franklin D. Roosevelt of the United States, Prime Minister Winston Churchill of the United Kingdom, and Generalissimo Chiang Kai-shek of the Republic of China (this was before the victory of Communist Party of

China). Joseph Stalin of the Soviet Union had refused to attend the conference on the grounds that Chiang Kai-shek, instead of Mao Zedong, was attending the meeting.

Regarding the Korean issue, the Cairo Declaration issued on December 1 stated that "in due course Korea shall become free and independent." The phrase "in due course" was presumed by the Koreans to mean "when Korea is liberated from Japan." President Roosevelt, however, maintained that Asian colonial peoples including Koreans were not ready to enjoy freedom and independence. Thus, they needed to be educated and trained under the guidance of the Allied powers over a considerable length of time in order to enjoy democratic rights and institutions. Apparently Roosevelt was not familiar with Korea's 5,000-year history of sovereign government, although it was not always one unified kingdom before imperial Japan annexed Korea in 1910. Japan took advantage of Taft-Katsura Agreement with the United States in July 1905, agreeing to Japanese control in Korea in return for American dominance in the Philippines. Furthermore, Americans were colonial people when they declared war for their independence against Great Britain and some historical notes reveal that some of the founding fathers of America did not even believe the majority American populace was ready to enjoy the freedom and democracy at the time. Nevertheless, Americans have been able to preserve their democratic system of government for over 200 years to date.

Korea had been a sovereign state for many centuries before it was taken over by Japan for only 35 years. Even during the Japanese occupation, the PGRK existed in Shanghai and later moved to Chongqing, China, when Chiang Kai-shek's Kuomintang government was pushed to Chongqing by the Communist Party of China. The PGRK was formed on April 13, 1919, as the de jure government of Korea following the Korean Declaration of Independence during the March 1st Movement of the same year following US president Woodrow Wilson's 14 points declaration. At this particular period Koreans had an unusual opportunity to look forward to a progressive and democratic government. This was because there were many capable and patriotic Korean leaders who recognized the key socioeconomic problems of the last days of the Joseon dynasty and were ready to change and build a democratic country under a well-drafted constitution. It's a misfortune for Koreans that Roosevelt was unfamiliar with Korean history and unaware of the determination of those Korean leaders who organized and maintained the PGRK under such arduous circumstances.

In brief the PGRK strived for the liberation of Korea from Japanese annexation that lasted from 1910 to 1945. They coordinated armed resistance against the Japanese army during the 1920s and 1930s, including at the Battle of Chingshanli in October 1920, and the assault on Japanese military leadership in Shanghai in April 1932. This struggle resulted in the formation of Korean Liberation Army in 1940, bringing together the Korean resistance groups in exile. The Liberation Army took part in Allied action in China and parts of Southeast Asia. Prior to the end of World War II, Korean Liberation Army was preparing an assault against the Japanese in Korea in conjunction with the American Office of Strategic Services, but the Japanese surrender on August 15, 1945, made the execution of the plan unnecessary. The preamble of the constitution of the Republic of Korea (ROK) recognizes the PGRK as the legal regime of the period between 1919 and 1948. The sites of the PGRK in Shanghai and Chongqing have now been turned into museums.

The Yalta Conference of February 4–11, 1945, attended by the heads of government of the United States, the United Kingdom, and the Soviet Union was convened in the Livadia Palace near Yalta in Crimea, USSR. Chiang Kai-shek of the Republic of China was not even invited to this meeting. As a matter of fact, Chang Kai-shek's Kuomintang government was on the verge of defeat in their civil war with Communist Party of China at this time. At this meeting President Roosevelt made a grave mistake by asking the Soviet Union to join the Allied forces in the Pacific War. Of course Stalin was delighted by the invitation and quickly agreed. This was three months after the German surrender. The Japanese military was in such terrible shape by this time that they could not continue fighting the Allied forces much longer. Yet it was the opinion of American policy makers at that time that the United States could not defeat the Japanese without

Soviet assistance. They grossly over estimated the strength of the Kwantung Army of Japan in Manchuria as well as the presumed Japanese determination to fight against the Allies "to the last man." The Kwantung Army at that time was no longer such a fearful force. As the situation began to worsen for the imperial Japanese Army many of its frontline units were stripped of systematically their best personnel and equipment and were sent to the Pacific theater to fight the US Army. By 1945, the quality of Kwangtong Army had fallen drastically as all the best men and materiel were siphoned off. These forces were replaced by militia, reservists, and cannibalized smaller units, all equipped with outdated equipment. This was the army President Roosevelt was so afraid of fighting without involving Soviet Red Army. It's obvious that American leaders were not very knowledgeable at all about the history and the geopolitical development in East Asian region.

The Potsdam Conference, July17–August 2, 1945, was attended by Harry Truman in place of the now-deceased Roosevelt, by Clement Attlee in place of Churchill (due to the loss Churchill suffered in the British general election), and by Soviet premier Joseph Stalin. Here the Allies decided to deliver an ultimatum to Japan for its unconditional surrender. Simultaneously the American and Soviet chiefs of staff worked out an agreement to synchronize military operations against Japan should Japan refuse to accept the Potsdam ultimatum. On August 8, the Soviet Union declared war on Japan and immediately began military actions against the Japanese. This was two days after America dropped the first atomic bomb, "Little Boy," on Hiroshima on August 6, 1945, and one day before the second atomic bomb, "Fat Man," detonated on August 9 over Nagasaki.

In the eyes of many who knew Joseph Stalin and the politics of the former Soviet Union like Nobel laureate Alexander Solzhenitsyn—who was a captain in the Red Army only to be rewarded with a term in the Soviet Gulag for dissenting with socialist thought—the decision of the United States to ask the Soviet Union to join the Pacific War against Japan was a big mistake. Of the Yalta Declaration, Solzhenitsyn wrote in *The Gulag Archipelago*:

"In their own countries Roosevelt and Churchill are honored as embodiments of statesmanlike wisdom. To us in Russian prison conversations their consistent shortsightedness and stupidity stood out as astonishingly obvious. How could they fail to secure any guarantees the independence of Eastern Europe? How could they give away broad regions of Saxony and Thuringia in exchange for the preposterous toy of a four-zone Berlin, their own future Achilles' heel? And what was the military or political sense in their surrendering to destruction at Stalin's hands hundreds of thousands of armed Soviet citizens determined not to surrender? They say it was the price they paid for Stalin's agreeing to enter the war against Japan. With the atomic bomb already in their hands, they paid Stalin for not refusing to occupy Manchuria, for strengthening Mao Tse-tung in China, and for giving Kim Il-sung control of one-half of Korea!"

I don't have in-depth knowledge concerning the situation in Europe during World War II, but concerning the Pacific War I absolutely agree with Solzhenitsyn. Roosevelt and Churchill yielded too much to Stalin for a short-term gain, which resulted in a very long-term loss and a cold war. Stalin got whatever he wanted and more, Eastern Europe, Sakalin Island, and North Korea, though Korea was intended to be the entire Korean Peninsula. Because Soviet Union became involved in post–World War II Korean affairs, it became impossible to build a noncommunist and unified Korea. The fate of Korea was already determined at the Yalta Conference. Extremely poor health of Roosevelt at the time may have weakened his desire to conduct a tougher negotiation with Stalin, the ruthless dictator who killed millions of people including many Russians.

In 2009, I read a Moscow news release reporting that a judge at a Moscow district court rejected a claim by Stalin's grandson Yevgeny Dzhugashvili, that Novaya Gazeta defamed Stalin in an April article referring to Stalin as a "bloodthirsty cannibal." Oh yes, indeed, Stalin was a bloodthirsty cannibal. Stalin certainly never cared about the welfare of Koreans; he imprisoned many thousands of innocent ethnic Koreans who lived in Russia in the Soviet Gulag; he expelled Koreans — the descendants of Koreans who had lived in Vladivostok since ancient times when Korean kingdoms like Goguryeo and Balhae used to occupy the region - to Kazakhstan; and he did not permit Sakalin Koreans, who were brought there for forced labor by imperial Japan during World War II, to return to Korea, their homeland after the war. Why should Stalin care about the welfare of Koreans in light of his motive to expand his communist ideals by placing the entire Korean peninsula under his control?

On August 9, 1945, a battle-hardened, one-million-strong Soviet force transferred from Europe attacked Japanese forces in Manchuria and quickly defeated the Kwantung Army. Then they continued their march rapidly into the northern part of Korea. They were supposed to defeat the Kwantung Army in Manchuria without permanently occupying the region. Korea was not even a part of the deal at Yalta.

Following large-scale attacks against Japanese troops in Korea on August 10, Soviet forces landed at Chung-jin and Na-nam in the northern Korean Peninsula. It seemed as though the Soviets could penetrate deep into the southern part of the peninsula while American troops were still in Japan 600 miles away from Korea. Realizing the urgent situation the American government proposed a military demarcation line along the 38th parallel in order to stop the Soviet advance. Stalin accepted the American proposal without objections. It's apparent that Stalin was planning from the beginning to place the entire Korean Peninsula under his rule by planting Kim Il- sung who was still in the Soviet Union as a captain of the Soviet Red Army. Accordingly Soviet troops occupied the area north of the line and American troops finally arrived in Korea in September south of the 38th parallel. This was done under the agreement that a joint control of the Allies was to be extended throughout the Korean Peninsula.

This was another lapse of judgment by the American leaders in trusting the Soviet leader and arriving in Korea almost a month later than Soviets, who had by then already swept the north. Thus the perpetual demarcation line of the 38th parallel was already drawn in 1945. There was no specific requirement for the Soviet Army to enter the Korean Peninsula, since there was no Kwangtung Army division stationed in Korea. By this time there was no chaos or confusion in the Korean Peninsula requiring Soviet troops' involvement because the clear agreement between the Japanese director-general and the Korean leader Lyuh Woon-hyung was already in effect to see to the safe return of the Japanese population leaving Japanese-owned properties in Korea for future distribution to Koreans and all Korean political prisoners were released from jail.

Lyuh Woon-hyung (May 26 1886–July 19 1947) was one of the most beloved and admired Korean leaders in recent Korean history. During this time his name was often mentioned when our neighborhood adults gathered in evenings in our home to discuss the future of Korea. That's why I remember his name so clearly. Lyuh was born in Yang-pyong, Kyunggi Province, son of a local Yangban (aristocrat) magnate. His pen name was Mong-yang for "dream" and "light." Lyuh began studying the Bible in 1907 and became friends with an American missionary, Charles Allen Clark, who helped him found Kidok Kwangdong School in 1909. In 1910, Lyuh freed all slaves owned by his household, radically defying Korean tradition. In 1911, he enrolled in Pyongyang Presbyterian Theological Seminary; went to China in 1914, where he studied English literature at the Gumlung Institute in Nanking and graduated in 1917; then he moved on to Shanghai and joined the PGRK.

In 1918, Lyuh met Charles Crane, a special envoy of the US president Woodrow Wilson in Shanghai and pleaded for Korea's independence. Crane's mission was to publicize President Wilson's "14 points" statement. In January 8, 1918, President Wilson set up the 14 points as a blueprint for world peace in a speech; the plan he set forth was to be used for peace negotiations after World War I. Lyuh learned about item 5 in the 14-point declaration calling for a free open-minded, and absolutely impartial adjustment of all colonial claims, based upon strict observance of the principle in determining all such questions of sovereignty the interests of the populations concerned must have equal weight with the equitable claims of the government whose title is to be determined.

Lyuh took Wilson's words at face value and believed Korea would be freed. At Crane's suggestion, Lyuh and Chang Duk Su wrote a petition for Korean independence for Crane to deliver to President Wilson. Crane suggested that Lyuh ought to send a Korean delegation to the Paris Peace Conference. Lyuh and company began a general peaceful uprising in Korea timed to coincide with the 1919 Paris Peace Conference, totally unaware of the secret pact of the United States, Japan, and France to exclude Korea and Indochina (a French colony at the time) from the Paris conference. In January 1919, Lyuh sent Kim Gyu-sik to the World Peace Conference to represent Korea. It turned out the 1919 Paris Peace Conference and Wilson's principle of self-determination was not for the oppressed peoples of Asia.

My search of the document revealed that there was no mention of either Korea or Indochina (Vietnam) in the 14 points although the names of other occupied territories are clearly identified (Romania, Serbia, Montenegro, the Turkish portion of the Ottoman Empire, and the Polish state). Ho Chi Minh's valiant effort to gain his nation's freedom from France was in vain and the Korean delegation headed by Kim Gyu-sik was rejected by the conference organizers.

The March 1st Movement inspired by Wilson's 14-point proclamation and the 1919 Paris Peace Conference cost Koreans dearly. Hundreds of thousands of students led by their Christian pastors and their leaders waved home-made Korean flags, Taegook-gi, and shouted "Long live Korea!" My intelligent grandmother documented many details of her relatives', her uncles' and cousins', and their church members' participation in this movement and the story of their arrest and torture by the Japanese police. Before she passed away she gave the thick document along with other historical documents on the local battles against many Hideyoshi invasions she had written to my father to submit them to the national library—the head of the library was a friend of my father—and Father delivered the documents to the library as she requested. The Japanese police and army attacked and burned Christian churches, fired on the unarmed students and arrested and tortured the marchers. About 6,670

Koreans were shot dead or beheaded, 14,611 were wounded, and 52,770 were arrested.

This was the first big blow to Lyuh for trusting the American government but it wouldn't be the last tragedy resulting from the American government decisions regarding its Korean policy. There is no clear historical record I could find about whether excluding Korea and Vietnam from his 14-point declaration was Wilson's own idea or the idea of the Republican majority in Congress who did not want to offend their colonialist allies, Japan and France. Since I am a great admirer of Wilson for his bravery in the era of colonialism it would be my greatest disappointment if Wilson had anything to do with this decision. I am aware of the controversy recently raised concerning Wilson's racism and I wonder whether Wilson had any knowledge about the secret pact of the United States, Japan, and France to exclude Korea and Indochina from the Paris Peace Conference.

The 28th President of the United States, from 1913 to 1921, Woodrow Wilson, the only US president with a PhD, was the leader of the Progressive Movement. He was clearly against colonialism and had strong principles. He served as president of Princeton University from 1902 to 1910 which overlaps Syngman Rhee's time at Princeton suggesting that he was probably aware of the struggle of Koreans to liberate Korea from Japanese rule at the time. Syngman Rhee published a book titled *The Spirit of Independence: A Primer for Korean Modernization and Reform.* As our parents, Wilson was a devoted Presbyterian; he introduced a profound sense of morality into international affairs, which obligates the United States to promote global democracy. For his sponsorship of the League of Nations, Wilson was awarded the 1919 Nobel Peace Prize. However he seemed to have suffered a great deal in implementing his progressive ideas domestically as well as internationally because of the intense opposition from the Republican majority in Congress. They did not want to offend their allies, colonialists, by implementing Wilson's policies. Could this be the reason why Korea and Vietnam was left out from the pact?

Lyuh took part in the establishment of the PGRK in 1919 and served as a member of Legislative Assembly. Like many others in the Korean independence movement Lyuh sought aid from both right and left since they needed funds to operate the PGRK abroad. He joined the right-wing Chinese Nationalist Party in 1924 and worked for Sino-Korean cooperation. In 1929, he was arrested by the British police for criticizing Britain's colonial policy and was handed over to the Japanese for imprisonment in Korea. Even the British police did not hesitate to hand over a Korean independence fighter to Japanese police. At that time imperialists like Britain ruled the world and those powerless independence fighters were up against their geopolitical power. This is how Lyuh was returned to Korea.

After three years he was released from the prison (1932) but the Japanese did not allow him to leave the country. Then Lyuh took on a variety of anti-Japanese activities in the areas of media and sports. In the 1936 Summer Olympics in Berlin a Korean marathon runner, Sohn Kee-chung, won the gold medal but Sohn had to wear a Japanese flag on his shirt because he had to represent Japan, since Korea was a Japanese colony at the time. *Joseon Joong-ang Ilbo*, of which Lyuh was the editor, ran the photograph of Sohn but removed the Japanese flag from his shirt. The Japanese closed down the newspaper and arrested Lyuh for this action. Lyuh's political views were a mixture of Christianity and Wilsonian-style democracy but he did not believe American-style capitalism was well suited to Korea considering the history of rebellion and social upheaval during the last days of the Joseon dynasty. He was very far from being a communist. He was an ardent sportsman who stayed fit by exercising, pumping iron and his robust good looks, his oratorical skills and easy charm drew many Americans to him.

When the Japanese were about to accept the Potsdam ultimatum, Endo Rysaku, the Japanese director-general in Seoul, approached Lyuh Woon-hyung and asked him whether he would be willing to form a political body to maintain law and order and guarantee the safety of the Japanese and their property. Rysaku was familiar with Lyuh's influence over the Korean populace and knew that Lyuh had organized an underground secret society named the

Alliance for Korean Independence in 1944 when Korea was still under Japanese rule. Lyuh agreed to ensure that their safety would be secured but not their property and on August 15 all Korean political prisoners were freed. Lyuh looked after the safety of all Japanese residents in the Korean Peninsula. Before the arrival of Soviet troops, the Committee for the Preparation of National Reconstruction was established by Yur Woon-hyong. It included moderate nationalists and socialists, extreme right- and left-wing politicians abstaining. The committee functioned as a central government, its local committees serving as local governmental units throughout the entire country. The country was running smoothly without any violence.

The North Korean defectors who witnessed what happened during this period testified that none of the Japanese living in the North at that time was harmed because of the policy of Lyuh's temporary central government set up to protect Japanese residents until Soviet troops entered the North of Korea. The Soviet troops terrorized and raped many Japanese women and killed most of their husbands. I remember my parents reading a book written by a young Japanese woman who fled the North with a baby on her back, without her missing husband, and returned to Japan. She described how brutal those Soviet soldiers were, raping young women with children and confiscating any valuables they were carrying.

On September 2, 1945, Lyuh's committee members learned that Korea had been divided into two military occupational zones. The 38th parallel was a line hastily drawn when Americans learned about Soviet troop movement down the Korean Peninsula after they defeated Kwangtung Army in Manchuria. On August 10, 1945, two young officers—Dean Rusk and Charles Bonesteel—were assigned to define an American occupation zone. Working on extremely short notice and completely unprepared, they used a *National Geographic* map to decide on the 38th parallel without consulting any Korean leaders because it divided the country approximately in half but would leave the capital, Seoul, under American control. The decision was hastily written into General Order No.1 for the administration of postwar Japan. It's a sad irony that a line drawn so hastily by two young American officers has determined the fate of Korean people.

After learning this terrifying news Lyuh and company quickly resolved to establish a Korean government before the arrival of American troops. They organized the first cabinet of the Korean People's Republic on September 14, 1945, including President Syngman Rhee, Vice President Lyuh Woon-hyung, Minister of the Interior Kim Gu, Minister of Foreign Affairs Kim Gyu-sik, and Minister of Finance Cho Man-sik. One conspicuous omission from the list is Kim Il-sung. Another omission is the Yenan Koreans: Kim Ki-bong, Kim Mu-jong, and other hard-line Communists like Park Hon-young. It's clear that Lyuh tried his best to create a government in which everybody could cooperate to build a unified Korea. Lyuh did not want a communist government in Korea. At the same time he did not think American-style capitalism would be suitable to post– World War II Korea. He wanted to ensure that the new government would be able to deal with problems like the Donghak Revolt. As the list of cabinet members reveals, Lyuh placed Syngman Rhee's name as the president and he made sure Kim Gu and Kim Gyu-sik, the president and vice president of the PGRK, held the most important cabinet positions. Obviously, Lyuh was not working hard to establish his own power base. He always tried to work with all moderate members and he had the support of majority of Korean populace.

At this time Kim Il-sung was still in the Soviet Union. Cho Man-shik, a Christian leader known as Korea's Gandhi, was the leader in the North at this time. Only one item, land reform, in Lyuh's proclamation scared a small group of wealthy landlords in the South. But some sort of land reform was critically needed because that was the main cause of the Donghak Revolt. Unlike a rich country such as America with a huge expanse of fertile land and plenty of natural resources, Korea is a small nation with very limited fertile land. More than half of the country in the east is mountainous. A nation where a very small percentage of the population owned all the land, exploiting the large percentage of hardworking farmers as their tenants, cannot sustain long-term stability as a nation.

*Photo 3: The above photograph represents the four most active
national leaders at the time of trying to rebuild a new democratic
nation after the liberation of Korea from Imperial Japan in 1945. The
upper left: Lyuh Woon-hung, the upper right: Syngman Rhee, the
lower left: Kim Gyu-sik and the lower right : Kim Gu.*

Chapter 7: North Korea under Soviet Occupation and Introduction of Kim Il-sung (1945–1948)

When my father heard the news that Soviet troops had swiftly moved southward from Manchuria and by the end of August had occupied the entire area north of the 38th parallel, he was wondering why we still hadn't seen any of the US military personnel in Korea. He was also wondering why the US military allowed the Soviet troops to move into the Korean Peninsula. Korea was not a part of the deal for Soviets to participate in the Pacific War. This was when the U.S. was the most powerful and respected nation in the world and the economic conditions in the Soviet Union were in shambles after World War II. Father, who was familiar with the history of Russian ambition surrounding the Korean Peninsula and Russia's desire for Asian expansion was already concerned about Russian involvement in Korean affairs. He said, "Korea is now between the two world powers of conflicting political ideology. Like shrimps caught between two angry whales, Koreans can now be crushed to death." His predictions turned out to be accurate.

When Soviets arrived in Pyongyang they found the provincial and local committees for the Preparation of National Reconstruction functioning as local governmental units under the Peoples' Committee of the North headed by Cho Man-sik. This committee had been well recognized as the primary ruling body in the North by the Central People's Committee in Seoul headed by Lyuh Woon-hyung before the establishment of Korean People's Republic. Cho was the respected and the most popular leader in the north due to his constant resistance to the Japanese. Soviet officers regularly met with Cho and tried to convince him to head the emerging administration in North Korea but Cho did not trust Soviets and did not approve communist ideals. But it was already clear what the intention of Soviet policy was regarding the Korean peninsula. Cho would have agreed to cooperate with the Soviet authorities only on his own terms of extensive autonomy. Cho's conditions were not accepted by the Soviet leaders. Despite his rejection of Soviet requests he was able to remain as chairman of Pyongyang's People's Committee for a short time. Soviet faith that

Cho Man-sik could become the North Korean leader with Soviet ideals diminished and new hope was placed on Kim Il-sung.

If there had been no interference by the Soviets in post–World War II Korean affairs in the North Cho would have been the leader in the north, not Kim Il-sung. Cho was a well-qualified and respected leader. He was raised and educated in a traditional Confucian style but later converted to Protestantism and became a Christian leader of the North. From June 1908 to 1913, he studied Law at Meiji Univ. in Tokyo. It was during his stay in Tokyo that Cho learned about Gandhi's ideas of nonviolence. Cho later used the same nonviolent opposition to resist Japanese rule. His nonviolent struggle against Japanese occupation was well known in the North when my parents were living in Pyongyang. That's when my father met with this Christian leader and he often mentioned what a decent and intelligent man he was and mourned Cho's painful fate in a North Korean prison when his former friends from Pyungyang came to visit our family in Seoul many years later.

In early September, Kim Il-sung, who was a captain in the Soviet Red Army, returned to Korea with Soviet troops. Kim led about 300 men who had been in Russia, collectively known as the Partisan Faction. He moved quickly to establish his power with the support of the Soviets. In late September, Hyon Chun-hyok, leader of another group of Korean communists in the North, the Domestic Faction, was assassinated. The members of this group were those who were in Korea during the Japanese occupation and fought for Korean independence. This was the beginning of Kim Il-sung's use of violent terrorist tactics and it was apparent from the very beginning that the ideology of communism was not Kim Il-sung's primary objective. Establishing his absolute power base in Korea by eliminating any rival authority that could confront him was his only objective. It was a gamble for Stalin to put his confidence in Kim Il-sung but the Russian leader recognized Kim Il-sung's ruthless character and Soviet-trained tactics and supported him fully to gradually put the entire Korean Peninsula under communist control.

On October 14, 1945, the Soviets introduced Kim Il-sung to the people in Pyongyang as a "national hero," apparently intending to make him the leader of Korea. What did Kim Il-sung accomplish for Korean independence to be honored as a national hero? Kim Il-sung was born in 1912 as Kim Song-ju in Pyongyang. In 1919, when Kim Il-sung was seven years old, his father moved to Manchuria with his family, where he operated an herb pharmacy. Kim Il-sung received a Chinese education from Badaogou and Yuwen schools, which taught him Chinese language and customs. In the autumn of 1929, he was arrested and jailed for participating in a subversive Chinese student organization and consequently was expelled from the school. This was a small, short-lived group of fewer than a dozen people, led by a member of the South Manchurian Communist Youth Organization. Kim Song-ju was seventeen years old.

In 1930, when he was released from jail, he did not return to school and he never finished his high school education. Instead he joined a Chinese guerrilla group to fight the Japanese in Manchuria. At this time he changed his name to Kim Il-sung. The exact reason why he changed his name is not known but it is more likely he was following Stalin's example of name changing to fit his new image. Stalin was born Josef Dzhugashvili but later called himself "Stalin," man of iron, which fitted his new strong image much better. Kim's immediate superior was Wei Zhengmin, who had the most influence over him. Kim held important positions in the Chinese Communist Party and attended the Seventh Congress in Moscow and this was his first introduction into the manipulative world of politics.

In June 1937 Kim's band attacked the Japanese police station in the town of Poch'onbo near the Manchurian border and killed a number of policemen. The division he commanded in the Chinese Red Army had only about 300 men. He carried out mostly hit-and-run operations, but during the winter of 1937, there were many more casualties. In the end the Japanese crushed these guerrilla groups. The fighters who survived including Kim and about 120 of his compatriots fled north to the Soviet Union in 1940. The Chinese and Korean guerrillas were trained by the Soviets in three camps in Vladivostok and Khabarovsk area. The Russians trained these men to form part of an international unit in case they had to fight the Japanese.

Kim Il-sung was appointed major in the 88th Division of this international unit of the Far Eastern Command of the Soviet army. During this time the Russians must have recognized his leadership talent. He was given political as well as military training. During this period he would have seen the way Stalin was running Russia; purges in action, how to deal with any opposition or dissent, the development of the cult of Stalin, and how Stalin negotiated with other countries. He could not have received a better training for later life and he took the opportunity to build up his connections with both the Russians and the Chinese. These alliances would prove essential in his political career later in his life. Strangely enough, Kim Il-sung had never been a member of the PGRK and had never worked with any of the Korean leaders during the Japanese occupation of Korea. He had always been with Chinese communist organizations and eventually he joined the Soviet Red Army.

Kim Il-sung strengthened his power with Soviet support and conspired to eliminate the nationalists under Cho Man-shik as well as the Chondogyo sect, the followers of an indigenous religion originally called Donghak. In 1860, Choe Je-u (1824–1864), an illegitimate son of a high government official, received a revelation that gave birth to Chondogyo in Korea. The message that Choe Je-u developed over the course of his four-year ministry (1860–1864) found many millions of followers in Korea, fueled the Donghak Peasant Revolt, and played a leading role in the independence movement against the Japanese. The name Chondogyo means "Heavenly Way Religion." The fundamental doctrine is that every human being is an embodiment of heaven and should be duly revered by others. Furthermore his teaching advocated universal equality and elimination of all forms of discrimination related to age, gender, education, and other social conditions. The religion provided social groups such as farmers, peasants, and the oppressed poor with a sense of worth and dignity as they harbored deep resentment against the privileges of aristocracy and official corruption. Chondogyo sect members were rooted in the peasant class not rich capitalists who exploited the poor. But that didn't make any difference to Kim Il-sung. He did not tolerate any other authority, not even the God people worshipped. He wanted to make people worship him instead and he became a godlike figure in North Korea even after his death. He soon became the first secretary of the North Korean Bureau established October 15, 1945.

Shortly after that Kim Il-sung took further steps to establish more local communist parties. This resulted in a series of bloody clashes between the rightists and leftists in Yongam-po and anti-communist uprising that erupted in many cities such as Shinuiju, Pyongyang, and in Hum-heung. Students, factory workers, and other young people in the opposing camp took up arms and caused more than 1,000 deaths. Between November 1945 and the early spring of 1946, the Korean communists supported by the Soviets dealt cruelly with the nationalists and others who opposed them. Small uprisings and riots of anticommunist Koreans occurred later but each time the Soviets and Kim Il-sung suppressed all opposition by killing hundreds and forcing thousands of Koreans to flee to the South. A new form of terrorism became the rule in the North, and the people who were freed from Japanese colonial rule were put under an even more oppressive rule by Kim Il-sung's communist regime.

The Moscow Conference was the next step to settle Korean issue among the world powers without the participation of any Korean leaders, considering Koreans as unintelligent colonial people who could not manage their own country. The Moscow Conference of Foreign Ministers—James F. Byrnes of the United States, Ernest Bevin of the United Kingdom, and Vyacheslav Molotov of the Soviet Union—met in October 1945 to discuss the problems of occupation, establishing peace, and other Far East issues. The communiqué issued after the conference on December 27, 1945, contained a joint declaration that covered a number of issues resulting from the end of World War II, and it was signed by all the foreign ministers of the three powers. On the subject of postwar Korea the communiqué directed that the rival US and Soviet military commands in Korea would set up a joint commission to make recommendations for a single and free government in Korea. This commission was treated with great suspicion on both sides from its inception. The most critical issue was the decision that a four-power trusteeship of up to five years would be needed before Korea attained independence.

I was too young at the time to understand what all the fuss and the commotion were about over this issue. But I was surprised when I saw my father getting very vocal about this particular communiqué because he had always been very careful not to get involved in any political party and avoided any political discussions. It seemed that he could no longer remain silent on this particular issue. He joined his church members in protesting the Moscow Conference decision, saying that the Korean people should be able to resolve Korean issues without the world powers' involvement.

When I read all the details of the Moscow communiqué, I could clearly understand why Koreans including my father were so furious about this particular communiqué. The Soviet Union had already consolidated its power in the North by planting Kim Il-sung. At the same time the Kuomintang government of Chiang Kai-shek began to falter in China. China was one of the four trustee powers they kept bringing up but Chiang Kai-shek's government was not even represented in this conference. Section IV of the Moscow communiqué titled "China," clearly revealed that the Soviet Union was closely monitoring the situation in China and was well aware of the communist takeover there. They even postponed their troop withdrawal from Manchuria to wait for the communist victory in China even though their task of defeating Kwangtung Army in Manchuria was already completed by August 15 1945. This was the political game played by the Soviets to buy time.

It's disappointing to learn that the American government was cooperating with the Soviets and being toyed with by Stalin's game. The nationalists in the North encountered many difficulties under the Soviet occupation and ultimately their opposition to the Moscow agreement brought about their downfall in early 1946 as Cho Man-shik was put under house arrest and many nationalists fled to the South. Sadly this was the end of one of the most respected Christian leaders since Cho never recovered his leadership position. He was eventually jailed and died in horrible and inhumane conditions. I remember reading a report about the intolerable conditions by a North Korean defector who was in the same jail with Cho. Cho spent his last days in a severely weakened state, buried in his own excrement, and died. Kim Il-sung didn't want to release Cho even in the last days of his life. Km Il-sung gradually consolidated his absolute power in North Korea with Stalinist brutality and by building up his character cult to crush all his political rivals.

After more than a half century, it's been demonstrated that the communist leaders of Russia can manipulate the policies of foreign governments to determine the fate of those nations and their people. Soviet Union created the three generation's of communist dynasty with the worst human right's abuse in North Korea by introducing Kim Il-sung, their well trained Red Army captain, as the national hero to help him to become the head of North Korean government. The KGB's skillful methods of manipulation are still alive and very far reaching. Look what they did to the U.S. 2016 Presidential election?

Chapter 8: The USAMGIK in South Korea and Lyuh Woon-hyung's Fate (1945–1948)

On September 6, 1945, finally 72,000 American troops under Lieutenant General John R. Hodge landed at Inchon and proceeded to Seoul. For the first time we saw American military men wearing cute little wedge caps ("garrison caps") in Jeeps on the streets of Seoul. Since majority of Koreans had never seen Caucasians except in movies, they all looked like movie stars to us and they were ardently welcomed by all Koreans as our liberators from Imperial Japan. The next day Japanese governor-general Abe Nobuyki surrendered to the Americans. The Japanese troops were disarmed quickly without any incident. The Americans had no knowledge of Korean history, culture, or economic and social conditions, and none spoke Korean. From the start General Hodge made a grave mistake. General Kozuki Yoshio, commander of the Japanese forces in Korea, warned General Hodge that Koreans were led by "communist agitators." Yoshio described Koreans as savages bent on obstruction of whatever the US force might do in Korea, and he offered his full cooperation in keeping Koreans under control. Beginning his assignment with this type of negative information prejudiced completing his mission successfully.

In the declassified document, IN THE SPHINX, A HISTORY OF ARMY COUNTER INTELLIGENCE CORPS (CIC) summarized by James L. Gilbert, John P. Finnegan and Ann Bray, they describe their Korean mission as a *terra incognita,* meaning unknown or unexplored territory. They also describe their major handicap as the lack of language skills and orientation to Korean culture. Despite the enormous effort and sacrifices of Lyuh to save the future of Korea, the CIC document described Lyuh simply as someone who had a small underground resistance force against the Japanese occupation who became the head of the Labor Party after the liberation. There was no mention of the Korean People's Republic he organized or PGRK. The CIC must have obtained this type of information from the same Japanese authorities living in Korea at the time. The CIC also conducted a liaison effort with several right-wing political youth organizations such as the North West Young Men's Association to gather important information on the Korean society. This is the same paramilitary youth organization comprised of North Korean refugees. General MacArthur's men describe them as nothing but murderous gangsters and ultra-right lunatics. If the CIC personnel really wanted to collect accurate information to understand the situation in Korea they should have directly communicated with Korean leaders like Lyuh Woon-hyung, Kim Gu or Kim Gyu-sik who had first-hand knowledge of Korean history and culture and were respected by the majority of Koreans. Why they chose the type of people they did to guide their mission bespeaks an existing prejudice against the Korean intellect and capabilities.

Unfortunately General Hodge was not much better than the CIC personnel. He was unaware that none of the Korean People's Republic, or PGRK members was a communist. Following Yoshio's suggestions General Hodge announced that all Japanese officials, including Governor-General Abe, would be retained in office temporarily in order to facilitate the administration of post–World War II Korean affairs in the South. This means that some 70,000 Japanese officials who were bitterly despised by Koreans remained in the government to help Hodge to administer Korean affairs. Further, Hodge outlawed the Korean People's Republic, organized with moderate and distinguished Korean nationalists who eagerly wanted to cooperate with each other to build a unified Korea. Hodge also dismissed the PGRK, the de jure government of Korea during the Japanese occupation, as the legitimate government of Korea. Then he established the US Army Military Government in Korea (USAMGIK) in September as the only government in the South. General Hodge didn't make any effort to listen to Lyuh's opinion before making his announcement. Obviously the American government had no respect for Koreans treating them simply as an Asian colonial people.

My father and his friends who were all well versed in Korean history were very disappointed and felt that this was an insult to all Koreans. Lyuh, who had worked so hard to build a unified Korea was devastated. He resigned from his post in the disallowed government. Then he formed the Working People's Party including more radical elements to continue to fight for the People's Republic. Koreans who had enthusiastically welcomed American troops as their liberators were disappointed. In fact their resentment against Americans grew rapidly. The first mistake Americans made was to see Koreans as Asian colonials who were not ready to enjoy independence, freedom and democracy and therefore had to be educated and trained under the supervision of the intellectually and politically superior Allied powers. The Allied powers included the Soviet Union, the United States, the United Kingdom and China. Meanwhile, Chiang Kai-shek's nationalist government of the Republic of China was already on the verge of falling to Mao Zedong's Communist Party. Stalin was well aware of this situation.

Sadly Koreans were denied the opportunity to build a peaceful and united nation even though Korea had many capable political leaders who were respected and beloved by the majority Korean people. They had intimate knowledge of the major problems of the last Korean kingdom in which the aristocratic class exploited the lower-class poor peasants and they were determined to work together to create a new democratic nation suitable for Korea, giving equal opportunity to all citizens. What a missed opportunity for the Korean people! Anyone can imagine the pain and disappointment Lyuh felt when Hodge outlawed the Korean People's Republic he so carefully organized without consulting him or any other Koreans leaders. The first two decisions Hodge made shortly after he arrived in Korea were dreadful, careless blunders by the U.S. government. And those actions were the turning point for many Koreans in trusting Americans as hope for the future. But this was not the end of the tragedy for this honorable and brave man, Lyuh Woon-hyung. The bright sunshine he had dreamt of for his new nation for many painful years was blocked by the thick black clouds of careless ignorance and disrespect.

In 2009, the newly elected American president Barack Obama spoke of the mistakes the American government has often made in foreign policy which ended up with disastrous results. He said this has happened because the American government has a tendency to dictate instead of listening and trying to understand a situation first before taking any action. The handling of post–World War II Korea is a glaring example. It would have been much easier for Hodge if he had recognized the Korean People's Republic and worked with its cabinet members that included moderate right and left politicians.

By this time Korean leaders who had fought for Korean independence abroad during the Japanese occupation of Korea were beginning to return home one by one. In October 1945, Syngman Rhee returned to Korea under American advice as a private citizen and not as a former president of the PGRK. He was nevertheless welcomed as a national hero by both Koreans and Americans, since he was known to be one of the leading Korean independence fighters and since he also served as the first president of the PGRK until he was removed due to irregularities in the PGRK's fund management. On his arrival he immediately created the Committee for Rapid Realization of Korean Independence that was joined by some 50 nationalist political parties. But the leftists did not join the group and continued to carry out their own agenda. Obviously Rhee's objective and the method of building an inclusive new nation were very different from that of Lyuh's.

Meanwhile, President Kim Gu and Vice President Kim Gyu-sik of the PGRK returned to Korea from China as private citizens because the USAMGIK refused to recognize the PGRK as the legitimate Korean government. Many Koreans including my parents and their friends rightfully felt that this was yet another insult to those who had sacrificed their lives for Korean independence for over 35 years. My father who had admired the successful democratic system of American government that had lasted so long began to wonder about many American policies toward Korea. He wondered, "Who in the American government is making all these misguided decisions that would certainly lead to a tragedy on the Korean Peninsula? If they don't know much about Korean history why doesn't somebody in the State Department read about real Korean history and learn instead of relying on the Japanese opinion of the Korean people?" He was disappointed and confused after waiting patiently for the Allied victory in the Pacific War to finally see a free and democratic Korea. It is certainly puzzling that Hodge and the US military command gave such credence to Japanese opinions of others having themselves learned of viscous Japanese brutality during the war.

Syngman Rhee (March 26, 1875–July 19, 1965) was born in Hwanghae Province into a rural family of modest means as the only son. Rhee's family traced its lineage back to King Taejong of the Joseon dynasty. (Taejong had helped his father, Yi Seong-gye, to overthrow the Goryeo dynasty by assassinating the powerful Goryeo official Jeong Mong-ju and established the Joseon dynasty in 1392). In 1877, his family moved to Seoul and there he received a traditional Confucian education. In 1894, he enrolled in the Baeje middle school, an American Methodist school, and studied English and journalism. Near the end of 1895, he joined the HyubSeong Club created by Seo Jae-pil, who had lived in the United States. He worked as the editor and main writer of the newspapers *HyubSeong HyeBo* and *Maeil Shinmoon*. During this period he earned money by teaching Korean language to Americans as my maternal grandmother did and he converted to Christianity.

In November 1904, Syngman Rhee moved to the United States. Rhee studied successively at George Washington, Harvard, and Princeton universities, earning his Ph.D. from Princeton. In 1911 Rhee returned to Korea under Japanese occupation as a YMCA teacher-evangelist but Japanese suspicions soon drove him back to the United States. From 1913 to 1940 he based his activities in Hawaii where he was principal of a Korean school and leader of a Korean expatriate faction called Tongjihoe (Comrades' Society). Rhee had a relatively easy and peaceful life in Hawaii compared to the lives of PGRK members living in China that was politically unstable since it was already undergoing a communist revolution and had to fight Japanese expansion. Rhee continued his vigorous campaigning for Korean independence. Rhee's status as a fighter and spokesman for Korea's cause was such that after the Korean independence uprising of March 1, 1919, he was named president of the PGRK in Shanghai. However his relations with other Korean leaders in Shanghai were strained. The PGRK accused Rhee of misappropriating its funds and he was impeached in 1925 and replaced by Kim Gu. But Rhee refused to recognize the action. Although Rhee had an impressive academic background and was educated in America he was inflexible and had an authoritarian personality. He could not work harmoniously with his colleagues to establish a unified democratic country. Unfortunately the American government did not recognize the negative qualities in Rhee's personality.

Kim Gu (August 29, 1876–June 26, 1949)—also known by his pen name, Baek Beom—has been generally regarded as one of the greatest figures in modern Korean history. He exiled himself to Shanghai, China in 1919 after the nationwide nonviolent resistance movement of March 1, 1919 was violently suppressed by the Japanese imperialist government. In Shanghai, Kim Gu joined the PGRK, which was determined to liberate Korea from Japanese occupation. In 1927, he became the president of the PGRK and was reelected to the office many times by the Provisional Assembly. He was the sixth and last president of the PGRK which lasted from 1919 to 1948. In 1931 he organized the Korean Patriotic Legion. One of the members of this legion, Yoon Bong-gil, ambushed the Japanese military leader - the commander of the Japanese army and navy, - who died in Shanghai on April 29, 1932. After escaping to Chongqing where Chang Kai-shek's nationalist government was established Kim Gu established the Korean Liberation Army commanded by General Ji Cheong-cheon. When WWII broke out on December 8, 1941 Kim Gu declared war on Japan and Germany and committed the Korean Liberation Army to the Allied side which took part in the fighting in China and Southeast Asia. Kim led the Korean Liberation Army in an advance on Korea in 1945. But days before the departure of the leading unit Japan surrendered and the war ended. Kim Gu was a right-wing politician, a strong anticommunist.

Kim Gyu-sik (January 29, 1881–December 10, 1950) was orphaned at a young age. He studied with the American missionary H.G. Underwood from the age of six, taking the Christian name Johann. Later he traveled to America, receiving a bachelor's degree from Roanoke College in 1903 and a master's degree from Princeton University the following year. In 1905 he returned to Korea, teaching widely, and fled to China in 1913 following the Japanese annexation of Korea in 1910. In 1919, Kim Gyu-sik traveled to Paris for the Paris

Peace Conference to lobby for Korean independence from Japan. He was sent by Lyuh Woon-hyung and Chang Duk-soo, who organized Sinhan Cheongnyeon-dang in Shanghai in the summer of 1919. His efforts in Paris were fruitless since the United States—even though its president Woodrow Wilson had championed the cause of national self-determination in his 14 Points—had no interest in upsetting its close ally Japan.

By October of 1945, the three former PGRK top leaders, Kim Gu, Kim Gyu-sik and Syngman Rhee were all in the South but sadly Rhee and the two Kims did not get along. Their personality clashes caused serious problems within the right-wing camp. Rhee made no effort whatsoever to work with either Kim Gu or Kim Gyu-sik. As my father always worried about infighting among different political factions as happened during the last days of the Joseon dynasty the political situation in the South was causing him great concern. The country was standing at a cross roads. We were thinking, "What if we choose the wrong way? What if we miss this chance? Do our leaders realize they have to work together to preserve our future?" However, ordinary citizens didn't have enough political influence to pressure our leaders or the US government to get together to make the right decision for the future of Korea – even if we knew.

For most of us life had to go on without knowing the future. The bone-chilling winter was approaching rapidly and it was time for Kimchang to prepare Kimchi for the winter. Kimchi s a traditional fermented Korean side dish made of vegetables with a variety of seasonings. Traditionally, kimchi is stored underground in jars to keep it unfrozen during winter and kept cool during summer. There are hundreds of varieties of kimchi made from napa cabbage, radish, scallion, or cucumber as the main ingredients. The most common seasonings include brine, scallions, spices, ginger, chopped radish, garlic, shrimp sauce, oyster sauce, and fish sauce. Kimchi has now become popular side dishes to those who acquired the taste of Kimchi in America as well as other regions of the world. Many American G.I.s loved Kimchi. When China had the bird-flu epidemic in 1996 Korean business men visiting China at the time did not contract the flu. People jokingly said that it must have been the spices in Kimchi that deactivated H5N1 virus. Young people were also getting married without delaying their marriage wearing traditional Korean customs. Thus the lives of ordinary people were going on as usual amid the pandemonium at the top. Life must go on as it always does.

Photo 4: Traditional Korean customs of bridegroom and bride at their wedding.

At the same time, the political saga at the top continued. As discussed in the previous chapter the Moscow plan was initially opposed by all Koreans in both the North and South. The *Dong-A Ilbo*, a leading daily newspaper that reemerged after August 1945, described the Moscow agreement as offensive and an insult to all Koreans. The Korean people having suffered an alien colonial domination for 35 years absolutely refused to accept another foreign rule whether it was for a short or a long period. Never has there been more Korean unity than at the time of the anti-trusteeship movement that began on December 28, 1945. In the South Syngman Rhee encouraged nationwide strikes and his never-cordial relationship with

General Hodge worsened. On January 3, 1946 the communists in both the North and the South suddenly changed their position to support the Moscow plan, realizing that the plan would favor Kim Il-sung with support from Moscow. But the nationalists who followed Rhee, along with Kim Gu and Kim Gyu-sik, fervently rejected the plan.

General Hodge felt that it was necessary to improve relations with Rhee so he established the 25-member Representative Democratic Council in February 1946, with Rhee as its chairman. But still the relationship between Hodge and Rhee did not improve. Rhee charged that moderate leftists such as Lyuh Woon-hyung used the council for their own political gain. Rhee, America's pick as the leader of the new Korea, was a major problem for Hodge. Rhee was unwilling to tolerate any other prominent Korean leaders' views but his own. The antagonism between the two grew even greater in 1946 when Hodge gave his strong support to Kim Gyu-sik and Lyuh Woon-hyung who formed the Coalition Committee for Cooperation between the Rightists and the Leftists, composed of moderate nationalists and socialists.

At this stage, Kim Gyu-sik and Lyuh realized the uselessness of Korean opposition to the Moscow plan and the work of the joint commission since the trustee nations considered Koreans to be simple colonials who were left without any power to veto the plans that were formulated by great world powers. As an alternative solution they declared that they would establish "a transitional government" in cooperation with the joint commission and they would secure Korean independence by unifying the rightists and leftists (May 1946–August 1947). Most Koreans heartily welcomed this new policy which, had it been implemented earlier in September 1945, might have contributed to the emergence of a unified and   democratic Korea before Kim Il-sung was brought in by the Soviets. But that didn't happen and the critical time was already lost. In the end General Hodge even tried to accept and secure Korea by unifying both the rightists and leftists despite Syngman Rhee's opposition. Although Hodge made many wrong decisions immediately after he arrived in Korea, he tried his best toward the end of his administration to establish a workable government in the South. Unfortunately his time had run out.

Syngman Rhee began harassing the Coalition Committee. On June 3, in the so-called "Jeongeup Speech," Rhee made a bombshell declaration. South Korea alone had to establish something like a provisional government or committee to get rid of the USSR above the 38th parallel. This was the first time that he announced his plan to establish a separate government in the South. He also visited the United States from December 7, 1946, to April 21, 1947, spending almost five months working to convince US leaders that the South should be given independent government status and be admitted to the United Nations. Until this time, the USAMGIK and Washington had already declared that a unified Korea was the primary goal. It was therefore obvious that Rhee's mission was contrary to the aims and purposes expressed by the United States. However, Rhee was given priority for his trip and was granted a long conference with General MacArthur to discuss the issue. It seems that Rhee was able to sway the United States and General MacArthur to support his idea to prevent the South from becoming a communist country. Rhee and his Korean Democratic Party mobilized the rightist paramilitary youth organization to explain the separate government plan to the Korean people. But the majority of Koreans did not support Rhee's Korean Democratic Party or it's plan. Most Koreans still wanted a unified country. This was revealed by an opinion poll compiled by the USAMGIK.

General Hodge desperately sought the support of moderate nationalists and leftists, including Lyuh Woon-hyung. The hostile antagonism between Hodge and Rhee worsened when Hodge, in October 1946, gave his strong support to Kim Gyu-sik and Lyuh Woon-hyung, who had by this time formed the Coalition Committee for Cooperation between the Rightists and the Leftists. Hodge also disclosed his plan to establish the South Korean Interim Legislative Assembly to replace the Representative Democratic Council that was largely made up of rich landlords. The South Korean Interim Legislative Assembly accomplished virtually nothing except the passage of a limited land reform and a franchise law endorsed by the new military governor, Major General William Dean, in August of 1947. Because he got virtually no cooperation from Syngman Rhee

Hodge encountered many difficulties in dealing with the Koreans as well as the Soviets, and became frustrated.

To make matters worse the proliferation of political groups was so chaotic and unmanageable that a majority of the Americans in Korea lost interest in further involvement and made plans go home abandoning any further concern for the Korean people's future. Realizing the ineffectiveness of trying to resolve the Korean question by negotiating with the Soviets, General Hodge finally adopted a plan to establish the South Korean Interim Government. Ahn Chae-hong, a moderate nationalist, who was a close associate of Kim Gyu-sik, was designated in early February 1947 as civil administrator. Only after the South Korea Interim Government was established, all Japanese officials retained in the government since 1945 were removed. As of August 1947, there were 3,231 Americans in the military government, of whom 2591 were military officers and 637 were civilians.

On July 19, 1947, in broad daylight, Lyuh Woon-hyung who had been mentioned as a possible candidate to head the proposed provisional Korean government was assassinated.

This event might have been related to Hodge's new policy involving Lyuh in his plan. His death was mourned nationwide by a majority of Koreans. He had given up his comfortable life, gave away most of his family fortune, freed the slaves, and dedicated himself to Korean independence and establishment of a unified democratic Korea. The major objective of Lyuh's political career was to resolve the fundamental problem of Korean society reflected by the Donghak Peasant Revolt at the end of the Joseon dynasty. But he was much too popular among majority of Koreans to stay alive in this cruel and inhumane political atmosphere. Although he was beloved by the majority of the Korean populace he had never been able to obtain support from extreme right and left politicians because of his desire to build an inclusive new nation from both parties by gathering moderate members who were willing to cooperate and work together.

When Father heard of Lyuh's assassination, he cried silently and went out in the dark to the nearby mountains to absorb this new event. He came home late at night with a simple flute made of native bamboo and played melancholic tunes deep into the night. Lyuh's assassin was a 19-year-old boy, Han Chigeun, a recent refugee from the North. It was a public opinion at the time that this 19-year-old boy couldn't possibly have his own political motive to kill Lyuh. Then, who would be the person behind this criminal activity? There were many assassinations but ordinary citizens could not find out any details about the truth about any criminal activities.

Recently a video of Lyuh's funeral scene has been uploaded to YouTube in which one can hear the cries of millions of Koreans shouting, "How could you leave us this way? Who is going to take care of our country now?"

Who was behind Lyuh's assassination? During January and February of 1947, Lyuh was busy trying to rebuild his People's Party which was destroyed by Park Hun-yong, a South Korean communist party leader. The plot to murder Lyuh began intensely as General Hodge, who was having lots of problems with Rhee, was turning to seek help from nationalists like Lyuh and Kim Gyu-sik. On March 17, 1947 Lyuh's bedroom was bombed but he escaped. On April 3, 1947 would-be assassins fired on his car, but Lyuh again escaped. On the night (July 18, 1947) before his assassination, Lyuh stayed at Jung Mu-guk's house for safety. At about 9:00 a.m., Lyuh left in a car for Kim Ho's house at Sungbuk-dong in order to say goodbye to his old friend Kim Yong-jung, a Korean American businessman returning to the United States that day. Kim Yong-jung believed that Syngman Rhee and Kim Gu lacked leadership ability or a majority political support base in Korea after decades of life abroad and believed that Lyuh was the right man to lead Korea. He was planning to discuss this situation with the State Department when he returned to the United States.

After parting with Kim Yong-jung, Lyuh phoned Nan-gu, his eldest daughter, and told her to get a clean shirt ready for him. He was on his way home for a quick change. Lyuh stopped by Jung Mu-guk's house briefly and left for his house in Geh-dong. He was to attend a friendly soccer match between Korean and visiting British teams as he was trying to make Korea a participant nation in the Olympics. Lyuh headed the Korean Olympic Committee at the time. When Lyuh's car slowed down at the Hyehwa-dong intersection a large truck suddenly pulled out from behind the police station and blocked its progress. Lyuh's driver slammed on the brakes and the car came to a screeching halt. The assassin jumped on the rear bumper and fired two pistol shots at Lyuh through the rear window. One hit Lyuh's back and came out of his stomach and the other went through his heart killing him instantly.

It was 1:00 p.m. The father of Korean democracy was dead, murdered by an impoverished refugee from the North. The shooter was eventually sentenced to death but he was secretly released. He took a false name and emigrated to Japan. Many decades later it was revealed that Lyuh's assassin, Han Chigeun, was a member of an ultra-right Youth Paramilitary organization. Very little information regarding this organization was known at the time but more than half a century later many details of these secret "Youth" organizations have been revealed a little at a time. The information can be found in autobiographies of US military personnel, previously silenced eyewitnesses, tortured but surviving victims, and declassified US Counterintelligence Corps (CIC) documents.

In this information age, anybody can post all kinds of story or "history" on the Internet and nobody checks the accuracy of their assertions, an ideal situation for historical revisionists. Consequently misleading information can confuse the younger people of South Korea with a variety of negative consequences. Thus I decided to be especially diligent in verifying the accuracy of available sources in detailing this book. I will discuss other findings of surprising and hard to believe activities of secret societies and how they conducted their criminal activities in later chapters.

Briefly, there is no evidence that the USAMGIK or the US CIC ordered those assassinations as some Koreans believe. That doesn't mean they were innocent bystanders. They apparently made no effort to prevent assassinations or civilian massacres in many cases. The USAMGIK disallowed both the Korean People's Republic and the PGRK and established the USAMGIK as the only legitimate government of South in Korea at the time. Therefore, it undoubtedly owned at least some responsibility for civil law and order. Why didn't the USAMGIK actively try to prevent political assassinations? Casual indifference or did it really care? Did they think those assassinations were just internal affairs? It must have known much more about the existence of criminal organizations than ordinary citizens did.

Under the USAMGIK, law and order was maintained by the CIC and the Criminal Investigation Division of the US Army, assisted by the Korean national police. At this time many Korean policemen and officers who had been in the Japanese police force were rehired to assist the USAMGIK and the Criminal Investigation Division. These unsophisticated men emulated Japanese brutality toward civilians and this contributed to the people's hostility toward the government. There were about 30,000 policemen toward the end of the American occupation. The judiciary was dominated by graduates of Japanese law schools and the Americans did not carry out any significant judicial or legal reforms.

The country was in economic chaos. The shortage of food, fuel, clothing, electricity, and other consumer goods coupled with a rapidly rising unemployment rate caused many serious problems. To make matters worse the severity of the winter of 1945–1946 was record-breaking. Prevention of epidemics and widespread starvation seemed to be the primary concern of the USAMGIK. The United States provided a $15 million loan and $409.3 million in relief funds between 1945 and 1948. The relief funds of the Government Appropriation for Relief in Occupied Areas (GARIOA) program prevented starvation and many deaths.

GARIOA funds were used to support an agricultural recovery and imported chemical fertilizers from the United States. American wheat flour was imported along with dried milk, medical supplies, and clothing. The UN Relief Rehabilitation Agency assisted, saving the lives of thousands of children and elderly. Because of the stubborn opposition of the members of the South Korean Interim Legislative Assembly who were largely landlords the USAMGIK failed to adopt a desperately needed land reform. Perhaps it was in educational and cultural fields that the Americans made their most significant contributions. The granting of freedom of thought, speech, and the press (which was significantly curtailed later by Syngman Rhee during the First Republic) at last liberated Koreans from various laws and restrictions that had been detrimental to the development of free education and culture.

Chapter 9: Our Family Life under the USAMGIK
(1945–1948)

Immediately after the liberation of Korea Father was offered a job as a bank president specializing in international business. The Korean financial field at that time could not find enough qualified people with knowledge in English to manage international business. The recruiter pressured my father to take the position telling him that he should not miss such a lucrative and rare opportunity. However, becoming rich had never been my father's goal in life. He was more like a philosopher and often talked about metaphysics. The financial field seemed much too shallow for him. He was convinced it spoiled men's otherwise pure minds. He thought that the best way to spend his life was to stay in academia and teach young people to become a historically knowledgeable future generation with good judgment for the welfare of the country. He chose to stay in academia and became a professor of English literature at Sookmyung Women's College which was located on the south side of Seoul.

The surrounding town had belonged to many Japanese people during the Japanese occupation. After the Japanese surrender, they were hurriedly packing up to return to Japan, some abandoning their houses. My parents found several very nice homes near Sookmyung Women's College. My mother wanted a home with a pretty flower garden in a quiet neighborhood away from the school but my father found a house located right behind the college dormitory with a large vegetable garden, almost one acre, and many fruit trees. I believe my father wanted fruit trees and a vegetable garden to help support his growing family. But mother's instinct was very negative about the moving into that neighborhood with unfamiliar people who seemed to be refugees from the North. She was also not very eager to leave a neighborhood where she had many good friends.

Although some refugees and many nationalists fled the North to escape communism more people fled to escape persecution. Kim Il-sung began arresting and mercilessly executing anyone suspected of being a Japanese collaborator. A big problem was that the USAMGIK didn't have any organization or special fund to take care of those refugees. The neighborhood homes were modest middle-class homes, not as nice as the one my father picked out, and the people who moved into the homes opposite our new home didn't seem like the type of people who could have afforded these homes. It was likely they just moved in when the Japanese residents moved out. It turned out my father's decision to buy this particular home at this location was an omen for our family and what would happen in this house and in this neighborhood five years later. There is a saying that women's intuition is very good but Father made the big decisions in our family.

When my father knocked on the door to negotiate the price of the house with the Japanese owner of the home, a former executive of a bank, he begged my father to move our family in right away for the protection of the owner and his family. They were afraid some other Koreans might try to confiscate their property before they were ready to return to Japan. I believe that was what was going on elsewhere in that neighborhood. My father, who was every inch a gentleman and did not believe in confiscating anyone's property even if they were Japanese occupiers of Korean property negotiated the price, paid for the house, and moved our family in before we sold our old home.

This new home had nine persimmon trees, a cherry tree, a sweet date (jujube) tree, a chestnut tree, an apple tree, a peach tree, grape vines, and a large vegetable garden. The downstairs had the master bedroom, a large tatami living room (a traditional Japanese-style room), a fancy guest room, a small maid's room, a bathroom, restrooms for men and women, and a kitchen. The upstairs had two large tatami rooms, a long corridor with shiny wooden floors, picture windows, and a deck with a distant view of the Han River. The front yard had all the fruit and flower trees. The side yard facing south was covered with a very thick reinforced concrete floor, which also served as the roof of the well-built bunker beneath—it could withstand most air raids. We could go down to the bunker by lifting the sturdy cover on this concrete floor. From the bunker, we could get out a door that opened to the vegetable garden. Since the house was built on a slight hill it looked as if it was sitting on the second level and the vegetable garden was on the ground level. It was a beautiful home except that as a Japanese style home it had thin walls that do not insulate the house adequately in cold weather. Each room needed a wood- or coal-burning stove to keep warm.

The USAMGIK was the official ruling body of the southern half of Korea from September 8, 1945 to August 15, 1948. During this period, the country was challenged by political and economic chaos. The US military was largely unprepared for administering the country arriving with no knowledge of the language, culture, history, or political situation. Thus many of their policies had unintended consequences. Waves of refugees from the North (approximately 400,000) and returnees from abroad also created more turmoil. Worst of all, inflation was skyrocketing. My frugal mother was having a hard time because what she saved very quickly lost its value. Mother used to buy bits and pieces of 24-karat gold with her little savings for emergency use since she could sell those gold nuggets at a higher price to keep up with inflation. Nobody was using banks to save their money. The USAMGIK was not organized to control inflation in Korea at that time—the country was too fraught with power struggles among different political parties.

The private college at which my father taught was having a hard time paying professors' salaries regularly, and our family often ran out of food or fuel to heat the house in the severely cold winter. Many times, we were out of rice and had to eat sujebi, a vegetable soup with a kind of impromptu pasta made from flour brought from America as an aid to prevent starvation. To make matters worse, the winter of 1945 was unusually cold and snowy and the inside of our Japanese-style home was particularly cold. When I went into the kitchen early in the morning during that winter to help my mother or our live-in maid, I used to notice very elaborate frost patterns on the kitchen windows frozen overnight from the steam generated from cooking dinner the night before. It exhibited various patterns of very distinct and perfectly symmetrical hexagons. I could see an ice forest with a snowy road among many tall trees standing on both sides of the road, all maintaining perfect fractal geometry. My mother used to wake me up by yelling at me saying, "What are you dreaming about standing there looking out that window? Hurry up if you don't want to be late to school again." (I was often late to school because I always went to bed very late, reading lots of books or studying and getting up late. I have always been a night owl not a morning person.).

After the awful first winter, my father was offered a presidential position at Chesin Communications Institute. It was not a private school but a college-level national institute so he decided to take the job because, unlike private schools, it didn't have problems paying regular salaries to its faculty members. A high-ranking US military officer, Lt. Colonel Stanley, was there to oversee the school management. Since my father was able to communicate with Lt. Colonel Stanley in English they got along very well. I remember the weekend trip our family took with him in his jeep to visit a couple of well-known Buddhist temples on the outskirts of Seoul. My mother prepared all kinds of food for this trip and he ate the same food as his lunch. One day after listening to a speech Father gave to the faculty and students Lt. Colonel Stanley was appeared very impressed with my father's oratorical skills even though he didn't understand Korean. He had been watching the reactions of the audience and praised my father for his eloquent speech. He was confident in my father's ability to manage that school so he put in good words for him to his superiors in the USAMGIK. He also helped my father financially, providing adequate budgets to improve the school's faculty, equipment, and facilities. At the same time Father was a very active and hardworking administrator, always full of energy. He knew it took many people to get all the school's necessary work done as rapidly as possible so he recruited better-qualified faculty members and paid regular monthly salaries without skipping even a month. Although he was not aware at the time, he also made some enemies by eliminating poorly qualified faculty members who then held grudges against him.

He was so successful in upgrading and building up the Chesin Communications Institute that in 1947 he was able to start another school on the same campus, a tuition-free Heungook middle school primarily for children of refugees from the North. Being a naïve, old-fashioned educator, he thought that they needed a good education and good guidance to become responsible citizens because he noticed that these youngsters seemed to belong to some sort of youth organization to support themselves and were doing the dirty work of powerful politicians. Being a simple, conservative educator, he didn't imagine the level of power the paramilitary organization had over civilians at the time. He didn't know that his goodwill effort was going to come back to hurt him and almost destroy his career only a few years later.

For my father this was an exciting time because he had full support from his supervising American army officer. Being able to build and steadily make progress with full financial support made my workaholic father very happy. The school even had a military jeep and a chauffeur, probably arranged by the American officer to help my father so he didn't have to struggle to get to work using the unreliable public transportation of the time. Meanwhile, our family's economic situation was gradually improving as well, because my mother could count on his salary every month. She began renovating the home. First, she converted the main bedroom and another small room on the main floor from tatami to a Korean-style ondol, with a warm floor heated from below so they wouldn't have to worry about another winter using coal-burning stoves. Burning coal inside the house not only made the rooms very dirty but was also dangerous on rainy or snowy days when there was incomplete combustion of the coal releasing carbon monoxide gas. A year later, my mother gave birth to her fifth child, the third son, Soo , a handsome boy taking after the maternal side's good looks and paternal side's bright brain.

My mother met a very nice Japanese lady in the neighborhood who was married to a Korean pharmacist and had two little boys. She didn't look like a typical, dainty Japanese woman. She was tall and very rugged looking and my father used to say she must be from the northern island of Japan, Hokkaido. She decided not to return to Japan and tried to learn the Korean language well enough to communicate with Koreans. She visited our home quite often to discuss many matters with my mother, usually in Japanese mixed with broken Korean. They became close friends.

Unfortunately the renovation work attracted the attention of some thieves in the neighborhood and our home was broken into three times in just one winter. They took everything valuable, including the beautiful Siberian tiger coats of Mother's, mine, and my brother's, all of which my father bought for us when we were living in Manchuria. When our family was living in Manchuria, Siberian tiger coats were very fashionable items in both Russia and Manchuria. Siberian tigers are one of the most beautiful cats on this planet but unfortunately their numbers are now dwindling because they have been hunted for their beautiful fur almost to extinction. The Siberian tigers are confined completely to the Amur region in the Far East where they are now protected. I would not wear a tiger coat even if I had one now. Since we hadn't seen anyone wearing tiger coats in Korea we thought it would be easy to trace the coats if the thief tried to sell them in the market but they never showed up while we were still living in Seoul.

We suspected that the thief who broke into our home was one of our neighbors. Their house was built like a duplex and we could see the activities inside of both homes from the second floor window of either my brother's room or my room, which were next to each other. It seemed that both units housed refugees from the North. We didn't know how they were making a living. They didn't seem to have jobs, and the government didn't have a subsidy program for refugees at the time. The unit on the left side housed a family consisting of a father, mother, and two young daughters while the home on the right housed an elderly lady with a daughter in her late twenties or early thirties. The daughter had a boyfriend who seemed to be a Korean army officer, probably also from the North. One day from the second-floor window of the room where my sister and I slept, I saw the father of the family living on the left side knocking on their front door around 3:00 a.m. with a big fat backpack on his back. I woke up to go to the bathroom but I looked out of the window because I heard some noise outside.

My mother reminded my father about this neighborhood with strange people and asked him to do something about it to prevent any more break-ins. In the neighborhood where we lived previously, we never heard of any home break-ins. So my father's chauffeur brought us a very smart and well-trained German shepherd as a guard dog. We named her Mary. She was indeed a very smart dog and she stopped our string of home break ins. At one time when I was walking Mary outside of our home, that neighbor of ours threw a piece of fresh red meat to Mary, probably to test her response. But Mary looked at the meat and looked at that man and began growling and barking instead of eating the meat. Mary was too smart for thieves to trick her with a piece of meat. This was another clue that the neighbor was up to no good.

Since our family's financial situation was slowly improving, my parents were now more relaxed and we finally began to enjoy our family life for a change. It's very important for a growing children's psyche to experience happy family life to remember later instead of a string of suffering. My father's inclination was toward the ethics and philosophy he had read in his college days including the ideas of ancient Greek philosophers like Socrates, Plato, Aristotle and the Chinese philosopher Confucius as well as the 18th-century German philosopher Immanuel Kant. Whenever my mother complained about money difficulties in managing the household with so many children he often replied with quotes from those philosophers and their ideas about material things.

In the spring the house was filled with the aroma of pale violet and white lilac flowers, my father's favorite fragrance. The yard was full of flowers: azaleas, cherry blossoms, the beautiful pink flowers from the peach tree, and white flowers from the apple tree. The small yellow flowers of Persimmon trees were almost invisible but when the persimmons began ripening they turned into beautiful bright red-orange colors. At night, we used to spread out the bamboo floor mat in the side yard over the concrete floor warmed by the strong sunlight during the day, and lie down side by side, watching twinkling stars, occasional streaks of falling stars, and the Milky Way. My mother would tell us the sad fairy tales of the forbidden young lovers who were only allowed to meet each other once a year on the Milky Way Bridge. While we were studying the patterns of stars in night sky, father pointed out to us the seven bright stars of the Big Dipper - four stars making up the bowl and another three making up the handle. The Big Dipper is called *Bookdu-chilsung* in Korean. There are many stories related to the Big Dipper. Stargazing was one of my favorite pastimes in those days.

On weekends, my father really enjoyed working in the organic vegetable garden, growing all kinds of vegetables: spinach, zucchini, squash, cucumber, eggplant, tomatoes, corn, and potatoes during the summer, and cabbage and radish in late summer to use to prepare kimchi for the winter. My mother raised chickens so we could have fresh eggs for protein. Although our house was within the city limit of Seoul the home was so large and with enough land that it was still possible to grow all those things. This way, my parents made sure they were self-sufficient enough to feed the growing family. Every spring when we woke up early in the morning, we saw very cute and tiny chicks hatched overnight and darting in and out of their mother's wings. All of them had only two legs, not four as in my kindergarten drawing. Our lives were flowing smoothly in peace for a while. Those are among the happiest memories of my childhood.

But there were unfortunate incidents. The country was still unsettled and many young people were in a terribly confused state. One May Day we received a frantic phone call from a faculty member at the school telling my father to get out of the house because a group of radical students who considered my father bourgeois were going to come to our home to attack him. Father listened very quietly without any comment and thanked him for the information, and hung up the phone. He was very calm, deep in his thoughts for a while, and finally said to Mother, "It's sad to see these youngsters wasting their time recklessly getting involved in politics without a good understanding. Someone has to give them guidance. What they need to do is to concentrate on their study and learn more to prepare themselves for the future and contribute to the society in the right way. We don't have enough skilled people in the country." But he made no effort to get out of the house.

Finally a group of students arrived and rang our doorbell. My father answered the bell, opened the door, invited them into the guest room and closed the door. Mother was so nervous and afraid they might physically hurt Father that she was standing right outside of the closed door trying to listen to the conversation. I was nearby worrying about what was going to happen next. There were quiet conversations going on in the room, mostly my father talking to those students. More than an hour passed. All of a sudden father yelled something very loud so Mother thought the students were physically attacking Father and opened the door to intervene. But all the students were sitting there quietly and Father was yelling at someone outside behind the front fence because they were trying to cut off a bunch of flowers hanging over the fence from the tree inside. So Mother was awfully embarrassed and closed the door. It seemed that Father convinced the students that what they really needed to do was study instead of getting involved in politics. I was very impressed by Father's skills to handle the very difficult situation. He was able to calm down those young fellows, a quality needed to be a good teacher.

Although the USAMGIK failed to establish a stable economy and unified Korea, it made notable contributions to improving the Korean educational system granting freedom of thought, equal rights for men and women, implementing programs such as speech classes, electing class presidents, and democratic ways of debating in the classrooms. Most of all, its educational system implemented freedom of speech in the press (President Syngman Rhee later imposed many restrictions). Father was delighted about this type of educational approach and for my part I loved speech class.

During this time, I was attending the Hyo-chang grammar school, learning Korean, history, math, geography, science, music, drawing, and physical education. I was doing very well at school, getting top grades in academic courses. My parents always made sure I did my homework every day. Father concentrated on our academic courses but not much on arts, music, or sports. Therefore none of us (eight children in all) chose a career in those areas. He was not very musical and had never been able to correctly sing the Japanese anthem the Japanese forced all students and teachers to sing every morning at school. Interestingly, however, he managed to sing the first verse of *"La donna è mobile"* ("The Woman Is Fickle") from Giuseppe Verdi's opera *Rigoletto* correctly. Apparently, he liked the meaning of the lyrics (*"This woman is flighty, like a feather in the wind; she changes her voice and her mind. Always sweet, pretty face, in tears or in laughter, she is always lying"*). My mother used to tease him about his lost first love which mother found out about from his old dairy written when he was a student in college. But he just laughed about that.

Father was a self-made man without any help from his family so he didn't show much sympathy when we complained about food or clothes. He had three mottos for us: (1) "Success is achieved 99% by perspiration and 1% by inspiration" (from Thomas Edison) (2) "Survival of the fittest I.E. you must be fit to survive in this world" (from *Origin of Species* by Darwin) (3) "Live by principle never bend, cheat, lie, or spy on someone for personal gain" (from the wisdom of many philosophers he admired). He despised Yi Wan-Yong, a pro-Japanese minister of the Joseon dynasty who signed the Japan-Korea Annexation Treaty, which placed Korea under Japanese rule in 1910. For his treason Yi was rewarded with a peerage in the Japanese *kazoku* system, becoming a *hakushaku* (count). My father also hated all other treasonous sycophants who yielded to Japanese aggression to secure a comfortable living by selling out their own country. While there have been so many brilliant, respectable and decent people in 5,000 years of Korean history, there were also more than acceptable number of despicable, murderous, and manipulative people who created enormous heartbreak, hardship and actually endangered the existence of the country we know today as Korea. Truly worthy of Operatic drama, so perhaps my father's love of Verdi is not surprising.

Father wanted to ensure that we prepared our lives to learn how to survive regardless of the conditions of society, but at the same time he made sure we never compromised our principles under any circumstance. He was an honorable man. I don't know how many men like him still exist on this planet. I had very clear and pragmatic lessons without any confusion from an early age and developed no illusions about life. My father's teachings helped me a great deal later in my life when I faced murky ethics in fiercely competitive corporate environments. I could have climbed the corporate executive ladder higher if I didn't follow Father's advice so closely. At one time during my long corporate career, one of my former bosses said " In addition to all your valuable contributions to the company, you could do so much better if you just play our game without questioning the reason why" I never betrayed my father's principles and I think I managed my life quite well. I have no regrets.

During the USAMGIK, Korean schools introduced democratic methods by electing a president of each class by classmates. The winners would debate certain subjects selected by the teacher. I was elected as the first president of our class. I was 9 years old. The class was very large by the standards of the day, 60 or 70 students. My class teacher, Ms. Nahm, arranged the desks in such a way that there was always at least one well-performing student in each team to help poor students keep up. For the debate, the teachers usually selected the subject, divided the class into two teams and let the 2 teams to debate on the given subject. One of the most interesting subjects was "Does Santa Claus Really Exist?" In my childhood I really believed he was real so I was on the pro side and the other team was con. Since this occasion was a demonstration for the school debate there were many faculty members standing in the back of the classroom for observation and evaluation. I explained very logically and made my position clearly understood. Eventually the other team gave in. All the faculty members were smiling and congratulated me for conducting a successful debate. My teacher told my parents I should become a defense lawyer when I grew up. Maybe they did not want to ruin our spirit since they never told me Santa Claus was a fairy tale.

There was another field in which I excelled - speech. For each assignment I wrote a draft, showed it to Father for his review; and he would edit the draft before I presented my speech. There were always a couple of paragraphs he inserted into my drafts that still remain in my memory: advising students (1) Concentrate on studying to learn more instead of wasting time with politics they were not yet equipped to fully understand; (2) Do not behave recklessly; (3) Avoid factional fighting and unite, giving examples of how factional fighting during the Joseon dynasty weakened the country to the point of being taken over Japan; and (4) Respect your teachers, parents, and elders.

Father hated any kind of violence. He was a peaceful man and teacher who believed in educating youngsters to become intelligent people with good judgment. He tried to prevent them from acting hastily and not be drawn to the mob. Maybe this is why I have never participated in any demonstration in my entire life. I always thought that I didn't have all the facts to make a solid judgment on many issues to participate in any demonstration. When I was reading *Leap of Faith*, a book written by Queen Noor of Jordan, I found a line that struck a strong emotional chord with me. She was spending time at the Mayo Clinic in Rochester, Minnesota, taking care of her dying husband, King Hussein. One day she went outside to take a break. When she looked up at the sky and saw one white goose among a flock of brown geese migrating north. She saw her husband as that white goose disappearing far away into the northern sky. It was an apt analogy for my father – a unique individual going his own way in violent dark days.

My father knew many people because he had been a teacher and a professor for many years in many places. In addition he and his Korean classmates from Kyung-sung University remained friends because there were so few in his graduating class. One day in 1945, shortly after the liberation of Korea, I accompanied him to Myung-dong, which was the main business district in Seoul. When we were walking down the main street and were stopped many times because there was always someone who recognized and greeted him. Some were his old friends; alumni members of Kyung-sung University and others were former students or faculty members he had not seen for many years. He didn't always recognize them until they explained who they were, where they met, and which school they attended when he was their teacher. They all seemed to be so glad to see my father again, as if they had found a long lost friend or a relative. I understood then who my Father was to many people.

Chapter 10: Emergence of Two Koreas and The Jeju Massacre (1947–1948)

General Hodge, unable to resolve the Korean problem, turned the Korean issue over to the United Nations. The UN accepted the proposal to establish an interim Korean government in the South departing from the Moscow agreement. Of course the Soviets were dead against the UN plan because they were afraid they might lose their controlling power over the Korean Peninsula. They had been slowly working toward creating a united communist Korea under Kim Il-sung. The struggle between the groups supporting the UN plan and those opposing it intensified. Throughout the South many bloody events took place.

Nevertheless the UN adopted a resolution on April 28, 1948, stating that the commission would observe the elections to be held on May 10, 1948, and that the elections were to be held in an unrestricted atmosphere and the democratic rights of speech, press, and assembly were to be respected and observed. In response, the communists in the South increased their activities in order to discourage the eligible voters from registering. They prevented the shipment of ballot boxes. The most intense rebellion took place on Jeju Island. The subjugation activities to put down the rebellion by the South Korean army, the Jeju security forces and the extreme right-wing Northwest Youth paramilitary unit resulted in the death of at least 30,000 persons - 10% to 15% of the island's population. Seventy percent (70%) of the island's villages was burned by the time the island was completely subjugated in the spring of 1949. At the time of the uprising the island was controlled by the USAMGIK although only a small number of Americans were present. It was only after November 30, 1994 that "Peacetime" control over the South Korean Armed forces was transferred to the South Korean Joint Chiefs of Staff. The brutal suppression of the islanders' revolt and the massive slaughter of the islanders were too extreme and inhumane to the eyes of many when the truth about the extent of the brutality was finally revealed many decades later.

Historically Jeju islanders suffered a lot and they were very poor on this isolated island. It was their extreme poverty that attracted them to the communist ideology. During the 500 years of the Joseon Dynasty, Jeju Island was a destination for exiles, political prisoners, and figures deemed undesirable by the central government. The descendants of those exiles make up part of Jeju population. One of the most distinct aspects of Jeju is its matriarchal family structures. The best-known example of this is found among the *haenyeo* ("sea women") who are often the heads of families. For centuries they earned a living from free diving—diving with no scuba gear—even well into the winter harvesting abalone, conch, and many other marine animals. Women were long prominent on Jeju as so many men left behind widows when their fishing boats did not return. Sadly, they made this fateful mistake of thinking that communism was the solution for all their problems.

Jeju islanders' strong belief in communist ideology is well described in the book *The Aquariums of Pyongyang: Ten Years in the North Korean Gulag* by North Korean defector Chol-hwan Kang. Kang's grandmother was born on Jeju Island but she had to immigrate to Japan as a laborer to make a living. In Japan, she met and married a rich businessman and lived well but she still insisted on moving her whole family to North Korea to dedicate herself to the success of communist ideals. When her husband disappeared one day and her whole family was sent to a labor camp she kept saying "There must be something mistaken because this is not supposed to happen in the communist system." The poor woman understand the reality and kept repeating the same sentence until the last moment she collapsed in the field died after her family was released from the labor camp, probably after her husband finally died in another camp.

Today, Jeju Island is one of Korea's most prestigious tourist destinations. Jeju Island is a UNESCO World Heritage Site and one of the new 7 Wonders of Nature. The mild climate, natural beauty, and fantastic seashore make it a popular destination for South Koreans as well as visitors from surrounding countries in East Asia. But the bones of men, women, and children who were victims of the massacre still lay silently in the sealed cave on Mt. Halla.

In spite of the communist terrorism the election preparations were carried out and by April 9, 1948, the last day of registration, 7,837,504 eligible voters - 79.7% of Koreans above the age of 21- had registered. Some 44 persons, including many candidates were killed. Nearly 100 were wounded. 68 voting stations were attacked by the leftist terrorists. But the actual mechanics of voting were generally satisfactory and the secrecy of the balloting was ensured according to the UN observers. In this first historic election in Korea 95.5% of registered voters participated. No party won a clear-cut majority. Rhee's National Society for Acceleration of Korean Independence won 54 seats. Nearly half of the 198 men elected were members of right-wing groups and a large number of the remaining members were suspected of being left-wing sympathizers. On June 25 the United Nations Temporary Commission on Korea certified the election results.

On June 12, a democratic constitution was adopted. On June 20 Rhee was elected the first president of the Republic of Korea by an overwhelming majority. On August 12 the United States recognized it as the government of Korea and on August 15, 1948, the Republic of Korea was inaugurated on the third anniversary of Korean liberation. On December 12, 1948, the UN adopted a resolution declaring "a lawful government of the Republic of Korea (ROK), the only legitimate regime in Korea," and it was recognized as such by the nations of the noncommunist world. This was a violent beginning of a nation.

The North Korean communists continued their game, political deception. In the North, the Supreme People's Assembly met on September 3, 1948 and ratified the constitution of the Democratic People's Republic of Korea (DPRK). It elected Kim Il-sung as premier and Pak Hon-yong, the notorious former chairman of the Workers' Party of South Korea, as vice premier and minister of foreign affairs. On September 9 the government of the DPRK was inaugurated. After recognizing the Communist regime on October 12 the Soviet Union named General Shtykov as their ambassador to Pyongyang. Without any doubt, the Soviet Union had no hesitation in recognizing the DPRK without any participation from South Korean leaders or the UN.

So it was the during the months of August and September of 1948, the Korean people witnessed the emergence of two separate governments, each claiming to be the legitimate government of all Koreans. The military demarcation line between the American and Soviet occupation zones became an international boundary- a new "iron curtain" across the Korean peninsula. More tragedies were certain to visit the Korean people because of the division of their country. This is why the three most respected Korean leaders, Lyuh Woon-hyung, Kim Gu, and Kim Gyu-sik, tried so hard to create one unified Korea. Unfortunately with the involvement of two massive world powers they lost their power, their dreams and their lives. These men remain beloved heroes of the majority of Koreans.

The liberation of Korea from Japanese colonial rule provided Koreans freedom to reconstruct their economy but the division of the peninsula and the political turbulence during the USAMGIK and the first ROK made it impossible to make any progress toward building a stable government and economy. The shortage of electric power and natural resources presented major economic difficulties. Ninety (90) percent of the electric power used by South Korea had been supplied by the North. South Korea had virtually no highly trained scientists, technicians, engineers, economic experts, or managerial personnel, thanks to the Japanese policy that did not allow Koreans to learn anything related to those critical fields. Political and social conditions were detrimental to economic growth, and the rampant inflation that was created by the Japanese leading up to World War II plunged South Korea into an even greater chaotic economic situation. South Korean farmers had almost no fertilizer to apply to their fields since the supply from the North was cut off. Rapid population growth due to a high birth rate and influx of refugees from the North brought additional economic problems. Shortages of food, fuel, and medical supplies threatened the livelihood of the people and created serious health problems.

The USAMGIK handed over a country in economic shambles to the Koreans in August 1948. The young republic faced many other economic problems. Uncontrolled deficit spending by the nation, particularly by agencies concerned with hunting down communists, inadequate tax collection, and the steadily increasing amount of currency in circulation sustained inflation, worsening existing economic problems. Between December 31, 1948, and January 1950, the government printed some $150 billion worth of currency, making the money practically worthless.

Photo 5: The bones of men, women, and children who were victims of the Jeju massacre have lain in this cold Daranshi cave on Halla Mt. on Jeju island for almost a half century. What is particularly tragic is that they were all burned alive by a fire set in front of the cave by the Jeju security forces.

Source:http://earthw.tistory.com/229.

Chapter 11: The First Republic of Korea and Assassination of Kim Gu (1948–1950)

Before the April 10 general election in 1948, my parents had an unexpected visitor at home, a candidate for the National Assembly, Hwang Sung-su. The country's first constitution was to be created by the National Assembly on July 17, 1948. Therefore this was a very important election to determine the fate of the nation. But my father had a lifelong policy of staying away from any political party. In addition, he was utterly disillusioned by the political assassinations at the time. He was very knowledgeable about factional fighting during the Joseon dynasty which victimized many innocent people. But he was still regarded as an influential person in our residential district by some local officials and they often recommended political candidates seek my father's endorsement.

Hwang Sung-su was the youngest candidate; handsome and eloquent. He was educated in the United States. Father was enchanted by his charm and his American style of campaigning to try to earn the trust of the people. This was unusual at the time because many other candidates were using intimidation and coercion to force people to vote for them. My father was delighted saying that we needed young and bright leaders who could change the old ways of selecting our representatives so he agreed to campaign for him. At the time my mother happened to be the president of the local Patriotic Lady's Association having been appointed by the local officials because the government was actively promoting such activities. My mother was also trying to make up for her husband's inactivity in participating in politics which could be misinterpreted.

I used to go to Hyo-chang Park with my little brother Soo whom I was babysitting to listen to Hwang's eloquent campaign speeches. I enjoyed listening to his persuasive and at the same time very informative speeches because speech was a part of our school program. Hwang was elected to the National Assembly of the First Republic of Korea (ROK) and later served as the leader of the Liberal Party before, during, and shortly after the Korean War. We didn't know then he was going to save my father's life during the Korean War. Like many other Korean politicians he didn't have a very long political career. We didn't hear his name in the political arena about four or five years after the Korean War. My parents often wondered what had happed to him.

During this politically chaotic period my father's nephew, Young-gi, the first son of my father's eldest brother was in Seoul attending Seoul National University majoring in French. He was tall and handsome with occidental features and he was often mistaken for an American or European when he was seen from a distance. My father was asked by his family to support his nephew's college expenses since he was the next generation's Kim family heir. So Young-gi used to come to visit our home once in a while, probably to collect the tuition from my father. Whenever he came he used to say that my parents belonged to the class of the bourgeoisie but his generation belonged to the proletariat. He believed Marxist theory would create a worker's paradise in Korea. My father, who was paying for his education, warned him that he'd better concentrate on his study and prepare himself to find a job after graduation rather than wasting his time wrapped in reckless political activity. Father also pointed out to him that his character would not last in a proletariat society because he had expensive tastes, enjoyed wearing stylish clothes, carried a fancy camera on his shoulder, and dated pretty college girls from well-to-do families.

In fact, he was dating a girl who was attending Sookmyung Women's College near our home where my father used to teach. Later he married her. But Young-gi didn't pay attention to his uncle's advice behaving as if he knew better. This was a politically turbulent and confusing time in Korea and many young people were cast about in many different directions without real knowledge of their own political ideology and without foreseeing the consequence of their actions. Young people are very emotional, easily indoctrinated, and fearless when fear might be a better choice. Hence they are very easily brainwashed and mobilized by ambitious political manipulators like Kim Il-sung, Mao Zedong, Stalin, and present-day ISIS clerics. And they often don't listen to their parents or family elders until it's too late. But then they are the ones who eventually suffer most from their actions so the circle does close in the end with tragedy.

This was a witch-hunting period in South Korea. Just as in the McCarthy period in the United States everybody had to be extremely careful what they said and with whom they should or should not associate. In a country established on democratic principles and having sustained a democratic government for as long as the United States this kind of atmosphere usually does not last long enough to do much damage. In the United States the Tydings Committee hearings were called to investigate McCarthy's accusations of numerous people as being communists. This was a subcommittee of the US Senate set up in February 1950 (the same year the Korean War broke out) to conduct "a full and complete study and investigation as to whether persons who are disloyal to the U.S. are employed by the Department of State." Many Democratic Party politicians were incensed at McCarthy's attack on the State Department of Democratic administration and hoped to use the hearings to discredit him. The Democratic chairman of the subcommittee, Senator Millard Tydings, was reported to have said, "Let me have him [McCarthy] for three days in public hearings, and he'll never show his face in the Senate again." This hearing effectively ended the McCarthy era in America.

Unfortunately in Korea at the time there was no mechanism available to investigate government officials, politically powerful people or organizations. Besides, there were not too many available jobs in those days for young people and the only jobs increasing in number were related to intelligence, the secret police, or detective work to hunt down communists or political enemies of the powerful people at the top. The easiest way to get rid of one's political enemies or to settle a personal vendetta was to accuse the enemy of being a member of the Communist Party, the Namno-dang. The accused would usually be destroyed.

Late one night, someone noisily knocked on our door. When my father answered, there was a man and two women standing there. One woman was my school teacher, Miss Nam, at my elementary school. The other woman was also a teacher at the same school. Since a part of a teacher's duty in Korea was to visit homes of their students Miss Nam had visited our home sometime before and met our parents. She was a very nice woman, a graduate of the best teacher's school in Seoul, but she was from a very poor family. My father recognized her right away but did not know exactly what was going on. Miss Nam wanted my father to notify her family, which was some distance away, that she had been arrested because of her activity in Namno-dang. She gave my father her parents' address, so my father agreed to notify her family of her arrest. He delivered the message early the next morning. We had no idea she was involved in communist activities but at the time it was not uncommon. When you are young and your family is very poor then Karl Marx's theory can be very appealing.

Some days later, when my father was walking down the short distance to his car where his chauffeur was waiting to drive him to work a man on the street was trying to say a typical morning greeting to my father, bowing and saying "Did you sleep well last night?" My father took off his hat briefly just to acknowledge by slightly nodding his head to this greeting without saying anything and went on to his car. My father saw another man standing nearby watching this process and he thought that was odd early in the morning when everyone was in a hurry to get to work. Since Father had many students at various schools where he taught many people recognized him on the street even if he did not necessarily remember them all. Later we found out the man who was greeting him that morning was a member of the Namno-dang. He was arrested at the time; the man standing nearby watching was a detective.

Apparently, someone who did not like my father for some reason was setting up a trap to accuse my father of being a communist under the theory that one who knows a Namno-dang party member must also be a member of Namno-dang. Using women's intuition, my mother thought something tricky was going on behind the scene and asked father to investigate what was going on at school, whether he had any enemies at school. But it was not Father's nature to suspect people even if someone was plotting to kill him. So he just shrugged it off saying that he had to replace some incompetent faculty members to improve the quality of education for students. But he didn't pursue the matter any further to find out whether somebody was building up a plot against him. This kind of dirty trick had been played to take over someone's job or carry out a personal vendetta in that witch-hunting atmosphere. Shamefully, this was a common practice in those days in Korea.

As I remember, it was during the first quarter of 1950, before the Korean War, that someone set fire to my father's school. Since this was during the first ROK under President Syngman Rhee, the American officer who gave full support to my father was no longer there to help. We received frantic phone calls from faculty members to inform us about the fire. When we went upstairs, we could see from our second-floor balcony intense red flames and black smoke in the moonless night sky in the far distance where the school was located. My father was not at home at the time since he was having a business dinner with some people at a restaurant. Someone finally located him and told him the terrible news. Father immediately went to see his school and saw it burning down. He broke down and wept. When he came home that night, his eyes were red and swollen from so much crying. This was the man who didn't cry when his parents passed away but witnessing his precious accomplishment reduced to ashes broke him down. He had worked extremely hard to build that school. He enjoyed doing it and was very proud of it. But my father had no idea who would want to burn down the school or why. At least he was hopeful that the local police could capture the criminals who were responsible for the fire.

But strange things were happening. The police arrested many innocent people, the type of people who had no reason to burn down the school - my father's chauffer and the school employees my father trusted. They were all later released due to insufficient evidence. Then the police arrested my father and tortured him to tell the truth about the fire. They asked him about a man from his hometown who was supposed to be a member of Namno-dang but father had no idea who that man was or how he was related to the fire. Maybe that was the man who tried to greet father one morning with a detective standing by watching when father was walking toward his car to go to work.

As mother predicted somebody was organizing a plot. They kept him in jail three days and released him for lack of evidence. My father didn't know what was going on and thought that it was a waste of his time to try to battle with unknown forces while he had the chance to start all over again. So he quit his job, the job he had been extremely successful at and loved so much. My father was getting tired of the political situation in Korea and was making a plan to leave Korea for a couple of years and spend the time at Harvard University, doing graduate work and thinking about what to do next. Mother thought that it was a good idea for his future career in a politically charged society.

I have always wondered who was behind the plot to discredit my father and burned down that school. I wanted to leave an accurate record of the incident as my tribute to my father. Unbeknownst to me my brother Soo who lives in Korea met Professor Chin Young-ok, who was writing the history of that school. He gave Soo a copy of my father's memoir covering his life as president of the school from 1946 to 1950. My brother said Professor Chin was a graduate of the school and admired my father's efforts and his contribution to the school. I was not aware such a document existed, because on June 25 of that year the Korean War broke out and I never heard any news about that school again until I left Korea in September 1959.

According to my brother Soo, the minister of Communications Department asked my father to return to Chesin Communications Institute in 1961 during the Second Republic of Korea under Yoon Bo-sun and Chang Myun. They wanted to establish order by cleaning up the mess created by student riots. This was right after a students uprising ousted Syngman Rhee. When father returned to that school in 1960 he wrote in his memoir of what had happened before the fire in 1950. Maybe he wanted to leave an accurate account of the incident. I am very thankful I finally found the facts in his memoir. It's shocking to find that the secret paramilitary youth organization even penetrated my father's school. What a lawless criminal society the first ROK government was! The leaders used North Korean youth and poor refugees to organize paramilitary organizations to eliminate anyone they didn't want alive. If you give power and weapons to immature youth odds are they will behave recklessly.

My father's memoir revealed the following facts:

He expelled 200 students in the early spring of 1950 from the Heungook middle school because those students entered the school to take advantage of its free boarding facilities but did not attend classes and they were not interested in studying at all. They were members of the Northwest Youth Association. My father, not knowing anything about the existence of this paramilitary youth organization and being a strict and principled educator, tried to convince those young men to concentrate on studying for their future. Regrettably, they ignored their principal's advice and continued occupying the school's limited lodging facilities depriving other serious students the opportunity of using the same facility. As a despicable act of revenge they wanted to accuse my father of setting the fire and of being a communist. Then the police had to arrest my father who was grieving for the loss of his hard-won accomplishment and torture him for three days, demanding that he locate a man from his hometown who was supposed to be a communist—but father had no knowledge of the man or how that man was connected to the fire. It just made no sense at all to my father. Strangely, the local police never made any effort to track down the real arsonists.

My father, who was a naïve educator, was unable to connect the dots to figure out that his young students were the members of a paramilitary right-wing terrorist youth organization run by Yum Ung-taek, receiving orders from powerful people at the top to eliminate rival politicians like Kim Gu and Lyuh Woon-hyung. I recall my father adding a tuition-free school, Heungook middle school, on the same campus where Chesin Communications Institute was located, using a part of its facilities to help poor youth, largely North Korean refugees, to give them an opportunity to study.

No wonder the local police were arresting innocent people who had nothing to do with setting the fire. The paramilitary youth organization under the USAMGIK and Syngman Rhee's First

Republic were very powerful political organizations. The local police department was nothing but their extended arm available to arrest and torture anyone they were ordered to. It's clear the students who were expelled from the school set that fire for revenge and tried to label their enemies as communists. But what would be the purpose of any communist to set fire to that school anyway? None of it made any sense.

I witnessed in my youth this kind of injustice in a society run by a bunch of criminals. I knew it was not enough to be an honest and hardworking person trying to live by the basic principles to avoid this kind of tragedy. You must know how to deal with situations of this kind. In this world, there are good and honest people, but there are also evil, dishonest, and highly manipulative people, who don't mind hurting anyone to satisfy their own goals. I realized that ordinary people of any nation without good and capable political leaders suffer tremendously. I wanted to find out who were the people instructing the paramilitary murder squads to kill rival political leaders.

The history of the ROK began in this turbulent environment, both domestically and internationally. Tragic events shaped the particular character of South Korean society. In the beginning, many anticipated it would be a unified, democratic nation. The Americans hoped to make the ROK "a beacon of democracy" in Asia, but there were many obstacles to such an outcome, both apparent and hidden. President Syngman Rhee, despite his impressive academic credentials, was an autocrat who commanded a rich democratic rhetoric. He was the president of a republic but harbored many imperialistic ideas. He did not tolerate any opposition; surrounded himself with men who were willing to obey his commands, he demanded an absolute loyalty from his followers. Many of his supporters were corrupt and incompetent, freely exercising nepotism and favoritism. Rhee was a 72-year-old man whose ambition was to create a modern, strong Korean nation. However, the relationship between the president and the National Assembly was not amicable.

Although Rhee's original cabinet members included those who were well educated abroad—such as the English-educated Chang

Taek-sang as foreign minister, German-educated An Ho-sang as education minister, American-educated Louise Yim as commerce minister, and American-educated Yun Chi-yong as home minister—it also included the progressive Cho Bong-am (formerly communist) as minister of agriculture. His appointments to government posts also included men who were regarded as former Japanese collaborators which aroused a storm of criticism that Rhee chose to ignore. After scrutinizing his appointees for any tendency toward insubordination or unreliability, in December 1948, only four months after the original cabinet members were appointed, Rhee carried out the first of his cabinet shake-ups that became a hallmark of Rhee's administration when he replaced Foreign Minister Chang, Home Minister Yun, Social Affairs Minister Chon Chim-han, and National Police Inspector Cho Byung-ok with men who were less inspiring and capable but more loyal to Rhee. The progressive Agricultural Minister Cho was dismissed in February 1949. Following the major defection of Western-educated leaders before and during the Korea War, the Rhee administration consisted mainly of Japanese-Korean educated individuals who were tradition bound and bureaucratically oriented. With frequent cabinet shake-ups, Rhee established his absolute control over the government making virtually all decisions in both policy and administrative matters by himself.

Facing the growing repressive tactics of the Syngman Rhee's administration, and looking toward the 1950 National Assembly election, the Hanguk Democratic Party merged with other moderate rightist groups and formed the Democratic National Party in February 1949, and it soundly defeated Rhee's proposal made in March 1949 for the postponement of the 1950 National Assembly election. The long-awaited land reform bill finally passed in May 1949 after the dismissal of the Agricultural minister, Cho Bong-am, in February because of his liberal views on land reform. However the rather liberal land reform bill was aborted by the Rhee administration and the conservative Land Reform Law that the Rhee Administration proposed was adopted by the National Assembly on June 21, 1949. In the political storm several national assemblymen, including Bo Il-hwan and Kim Yak-su, were arrested for their communist linkage and with alleged violation of the National Security Law.

In the midst of a growing anti-Rhee atmosphere Kim Gu, the leader of the Korean Independence Party, was assassinated in his office on June 26, 1949, by Ahn Doo-hee. Kim Gu's assassin, Ahn Doo-hee, was arrested shortly after the murder and his name was all over the newspapers. The assassin was identified as a lieutenant in the Korean Army. Kim Gu's supporters had seen Ahn in Kim Gu's company frequently as if he admired and loved Kim Gu like his own father and Kim Gu trusted him like his own son. It appeared that he was spying on Kim Gu and looking for a chance to murder him. But the newspapers did not report any further information at the time as to why he killed Kim Gu or who ordered the assassination. Kim Gu's murder was only one of the many political assassinations that took place during the USAMGIK and the first ROK. The general public was never informed of any details as to who ordered all those killings or who was funding the murder squad that seemed to exist. There were only various rumors and guesses floating around.

It's hard to believe that I had the privilege of meeting Kim Gu by chance after he returned to Korea when my elementary school class was in Ui-dong for a field trip to appreciate and enjoy nature's beauty. He was there with three or four other men leisurely strolling around and chatting and enjoying the beautiful environment of his home land he had not seen for such a long time since he left in 1919. When our teacher invited him to take a picture with us he was delighted to sit in the middle of our class to take a picture. I was much too young to appreciate his enormous stature in Korean history at the time. I asked my brother Soo in Korea to find that photo for me to place it in this book, but he could not find it in any of our remaining family albums. Unfortunately the photo appears to have been lost. During the Korean War, my mother tried her best to save all our family albums when we moved out of our home in a hurry but it was impossible to carry all of them without a car. It's a sad story because many of our precious memories are forever gone. Unlike material things you cannot relive the past.

Chapter 12: The Blind General and His Paramilitary Murder Squad (1946–1950)

More than half a century has gone by since, and the powerful political leaders of the chaotic period of the 1950s have all left us for another world, whether heaven or hell, and much formerly classified information has now been declassified. More importantly, people who witnessed the crimes are no longer afraid to speak up without being punished severely and the people who actually committed certain crimes are now forced to confess by the civilian governments' Justice System. Thus it has become much easier now to piece together all the broken pieces of information to write an accurate history and finally vindicate those innocent victims of that terrifying period in South Korea.

I obtained a summary of the declassified information that covers the history of the US Army's CIC during World War II and the early Cold War in Korea, a classified 30-volume publication prepared in the late 1950s by Major Ann Brady and others at the CIC and printed in 1959. The document contains the history of the CIC until 1950. A declassified (sanitized) version of the official history is now available at the National Archives and Records Administration. I also obtained copies of Major George E. Cilley's report to US Army headquarters intelligence chief in Washington, DC, dated July 1949. I purchased the book titled *In the Devil's Shadow* by Michael E. Haas, published by the Naval Institute Press in 2000, as well as D. Nichols's autobiography *How Many Times Can I Die?*, the life story of a special intelligence agent for the US Air Force and memoir of his activities and contributions to the Korean War (this book is out of print but it's available from the Library of Congress in Washington, DC, and there are two other copies still extant, one at the US Air Force Academy library and another at University of Alabama library). I was able to obtain a digital copy of this book from the original publisher. I also found additional information from various other sources such as old and more recent articles written by foreign correspondence who were in Korea during the Korean War who witnessed atrocities, more recent Korean newspaper articles they were unable to publish before in the fear of being shut down. After reviewing all the relevant materials I was shocked to realize what was really going on in South Korea during the USAMGIK and the first ROK under Syngman Rhee.

Major George E. Cilley, in his report to the US Army intelligence chief in Washington, D.C. on Kim Gu's assassination described Yum Ung-taek, nicknamed the "Blind General," as the most colorful and the most malignant man. He described Yum's Baikyi-sah (white-clothed warriors) organization as nothing but a underground network of assassins, murderous gangsters, and ultranationalist lunatics. Yum told Major Cilley that he was betrayed by a Korean compatriot he had trusted and respected, so he wholeheartedly hated him and would not hesitate to kill him once the order came down from above. It turned out the man who fingered him to Mao's security was Kim Gu. Thus, Major Cilley believed that it was Yum's agent of the paramilitary organization that killed Kim Gu. Ahn Doo-hee was indeed one of Yum's agents, belonging to Cell number 1 of the Special Attack Corps; he was also an informer for the CIC and later its agent. There has been no confirmation or denial of Cilley's report but it was his belief that the assassination of Lyuh Woon-hyung was probably carried out by this underground organization as well. It's interesting to find that most of Cilley's reports were written as third party observations.

Evidently Cilley didn't know Yum's past very well and was impressed when Yum told him that he could speak French, German, and English fluently but always used interpreters to hide his real identity in order to conduct his secret paramilitary activities. Scanning through Yum's background there is no possibility Yum could have acquired multilingual skills as he claimed. It's hard to believe that this kind of psychotic and delusional person was allowed to run the youth paramilitary organization even with help from powerful right-wing politicians. It was Shin Ik-hee who introduced Yum to the US CIC and to General Hodge in order to ask for funds for Yum's operation suggesting that they could provide intelligence on North Korea to the US CIC. Right-wing Korean politicians Shin Ik-hee and Yi Bum-suk, who served later as the prime minister of the first ROK under Syngman Rhee also asked General Hodge for financial aid to establish an anticommunist youth corps in preparation for an anticommunist army.

General Hodge was trying to secure consent from General MacArthur and the US Department of State on this issue but this was only after-the-fact approval since the Korean Youth Corp had already been established on October 6 while his requests for approval began on October 28. But John Carter Vincent, Director of the Office of Far Eastern Affairs in the State Dept. clearly opposed this plan. General MacArthur appeared to adopt the State Dept. position as well saying, "This suggestion is believed to be unfeasible." As a result General Hodge sent Korean-American US CIC sergeant Lee Soon-yong to Shin Ik-hee with the message that Shin's action committee would be disbanded unless Shin agreed to provide intelligence on North Korea to the US CIC. It was agreed that Yum's Baikyi-sah militia (the white clothed warriors) would work for General Hodge collecting intelligence on North Korea.

Yum's American contact was US Army Major Whittaker who headed the US CIC detachment in Seoul at the time. Major Whittaker acquired a training camp for Yum. By May 1946, Yum had ten agents trained at this CIC-provided training camp. They were sent to North Korea, two per province. Their mission was to collect information on military installations, personnel strength, ordinance, and so on. Major Whittaker gave Yum a list of specific kinds of information that the Americans wanted. So those poorly trained Koreans went to North Korea for intelligence gathering for the US CIC and most of them never returned having been captured and either killed or broken.

It's clear that the US CIC connection to Yum had nothing to do with the assassinations of Lyuh Woon-hyung or Kim Gu. The US CIC was only interested in obtaining information on North Korea at the time through Yum's organization as recommended by Shin Ik-hee. It is disappointing to find that the USAMGIK or the US CIC cooperated with this organization of ill repute and did not try more diligently to prevent the political assassinations that took place during their administration. They seemed to have just watched the show, collecting information and reporting to their headquarters. Apparently this policy was a disaster since they did not receive any valuable information on North Korea and lost Korean leaders who had support from the majority of the Korean population.

According to the ROK Ministry of National Defense, from September 1945 to January 1948, about 803,000 refugees came from the North. This swarm may be divided into two groups. One group came to the South to study or to find work; while the second came because of their strong anticommunist ideals. Many of the latter group became members of the rightist paramilitary organizations. It served them well, since there were not many jobs available to support them at that time. They formed the most aggressive anticommunist youth organizations ultimately organizing a strong corps, the Northwest Youth Association, on November 30, 1946. This group participated in the Jeju Island massacre as well. This is the same group that burned down my father's school to settle a personal vendetta and convinced the local police to arrest innocent people, including Father, accusing them of being communists and responsible for destroying the school. Based on all the available information, it seems likely that it was not the American CIC who ordered Lyuh Woon-hyung's murder - it was more likely Korean political power players at the top who used Yum's murder squad to eliminate rival politicians.

Who was this character named Yum Ung-taek? I never heard of his name and his name never appeared in any newspaper when I was growing up in Korea, probably because his secret terrorist organization was well protected by the powerful political machine. Over the years Yum's identity and the history of his clandestine criminal activities have leaked out little by little. Yum began his career as an aspiring Korean nationalist officer in China. He was a cadet at a military academy for Korean nationalists in China when he instigated a student riot over the stipend paid by the school. It was Kim Gu who arranged with Chang Kai-shek to allow Korean cadets into a special class at the Nanking Military Academy and the first class of Koreans started in December 1933. Consequently Kim Gu was not pleased to hear of Yum's riot over the stipend; it created a problem for Chang Kai-shek and he ordered Yum arrested and punished. But Yum managed to escape to Shin Ik-hee's house and stayed there for a while in Nanking. Then, he joined Chiang Kai-shek's notorious and brutal secret service organization, Namyi-sah. While on a spy mission for Namyi-sah, Yum was captured by the Japanese and unable to ride out the torture, Yum confessed and agreed to spy for the Japanese. The torture he received in the Japanese prison left him almost blind so the Americans nicknamed him as the Blind General.

Arakawa Takejo was the Japanese detective who caught and broke Yum Ung-taek. Arakawa had Yum spying on Koreans fighting for Korean independence in Pyongyang when Japan surrendered to the allied forces in 1945. Yum's cover was broken and he was put in jail, but due to a bureaucratic mix-up the Soviets released him. He escaped to Seoul in November 1945 and formed Baikyi-sah, modeled after Chiang Kai-shek's Namyi-sah. Yum reconnected with his old mentor Shin Ik-hee, and other right-wing extremists. Shin Ik-hee was a right-wing politician and a public figure in South Korea who later served for two terms as the speaker of the National Assembly. More recently declassified US documents show that Yum indeed provided intelligence to US CIC agents in Seoul and received financial and other support from the Americans. Yum's agents indeed infiltrated the military police and civil organizations in South Korea and collected intelligence for the CIC. Yum was trying to hide his shameful past as an informer for the Japanese but Kim Gu knew all about his shameful past. No doubt Yum was very happy to send out one of his agents to assassinate Kim Gu as soon as such an order came from above.

There are many indications that Syngman Rhee was deeply involved in Kim Gu's assassination. Rhee must have used Ahn Doo-hee to get rid of Kim Gu, who was his number one political rival at the time. Although Kim Gu didn't have real political power at the time, he was far more popular among the general public and that created a headache for Rhee. Although Ahn Doo-hee was convicted of the assassination and sentenced to life in prison shortly thereafter his sentence was commuted to a term of 15 years by then newly elected Korean president Syngman Rhee. At the outset of the Korean War in 1950, Ahn was released from prison, having served only one year of his 15-year sentence. Upon his release Ahn was reinstated as a military officer. After serving under Rhee during the Korean War, Ahn was discharged in 1953, having attained the rank of colonel. After Syngman Rhee fled Korea in response to the April Revolution of 1960 Ahn went into hiding living under an assumed name for many years until he was eventually found and killed by one of Kim Gu's followers.

Four decades after Kim Gu's murder on April 13, 1992, a confession by Ahn Doo-hee was finally published by *Dongah Ilbo*, a Korean newspaper. I don't know how long they had this information but they unable to print it. In the confession Ahn claimed that the assassination of Kim Gu had been ordered by Kim Chang-ryong, who served as the head of national security under Syngman Rhee. He was the same man who tortured my father to extract a false confession to confiscate our home. We had no idea about this man's powerful connection. How could it be true that our family was up against this bloodthirsty right-hand man to the president of the nation! The more I learned about the details of the hidden history of South Korea during the politically turbulent years the more I felt a chill down my back. We didn't learn about these kinds of details for almost half a century.

It's no surprise that Lyuh Woon-hyung's assassin, the 19-year-old North Korean refugee Han Chigeun, also belonged to Yum's organization. Han was sentenced to death when he was arrested but he was secretly released. Then he took a false name and emigrated to Japan. Yum's ultra-right paramilitary youth murder squad seemed to have had quite a record of accomplishments.

Yum's organization had been in operation until the US CIC's role diminished and the Korean government established its own spy agency: the South Korean Higher Intelligence Dept (HID). Some 100 of Yum's agents joined HID and Yum's training center was taken over by HID in 1948. In February 1949 an emissary of General Willoughby, General MacArthur's intelligence chief, came to see Yum with an urgent request for intelligence on North Korea and promises of future cooperation. It's really disappointing to learn that a high-ranking U.S. intelligence officer was relying on a lunatic like Yum for such important intelligence. Consequently, the Korean

Liaison Office (KLO) was established on June 1, 1949. The few remaining members of Baikyi-sah became the founding members of the KLO. In June 1950, during the Korean War, Yum was captured by North Korean military personnel in Seoul and was killed in an air raid conducted by American air force while being transported to Pyongyang.

Chapter 13: Lawrence of Korea and the Suwon Massacre (1946–1957)

In 1962 a famous film brought forth a British Lt. Colonel T. E. Lawrence (1888–1935), who played a liaison role during the Arab revolt against the Ottoman Empire (916–1918). Lawrence was a highly educated and brilliant man and a prolific writer (his major work, *Seven Pillars of Wisdom*, is based on his experiences in the war). His flamboyant writing style, along with the variety of his activities and associations, has made him an object of fascination throughout the world as Lawrence of Arabia.

But there is another historically conspicuous character nicknamed "Lawrence of Korea" by the US CIC members in the South Korean theater: Colonel Donald Nichols. However Colonel Don Nichols was a far cry from T. E. Lawrence in his credentials as an intelligence officer. Nichols also wrote an autobiography, *How Many Times Can I Die?* It was his life story as a special intelligent agent in the US Air Force and involvement in the Korean War.

In his book *In the Devil's Shadow*, published in 2001 by Naval Institute Press, Michael Haas describes Nichols as a most amazing and unusual man and refers to his activities in Korea as a one-man war. Haas himself is a retired colonel in the US Air Force and served in the Special Forces and psychological operations units. He is a graduate of the Naval Postgraduate School with a master's degree in national security affairs. His book describes how much General Earle E. Partridge, commander, Fifth Air Force, knew about Nichols's activities in Korea and critical decisions concerning Korean affairs. General Partridge first met Master Sergeant Donald Nichols in 1948, soon after he arrived in Japan to assume command of the Fifth Air Force. Although Partridge received periodic briefings from Nichols during the subsequent two years leading up to the war he admitted later that he had very meager knowledge of Nichols's activities in Korea during the prewar period. He wrote, "Nichols's world was found in the mean streets and back alleys of prewar Seoul, a long way from the plush offices at Fifth Air Force headquarters in Tokyo". It's apparent again that US intelligence officers were aware of Nichols unusual activities in Korea but carefully avoided questioning him about how he was gathering information they needed in Korea, detecting some tricky and unlawful activities.

When the war broke up, Partridge had to understand more details in Nichols's operation in the summer of 1950, and he was startled at what he found. He described what Nichols had established on the Korean Peninsula during the prewar years as the most efficient and successful special operations of the war although Nichols's method of information gathering was rather bizarre. But Partridge's problem was that neither the newly arrived Central Intelligence Agency (CIA) nor the Far East Command's army intelligence team could compete with the quality of sensitive information generated by Nichols's contacts. Nichols established a deep penetration during his agent's years throughout the Korean Peninsula. By 1950, Nichols had access 24 hours a day to both General Partridge and South Korean president Syngman Rhee. They also knew of a host of shadowy Asian characters involved but they didn't want their names to be published anywhere. Although Nichols had only a sixth-grade education, he considered himself a master spy whose warnings accurately predicted within days the North Korean invasion of South Korea. But Nichol's warnings were totally ignored at General MacArthur's headquarters.

During the Korean War, Nichols personally organized and led a daring helicopter mission deep into enemy territory to strip parts off a downed MiG-15 fighter the most highly sought intelligence prize of the war. Knowing well Nichols's world had a side worrisome and uncomfortable, Partridge and others still relied on Nichols time and time again when they became desperate for results or information without questioning his methods or when the need was too sensitive to put in writing. As President Rhee's trust in Nichols grew Rhee took the highly unusual step of placing selected South Korean coast guard and air force personnel under the command of the American sergeant. He emerged three years later as a legend in South Korea's most powerful military and intelligence circle. This was a big puzzle even to the US special operators who worked for him and to this day remains virtually unknown to the American public.

In his autobiography, Nichols brags that "By this time [1947–1948] our unit was really moving in 'high, very high' South Korean government circles. All doors were open to us. In those days no one in this area knew or even thought about Positive Intelligence. We invented it for this area and taught others, as we saw fit, for our own benefit." Nichols's unit was Subdetachment K, 607th CIC, stationed at Gimpo Airfield on the western outskirts of Seoul. After reporting to the subdetachment in June 1946 Nichols soon began making effective and extensive use of Korean civilians to establish a covert network throughout the length of the politically troubled peninsula. Evidently, Syngman Rhee used Nichols to further his political ambitions and Nichols took advantage of this opportunity to become his confidant. He went after the Korean "communists or accused communists" i.e. anyone opposed to Rhee in South Korea. Nichols ran a large spy enterprise for Rhee and the US Air Force in Korea as early as 1948 and participated in the killing of many "communist (accused) leaders" in South Korea. General Partridge carefully avoided questioning Nichols about much of what he was doing.

From 1947 to 1948, Nichols traveled to Pyongyang disguised as a supply convoy commander for the US mission in Pyongyang. Nichols expanded his counterspy operation with full personal support from Syngman Rhee. On March 31, 1947 Nichols traveled through North Korea disguised as a World Federation Trade Union delegate. In 1948 and 1949 Nichols placed several moles among the ruling group of the South Korean Comunist Party (Namno-dang) in North Korea and received high-level intelligence on North Korea's war plans including the exact date of the invasion. Nichols supplemented human intelligence with aerial reconnaissance obtained by South Korean pilots in L5 observation planes. However, his intelligence reports fell on deaf ears in Tokyo and Washington.

How did Nichols become Lawrence of Korea? On June 28, 1940, Nichols joined the US Army Air Corps. He was assigned as a truck driver to Company F, 30th Quartermaster, MacDill Air Base in

Tampa, Florida. In January 1942, he was sent to Karachi, India, to maintain several thousands trucks on the 4,000-mile supply line from Karachi to Chiang Kai-shek's wartime capital, Chongqing. Nichols's unit, the 1603rd Echelon Automotive Maintenance and Supply Co. had to improvise to keep the fleet in operation. In April 1945 Nichols returned to the United States on a medical leave and was reassigned to Camp Waco, Texas, and a few months later to the Army Air Corp Base at Kearns, Utah. He was a 1st sergeant assigned to a casualty unit. It was here in Mormon country that he became a Mormon.

Nichols reenlisted in October 1945 and was sent to Guam as a master sergeant in charge of the motor pool at a B-29 base—the 31st Air Service Group. In April 1946, Nichols volunteered and received training as a special intelligence agent (CIC) in Tokyo. He graduated on June 29, 1946 and Niclos was assigned to the three-man "K" sub-detachment of the 607th CIC. The unit's mission was to guard the US Air Force base at Gimpo and other areas of South Korea. One of Nichols's duties was to "look over" Syngman Rhee, who evidently was chosen by the Americans as the South Korean leader from the beginning but was not fully trusted. Nichols and Rhee became close personal friends. Rhee provided funds and manpower to Nichols in order to facilitate extermination of Rhee's political enemies as "communists." This "duty" fell nicely into Nichols's scheme of things. Nichols was able to expand his little empire rapidly and to intimidate and control many political and military leaders of South Korea—including Syngman Rhee.

Nichols wrote in his autobiography:

> "I had complete access to the Republic of Korea government from its highest echelons to the bottom line. I soon learned one of the most effective ways to control high-level politicians is through a state of fear. Everyone has a skeleton to hide; find out what, where, or who it is, and you have your man more-or-less under control. I used this tactic with any official I couldn't win over by sheer friendship and magnetism."

Nichols details various methods of torture and extermination of the "communists" used by the American and the South Korean agents under his command. When the war broke out, Nichols' unit was based at Pupyon in Seoul and he was the last American to leave Seoul. On his flight south, he participated in (he said in his book he merely witnessed) one of the worst massacres of civilians in the war: some 1,800 civilian prisoners were systematically shot to death by Nichols's Korean employees at Suwon.

Nichols continued:

> "I stood by helplessly, witnessing the entire affair. Two big bulldozers worked constantly. One made the ditch-type grave. Trucks loaded with the condemned ["communists"] arrived. Their hands were already tied behind them. They were hastily pushed into a line along the edge of the newly opened grave. They were quickly shot in the head and pushed into the grave. I tried to stop this from happening; however, I gave up when I saw I was wasting my time. I was the only foreigner there. I think I'd rather have gone with the dead and gotten it over with quick and easy—then I wouldn't have these terrible nightmares. The worst part about this whole affair was that I learned later that not all the people killed were communists. The least I could do is to make a photographic record of this stinking episode. Then the manner of their deaths would never be disputed or falsely blamed. These photos I still guard, as I have since that miserable day in July 1950, so that they would not fall into hands that would misuse them for false or treasonable motives, personal gains or exploitation."

This photo of the massacre of civilians is indeed included in his book. One of the photos floating around on the web as the Bodo League massacre looks identical to the photo I saw in his biography describing Suwon massacre. I believe that photo is incorrectly labeled. Nichols continued his service in Korea for Rhee until 1957. He was finally removed from his command in November 1957 because of many complaints about his activities and was sent back to the US awaiting investigations. I could not find the details on this investigation. He was finally discharged in 1962.

Unfortunately, the Suwon massacre was only the beginning of many civilian massacres that took place shortly after the outbreak of the Korean War as described in the following three chapters. Many decades after the war, the shocking details of the government-sponsored atrocities finally surfaced. The South Korean military ordered "preemptive apprehension" of suspected leftists nationwide. Thousands were detained and sorted into four groups, labeled A, B, C, and D, based on the perceived security risks each posed. On August 30, 1950, a written order by a senior intelligence officer in the South Korean navy instructed Jeju's police to "execute all those in groups C and D by firing squad no later than September 6." There seemed to have been no end to those poor islanders' sacrifices. For almost 50 years after the uprising it was still a crime punishable by torture and a lengthy prison sentence in South Korea to even mention the events. The government had largely ignored the event. Of course, we didn't know any details about all those atrocities because they were well-hidden government-sponsored war crimes for many decades.

In 1992, President Roh Tae Woo's government sealed up a cave of Mt. Halla, the beautiful sleepy volcano where the remains of massacre victims including women and young children had been discovered. In October 2003, President Roh Moo-hyun, the third civilian president and the ninth president of South Korea, finally apologized to the Jeju islanders for the brutal suppression of the uprising declaring that "Due to wrongful decisions of the government, many innocent people of Jeju suffered many casualties and their homes were destroyed." Roh Moo-hyun, as South Korean president, had made the first apology for the 1948 massacre. In March 2009, The Truth and Reconciliation Commission confirmed its findings that "at least 20,000 people jailed for taking part in the popular uprisings in Jeju, Yeosu, and Suncheon, or accused of being communists, were massacred in some 20 prisons across the country" when the Korean War broke out.

Chapter 14: Korean War and the Bodo League Massacre (June - July, 1950)

My father always described the history of Korea in one word: Yongdu-Sami, Dragon Head and Snake Tail. He meant to say that Korea began as a very large and strong nation stretching far north into Manchuria and Vladivostok like the big head of a powerful dragon, but it gradually shrank into a tiny nation like a snake's tail, one half of the peninsula in the South. His discontent with his own country's history and with continuing chaos in the nation made him greatly admire the work of the founding fathers of the United States who created a successful democratic system of a government. He believed that absolute monarchial systems in which supreme power is lodged in a monarch - one individual for life - are fundamentally flawed. This was the common form of government in the world during ancient and medieval times but it lasted even longer in Japan, Korea, and China, in fact until the 19th century. My father blamed the inability of the dysfunctional monarchial system and the continuing infighting of the last Korean dynasty for failing to protect the country from Japanese takeover.

My Father believed that the founding fathers of the United States who signed the Declaration of Independence and participated in drafting the Constitution are not only American heroes but they also changed the political paradigm of the world. Father was also very impressed by the rapid progress made in American technology and often talked about Thomas Edison's achievements quoting his motto "Success is achieved by 99% perspiration and 1% inspiration" to make sure we didn't become disappointed when we didn't succeed in our first efforts in our school work. My father wanted us to emulate Thomas Edison (1847–1931) because Edison was famous not only as a prolific inventor and a good businessman who developed many devices that greatly improved human life around the world but was also one of the first manufacturers to apply the principles of mass production which was a key to America's industrial success. Edison proved that persistence after failure could also lead to success and that protecting inventions by patenting can make you rich as well. Edison held 1,093 U.S. patents in his name, as well as many patents in the United Kingdom, France, and Germany. (Apparently, my father, who always admired a person's character as the most important factor, did not know much about Edison's nasty temperament and vendetta against Nikola Tesla and Westinghouse Electric Company.)

It was always father's dream to spend some years in the United States to learn and observe how American democracy had worked so successfully and at the same time to do graduate studies at Harvard University in Cambridge, Massachusetts. He was like a professional student with an inquisitive mind and a desire to learn new things and gather new knowledge. He also felt that the education he had received under Japanese control was very restricted and inadequate, but he hadn't found a suitable time to fulfill his dream because he had to support his family.

Since he had connections in the Department of Education, he was in the middle of making necessary arrangements for a cultural exchange scholarship program for Korean educators to leave for America after my mother delivered their sixth child in late July. The time was just right for him to pursue his dream because the family was living in a beautiful home; we were financially comfortable; and there was a self-sufficient vegetable garden, fruits from the fruit trees, and my frugal mother had learned how to manage the family finances adequately by then. My father was excited about his prospects and Mother also thought it was a good development for his career in a highly politically charged society. At this time, I had just completed seventh grade, the first year in middle school, and my brother John was still in elementary school.

It was a peaceful Sunday, June 25, 1950 and the house was filled with fragrance from white and violet lilacs in the yard, my father's favorite flower. I was on the balcony of the second floor in our home, watching the distant view of the Han River and the ever-changing animal silhouettes formed by white clouds in the blue sky I habitually enjoyed while lying down at the edge of the balcony rail on the roof. All of a sudden, my parents rushed home from morning church service and told us that North Korean forces had crossed the

38th parallel and were invading South Korea. We didn't have any details of the North Korean invasion at the time but I learned many years later from General MacArthur's autobiography that North Korea invaded with an estimated strength of 6 infantry divisions, 3 brigades, and 200 tanks with supporting units of heavy artillery. They invaded early in the morning overwhelming the South Korean advance post at the 38th parallel.

My mother was eight months pregnant with her sixth child at the time and we had no family car. In fact no family I knew had a family car those days. This was a really helpless and panicky situation. We turned on the radio (no TV was available in Korea yet) to listen to updates on the progress of the war. We heard no encouraging news but only very confusing statements. President Rhee encouraged the citizens of Seoul, the nation's capital, to remain calm in the city and assured us that the government would defend the capital.

My father prepared our bunker just in case there was an air strike. We were glad we had the sturdy bunker for protection. Everybody was running around hysterically not knowing what to do or how to escape. Korea is a very small country so the enemy could reach Seoul in hours if they moved at high speed. Two days after the invasion we heard a thunderous explosion that shook our house. We learned later that it was the sound of the Han River Bridge being blown up to prevent enemy tanks from crossing. We also learned that President Rhee himself had already left Seoul as soon as the war broke out and established a temporary government in Daejeon. Not only did destroying the Han River Bridge prevent thousands of citizens from escaping from Seoul to flee from the North Korean forces but also those who were already on the bridge at the time were all drowned. When my father heard this news, he was very upset about the deception by the president of the nation. He said that Syngman Rhee had lost the people's trust as president and would come to regret this later. If we had owned a car, our family might have been on that bridge at that time and drowned in the river like the others.

On June 28, Seoul was already in enemy hands. In the early morning of the 28th, someone was knocking at our door shouting for everyone to hear, "All of you come out! Seoul has been liberated by North Korean soldiers!" When my parents opened the door it was none other than my father's nephew Young-gi who was a student at Seoul National University majoring in French at the time. Our parents had no knowledge where he had been for a long time since he hadn't come to visit us for quite a while. I remember he used to accuse our parents of being bourgeois and said his generation belonged to the proletarians. Father used to advise him not to act recklessly due to the trend of mob psychology of young people and to concentrate on his schoolwork and get a job after his graduation as a diplomat to France. My impression was that Young-gi didn't pay much attention to father's advice.

Young-gi told us that he was in jail for many months because he was a member of Namno-dang and was just released from the jail because all the jail doors were opened after Seoul was taken over by the North Korean force. My mother said, "Oh my God, our neighbors are going to think we are communists. Why is he coming to our home making such loud noise?" Unfortunately, this incident had already given a wrong impression of our family to our neighbors. I suppose our home was the closest place to the jail from which he was just released, so he came to wash up and change.

Our parents began worrying about the safety of my aunt's family. They lived on the north side of Seoul, Dongsoon-dong. My aunt, who was my mother's sister was married to one of my father's previous students whose family were rich landlords in Hwanghae Province near the 38th parallel but still within the South Korean territory. Father went to visit my aunt's family to find out how they were doing. My father confirmed that they were all alive and safe. On his way back home near the Seoul train station he heard an air-raid siren so he ducked behind the wall of the Sebrance Medical Center. He heard a big bomb explode nearby and felt a strong shock wave. When it was over he came out and saw the woman who had been walking right in front of him dead on the street. An American plane had dropped a bomb because there was a North Korean tank and soldiers in front of the Seoul train station. Thus Father knew the Americans were getting involved in this war but he didn't know the details about how many other countries were following suit or what was happening at the United Nations. There was no way to obtain accurate news. Father was very shaken by this incident at the Seoul train station and hurried home to check on us to see whether we were still alive. We could have lost Father on that day and my religious mother thanked God for saving his life.

Before the war my father learned about how American forces withdrew from South Korea in 1948 leaving poorly trained South Korean units along the 38th parallel; they had only light weapons, no air or naval forces, no tanks or artillery or other essentials needed by a fighting force. The decision to equip and organize them that way had been made by the US State Department to prevent South Korea from attacking North Korea. We will never know why it never occurred to the US government officials and CIA that North Korea could attack South Korea instead. It was a fatal error not to prepare South Korea to defend itself against such an attack.

The president of the first ROK, Syngman Rhee, had spent all his time and effort in creating more police forces and paramilitary youth organizations to eliminate his political enemies and root out suspected communists in South Korea instead of strengthening military forces to defend the country against a possible invasion from North Korea. Kim Il-sung consolidated his power by horrendous suppression of anticommunist forces and then began advocating immediate withdrawal of all foreign forces from Korean Peninsula, preparing to invade South Korea. During the same period, the Soviet Union totally ignored the UN peace code. They trained the North Korean Army and supplied necessary military equipment, not only to defend them but also to invade South Korea. The result was that 100,000 US-trained South Korean troops, with few weapons besides rifles, were opposed by a Soviet-trained North Korean army of 200,000 men equipped with every modern implement of war.

There were some noisy victory parades on the street organized by local people, many from the poor working-class laborers but also some teachers and high school and college students. This is how the communists used underprivileged people like farmers against land lords, factory workers against factory owners. Sometimes they turned students against their teachers, and even children against their own parents, giving them new status as revolutionaries. But after they achieved their goal, they gradually pushed those naïve people back and ignored them or even suppressed them.

Soon after some kind of temporary wartime police showed up here and there, most of them from North Korea but joined by some local people to keep law and order. They were distributing very large photos of Kim Il-sung and flyers telling us what to do – instructing all students and teachers to return to their designated schools, adults to attend evening political reeducation lectures, and so on. We were relieved in a way that they were unable to continue enforcing all those rules on us because of ever-increasing bombing by American planes. Radio stations continuously played North Korean revolutionary music and reported how far south their forces were advancing every day. Father was trying to find a radio station to listen to broadcasts from Japan or any English broadcast from abroad without success, may be because the radio we had was not sophisticated enough to receive transmissions from abroad.

It was only after the war that we found more details about what had been going on while our family was in the dark in our bunker. Quick decisions were made in Washington that Sunday afternoon, June 25, 1950. At the request of the United States, UN Secretary-General Trygve Lie called the UN Security Council (UNSC) delegates into a special session. The Russians did not have a delegate present. They were boycotting the UN in protest against the membership of the Chinese nationalists but the deeper reason for the Russians not attending the meeting was to avoid the questions of whether Russia knew about this invasion beforehand, approved it, and supplied military equipment to the North Korean army.

According to my research Stalin thought that the time was not right and he didn't want to get involved in a war with the United States, but Kim Il-sung convinced him that the war would be a very short one because he was aware that the South Korean military was poorly equipped, that the US military forces had already withdrawn from South Korea, and most of all, that the US secretary of state, Dean Acheson, left South Korea out of the US "defensive perimeter" in Asia during a speech in Washington, DC, before the National Press Club on January 12, 1950. Dean Acheson's decision might have had something to do with General Hodge's terrible experience in South Korea because of the never-ending conflict between right- and left-wing politicians and Syngman Rhee's lack of cooperation to achieve any political goals General Hodge was assigned to achieve under his administration. No matter what the real reason behind Dean's speech, it assured Kim Il-sung that the United States would not commit troops should North Korea invade South Korea. If the Russians had come to the UNSC that day the outcome of the Korean War could have been very different since they had veto power.

This was a time when the United States was a highly respected world power after World War II and had great influence over UNSC decisions. The United States took advantage of this opportunity to propose a resolution condemning the action of the North Korean forces as a breach of the peace and called for the authorities of North Korea to withdraw their armed forces to the 38th parallel. Of course, the North Korean authorities had no intension of withdrawing.

On June 27, the UNSC met again and passed another resolution, concluding that "urgent military measures are required to restore international peace and security," and recommending that "the members of the UN furnish assistance to South Korea to repel the invasion." The US was able to organize an impressive coalition to repel communism and protect freedom and democracy in Asia. Until this day nobody seems to know for sure why President Truman changed his mind and got involved in the Korean conflict after his secretary of state had already left Korea out of the US defensive perimeter in Asia. This must have been a big surprise to Kim Il-sung.

After the war we found that approximately 150,000 foreign servicemen fought in this war and 14 foreign nations sent ground forces to Korea. Australia, Canada, New Zealand, and the United

Kingdom made up the British Commonwealth forces. Luxembourg, Belgium, Colombia, Ethiopia, France, Greece, the Netherlands, the Philippines, and Thailand had battalion-sized units attached to US Army divisions, and Turkey deployed an infantry brigade. Eight foreign nations deployed more than 100 naval vessels including carriers, destroyers, cruisers, frigates, landing ships, tankers, and other utility craft. Foreign naval vessels participated in the Inchon landing; the evacuation of the UN's ground forces from Nampo, Hungnam, and Wonsan; shore bombardment of North Korea's coastlines; and patrols of the sea lanes of communications to South Korea. The 77th Fighter Squadron of Australia was the first foreign unit to arrive in Korea, on July 2, 1950. It was attached to the 35th US FG. South Africa's Second Fighter Squadron was attached to the US18th FG. It provided close air support to UN forces. Australia, Canada, Greece, and Thailand provided air transport units to the UN's command. This was an impressive coalition the United States was able to put together to fight communist expansion in Asia.

On June 28, Seoul was already in North Korean hands and the ROK government moved its temporary headquarters to Daejeon. On June 29 General MacArthur landed in Suwon, 20 miles south of Seoul, reached the Han River by Jeep, and witnessed the bridge being blown up by the ROK government to prevent the North Korean tanks from crossing. He felt that there was nothing to stop the communists from rushing their tanks straight down from Seoul to Busan at the end of the peninsula, and the entire Korean Peninsula would then be under Kim Il-sung's control. He decided that even with air and naval support, the ROK force could not stop the North Korean force's rapid southward advance without involving his own troops. Within 24 hours, President Truman authorized the use of ground troops. It was critical to slow down the North Korean forces before they conquered all of Korea.

Our family was still stuck in our bunker in Seoul without knowing all this was going on. We could not go anywhere even if we had a car. Where could we go to escape from the North Korean forces? ROK is smaller than half the state of California. But if we stayed at home we had at least some food hidden away and we had the vegetable garden and many fruit trees to depend on. A few days later one of my father's former students from Pyongyang, Hahn Gilhyun, came to our home and wanted to stay upstairs for a while. He was a tall, nice-looking fellow who fled North Korea after Kim Ilsung took over and was living in Seoul. He visited our parents once in a while but our parents had no idea how he was making a living. My father thought that he might have been involved in Syngman Rhee's intelligence service since that's how many young North Korean refugees made a living in the ROK those days. Now, he was trying to hide from the North Korean force by hiding in our home. As always, my parents never refused to help anyone, especially his former students, so they just let him stay upstairs, sharing our food, whatever we had.

As an unexpected misfortune to our family, one small North Korean battalion moved into the Sookmyung Women's College dormitory, just behind of our home within a few weeks. This could become a US bombing target, destroying our home or otherwise complicating our lives, but there was absolutely nothing we could do to prevent it. There were about 300–400 soldiers since that dormitory could not accommodate any more people than that. This was the second time my mother reminded my father about the poor location and neighborhood of our house that he insisted on buying, but it was too late to regret. My parents seemed to have an anxious feeling that some bad fortune was building up. We were stuck with the situation and had no choice but to leave our fate to God. Whatever was going to happen would happen and all Mother could do was to pray to God every day to protect the fate of our family. We had no idea what kind of tasks the military unit in our neighborhood was assigned to do. Apparently, they didn't belong to the infantry division as frontline fighters, but rather they were there as a support group for the purpose of gathering information or monitoring the civilians behind the front line.

The very next day I heard our front door bell ring and I went to see who was at the door. It was a nasty looking short man, a North Korean military officer. He might have been a major or a lieutenant colonel but I couldn't tell for sure because they didn't have the same type of badges as ROK or U.S. Army officers wore. I thought that he was the highest-ranking officer of the unit that had just moved into that dormitory. My father was not at home because he had gone to the local farmer's market to buy some food. My mother and I were at home with my sister, Oak, and three brothers (John, Churl, and Soo). Mr. Hahn was still upstairs hiding in our home. I was very nervous but I composed myself quickly, smiled at him, opened the door and greeted him, saying "Welcome comrade, is there anything we can do for you?" As soon as he walked into the yard, our German shepherd, Mary, began barking at him very violently. She was a very smart dog, so she always had a good instinct to recognize bad guys. The North Korean officer became very angry with Mary; he pulled out his pistol, aimed at the dog, and was ready to shoot. I was terrified but, not realizing, I instinctively blocked him from shooting by standing between Mary and him, begging him not to shoot the dog. At the same time, I kept telling Mary to get into her little doghouse and she finally seemed to realize the dangerous situation and went inside. Mary was on a chain all that time, so she could not have possibly bitten him anyway unless he went close enough to her. But this smart dog stopped barking at him when she saw the pistol aimed at her. The officer calmed down a little and said he wanted to look around the house. My heart was pumping very fast now and I was trying to recover from the shock.

Because of all the noise outside my mother looked out to see what was going on. As usual, my mother was always very quick to assess the situation and she used her diplomacy. She invited him in and served him tea. He just sat down at the edge of the hallway where the sliding glass door was opened but he didn't drink tea. Maybe he was trained not to drink tea offered by a stranger or he simply didn't trust us. Mother told him all about my father's nephew, Young-gi, a high-ranking member of Namno-dang although we didn't really know how high a position Young-gi was holding or what he was actually doing in the party but that was enough to cool down this mean guy's attitude toward us. Then he said that he wanted to check out our house because someone launched light signals aiming high up into the sky from our vegetable garden the night before, probably to signal the U.S. planes the location where this North Korean unit was staying.

We had no knowledge of that and were terribly worried about him inspecting the whole house because Mr. Hahn was still upstairs. Mother reminded him that we lived just next door to them and if the U.S. plane dropped a bomb, our own house could have been the direct hit and we would all be killed. Why should we do such a stupid thing? He became more relaxed after listening to mother's explanation and left our home without further home inspection. We were able to breathe at last after he left us.

Right after that incident Hahn decided to leave our home to avoid further risk. He felt it was too dangerous for him to stay next to the North Korean military unit. We never heard from him again. When my father returned home, we told him about the incident with the North Korean officer and our dog Mary. He said that dogs get very frightened during the war, especially at the noise of a bomb blast, so we should get rid of the dog anyway. He decided to return the dog to his former chauffeur who brought us the dog if he could find him in his home. Next day my father left the house with Mary on a chain. Mary kept looking back at me as if she knew that was the last time we were going to see each other and I felt very guilty letting her go not knowing her fate. I cried. I can still see her looking back at me till this day. She served us well for many years as our watch dog and finally ended a series of burglaries that took place before she joined our family and we had to let her go this way. War is cruel not just to humans but to animals as well.

A couple of days later a group of people, including our neighbors living across from us knocked on our door and asked us how much rice we had in the house because we now had to share food with all our neighbors. My mother was 8 months pregnant and we desperately needed to keep some rice and some nutritious food for her to recover after delivering a baby but we had to give away a good portion of what we had. Mother said again what kind of neighbors we had. She was sure they hid their own rice in their home and came to get ours. This was not all. The people who occupied the local political office found my mother's name as the president of the patriotic ladies' society during the 1st ROK under Syngman Rhee. They called on her in order to interrogate her. She again used Young-gi's name as the high-ranking Namno-dang member in our family and was released, but they insisted that she had to serve in the same capacity under their communist government. She had to distribute some of their flyers for them a couple of days but she used her late pregnancy as an excuse to resign.

When a government keeps changing hands from one side to another it makes civilian lives very difficult because they have to cooperate with each government to survive. Most people don't want to get involved in politics and just mind their own business, work hard and make a living to support their family but unfortunately that's not always possible. This is the tragedy for ordinary people living in unstable countries when they are dragged into political activities they try so hard to avoid.

A few days later I saw someone behind the fence picking peaches from our tree so I yelled saying "Who is there stealing our peaches?" I went to see who was behind the fence. To my surprise, they were two young North Korean soldiers who were staying in the dormitory. I could not tell their ranking since they were not wearing the top but just the bottom of their uniform but I could tell they were definitely not officers. Maybe they took off their top uniform to cool off because July weather was hot and humid. I had to apologize right away and said they could take as much as they wanted. They were very young, either late teens or early twenties, and didn't get nasty toward me for yelling at them.

After this incident, those young soldiers came to visit us once in a while to pick more fruit from other fruit trees and chat with us. They said they were drafted from school to be trained and join the war to liberate the south. Not to be accused of spying on them our parents never brought up any political discussions with them. Unlike the nasty officer who came to inspect our home, those boys never talked about politics or tried to promote their communist ideology to our parents. They just wanted to pick some fruit to supplement their poorly balanced army diet.

That became more apparent one afternoon when our family members were all working in the vegetable garden picking zucchini, cucumber and corn. The second lieutenant of our military neighbors, who looked a lot older then the rest was standing just outside of the kitchen of their dormitory which was located immediately on the other side of the wire fence of our vegetable garden. He asked my mother whether they could trade their salty mackerel preserves for some fresh vegetables, tofu, bean sprouts and zucchini in the market. They were sick and tired of eating the same military rations of salted mackerel, probably with rice and kimchi, everyday. Mother told them where the closest market was and he sent their cook to the market.

Now bombs were falling every day. My father turned on the radio and tried to find out how the war was progressing but there was continuous propaganda, music and the news of another southern city overtaken by the North Korean Army moving rapidly through Suwon, Daejeon, Chonju, and down the southern end of the peninsula. Since we had no access to foreign radio stations we just had to rely on rumors or leaflets. Every day there were unknown people diligently distributing leaflets of propaganda. Huge photos of Kim Il Sung, referred to as the great leader, were posted on every wall including ours. These people seemed to belong to a group organized for spreading propaganda to indoctrinate the South in communist doctrine.

Mother's delivery day was quickly approaching but many hospitals were shut down and it was very difficult to find any obstetrician during the war because of the continuous bombardment. Fortunately Mother knew a midwife and asked her to come and examine her and deliver the baby when it was due. What she found in her examination was very alarming. The midwife discovered that the baby was in a reverse position, head up and legs down. This might have been the result of so many trips mother had to make up and down to the bunker using a steep ladder because of air raids. The midwife notified her that a normal delivery was not possible. My parents were getting panicky and asked for her advice. The midwife said she might be able to turn the baby little by little every day by grabbing the fetus's head and the legs in the uterus to reverse the position so that the head would come out first, during the delivery. My parents had no choice but to accept her plan, holding their breath and praying to God for the best outcome. Mother's face and body began to swell to a dangerous point and it was difficult to predict the dangers of a safe delivery.

July in South Korea is hot and humid. Mother was expecting the delivery any time. The midwife informed us that she had been able to reverse the fetus's position in the uterus and she was expecting the head to come out first just like a normal delivery.

On the evening of July 31, Mother went into labor. My father brought the midwife home and covered all the windows with double-layer black curtains to block the light in case of an air raid thereby preventing our home from becoming a target. In addition we avoided using a very bright light for fear that it might still leak. The night was deepening and there was another air-raid siren. Soon after we heard a rocket explosion nearby and then we heard the baby's cry. A boy was born, my parent's sixth child and the fourth son. Mother was still alive. Father named this boy "Suk". When I think of the situation now I know it was probably a miracle mother survived. But I was too young to fully aware of the seriousness of the situation at the time. The next morning, we saw a rocket-damaged house on the other side of the women's dormitory and heard that several people in the house were hit by the rocket and died. The rocket could have been aimed at our home because of some leakage of the light but missed a little and hit that house instead. But nobody really knows. Not that it matters to those who died.

Mother was thankful and said God had saved us for the second time although she had a really hard time recovering. Unfortunately it was a hot summer and we could not provide a cool and comfortable environment for her. Besides, we did not have enough nutritious food to help her recover after childbirth. Every day she ate rice with the same seaweed soup boiled with some dried shrimp Father saved for her. Her face and body were swelling even further and the midwife said she might have contracted an infection during delivery because of the conditions, but she did not have proper medicine to treat her.

Father had a doctor friend, a classmate in Seoul, but he could not find him. We just had to rely on Mother's immune system to fight the infection. Would there be God's help to save Mother once more? We all prayed every day. Her swelling gradually went down to a normal level. She went through a great ordeal, yet she still survived! It's a miracle such a delicate woman could endure such hell. But such is war and vulnerable civilian lives trapped in war.

It was August now and the news reports were that every city had fallen into the hands of North Korean forces except Busan, which is at the southeastern tip of the Korean Peninsula. This meant that my maternal grandparents' city, Gwangju, was also taken. So my father said, "Even if we escaped Seoul somehow and reached Grandparents' home in Gwangju, that would not have made any difference now." He could not believe that the powerful US Army with superior air power was being defeated so rapidly by the North Korean Army. At the same time he began to worry about how to make a living to support his family in the future. After all, he was an English literature professor, undoubtedly a subject the North Korean government wouldn't want to include in its university curriculum. Besides, father was also aware that communist revolutionaries hate intellectuals; people they cannot easily brainwash.

About this time Professor Sohn, a professor at Sookmyung Women's College, contacted father to meet with him to discuss the school curriculum to see whether English literature could be included. Since the school was within walking distance my father went there a few times to chat with Professor Sohn. Of course, there were no classes or students at that time partly because of intensive bombing and partly because it was during the summer recess. But shortly after, he stopped going there because the North Korean government was trying to send all teachers and professors in the South to Pyongyang for reeducation and training. That's the last thing he wanted to do - leave a wife in poor health with six kids, in the middle of a war. Because of constant American air raids, fortunately for us, they could not mobilize their police force to come after everybody to enforce their policies of reeducation of communist indoctrination. To these people, the welfare of individual families was not a priority but infusing the communist doctrine was.

American planes were getting pretty good at targeting the schools where the North Korean military was storing their military supplies. Although our parents were also worried about the dormitory being hit because North Korean soldiers were still there we had no other place to go with our large family. We were leaving our fate in God's hands. We were completely isolated from the outside world in this small bunker. One day, I dozed off and had a dream; our family members were in an immense place where colorful butterflies were flying over beautiful flowers. It was a very peaceful place. It's strange that we were not talking at all. I was lying there looking at the blue sky where white clouds were slowly moving and continuously changing their animal silhouettes. Unfortunately a nearby bomb blast sound woke me up and I was back to reality in the bunker.

Many decades later I learned what was going on outside of our bunker. The South Korean government moved to Daejeon shortly after the outbreak of the War. There in Daejeon, President Syngman Rhee ordered the execution of people related to either the Bodo League or the South Korean Workers Party on June 27, 1950. This was a confession from Kim Mansik, who was a military police superior officer at the time. Retreating South Korean forces and anticommunist paramilitary groups executed the alleged communist prisoners along with many of the Bodo League members. Of course, the executions were performed without any trials or sentencing. When Seoul was recaptured in late September, 1950, an estimated 30,000 South Koreans were summarily deemed collaborators with the North Koreans and shot by ROK forces. A mass execution of 3,400 South Koreans also took place near Busan that summer. In many seaside villages victims were tied together and thrown into the sea to drown. Retired South Korean Admiral Nam Sang-hui confessed that he authorized 200 victims' bodies to be thrown into the sea, saying, "There was no time for trials."

The Bodo League massacre was clearly a war crime. Many of the dead were civilians who had no connection with communism or communists. Estimates of the death toll vary. According to Professor Kim Dong-choon, commissioner of the Truth and Reconciliation Commission that was established after the civilian government was restored; at least 100,000 people were executed on suspicion of supporting communism. Others estimate closer to 200,000. The massacre was wrongly, and intentionally, blamed on the communists for four decades and the South Korean government concealed the atrocity. Survivors were forbidden by the government from revealing it. Doing so meant being branded communist sympathizers. Public revelation also carried with it the threat of torture and death at the hands of military police. During the 1990s several corpses were excavated from mass graves resulting in public awareness of the massacre. This is why history didn't record the atrocity well into modern history and well beyond the period allocated to the Korean War.

How was Bodo League created? In June 1949 the South Korean government accused independence activists of being members of the Bodo League. Noncommunist sympathizers or political opponents of Syngman Rhee were also forced into the Bodo League to fill enlistment quotas. Syngman Rhee had about 300,000 suspected communist sympathizers or his political opponents enrolled in an official "reeducation" movement known as the Bodo League (or National Rehabilitation and Guidance League) on the pretext of protecting them from execution.

Photo 6a: Retreating South Korean soldiers walking among the bodies of Bodo League victim. At Daejon in July 1950. Photo by U.S. Army Major Robert Abbott in July 1950. Photo in Public Domain)

Photo 6b: This U.S. Army photograph, once classified "top secret," is one of a series depicting the summary execution of 1,800 South Korean political prisoners by the SK military at Daejon, South Korea, over three days in July 1950. Photo by U.S. Army Major Robert Abbott in July 1950. Photo in Public Domain.

Chapter 15: Threshold of Life and Death
(September–October 1950)

September arrived and the weather was getting cooler. We were running out of food. Father, between air raids, planted cabbage and radishes and some other vegetables that can grow in cool weather saying that we might be able to survive on soybean soup, kimchi, barley, and unprocessed wheat until the war was over. We noticed that some of our neighbors had broken into our vegetable garden at night and pulled out vegetables from the root leaving empty spots here and there on the ground but we could not even investigate to find out who stole our vegetables because communists do not recognize private ownership. The wire fence surrounding the vegetable garden was flimsy and it was very easy to break in. We ate steamed zucchini leaves, wrapping them around steamed rice or steamed barley with a drop of boiled soybean paste. When I complained that I didn't have any appetite to eat that kind of food my father used to say, "If you starve for three days, your appetite will return. Soybean is a good source of protein and barley has lots of vitamin B (thiamin, riboflavin, niacin, and folic acid) to help your brown hair turn black." To train us how to survive through difficult times my father didn't usually show much sympathy. Mother collected sweet dates (jujube), chestnuts, and persimmons from the trees on our land to supplement our poor diet.

By mid-September we needed to know what was really going on at the war front, how we were going to live, and for how long. Our lives were passing by every day in our isolated family bunker without learning anything new or doing anything constructive. It was a really monotonous, unproductive, and unexciting life and I was beginning to wonder why people wanted to continue such monotony. What's the use? I asked myself at times; I could not stand it much longer.

One day very late at night, someone loudly knocked on everybody's door, yelling and screaming that Busan had finally been taken and the whole country was united under Kim Il-sung. Mother thought that was really odd. She said "Why couldn't they wait until morning to report such good news if it really happened?" Early next morning we heard distant thunder, not sounds of bombardment but sounds that seemed like naval artillery striking inland targets. Father recognized immediately that the Allied forces might be attempting an amphibious assault in Inchon. We could see the sudden increase in activity of the North Korean military unit staying in the dormitory, trucking out soldiers in a hurry, leaving the place empty. Were they going to Inchon for a battle or retreating?

I learned more details after the war about what was really going on during those months. When the war broke out unexpectedly and suddenly General MacArthur had to come up with a strategy in a hurry. In the beginning he used only air power, hoping that displaying that strength might fool the North Korean military into believing that he had greater resources than he did. That's how he gained 10 days before the North Korean forces reached Suwon as the pivotal point. By that time he was able to bring in the 24th Division from Japan under Major General William Dean. Dean fought a desperate series of isolated battles in which a large part of that division was destroyed. This was when we saw American prisoners in Seoul.

Then the North Korean commander realized that he had been fooled by the appearance of force so he moved rapidly to make up for lost time. But by that time MacArthur had established the Eighth Army commanded by the four-star general Walton Harris Walker. The North Korean forces still had enormous superiority in manpower they could use to exert heavy pressure against General Walker's men. On July 7, General MacArthur asked the joint chief of staff in Washington for reinforcements but was denied because a suitable US military posture in other parts of the world had to be maintained. It was a matter of "priorities". The Far East was again at the bottom of the list. The UNSC directed the establishment of a united Korean command and President Truman named MacArthur as commander in chief. ROK President Syngman Rhee signed his government's approval of his appointment. By July 20, the period of piecemeal entry into action was over. The North Korean force's great chance depended upon the speed with which they could overrun the South once they had broken the Han River line.

Bloody fighting took place during the months of July and August and the fierce attacks on the Allied forces by the enemy were repeated. By the end of August the ROK force had been reorganized, and five small ROK divisions were fighting under General Walker's direction. A brigade of the First US Marine Division had also joined the Eighth Army. The UN forces made a plan to withdraw from Daejeon and take the battle to the Nakdong River. At Yongdog, after a bitter four-day struggle the North Korean force overwhelmed the UN position and forced a withdrawal further south to an extended beachhead around Busan. Although there was continuous bombing, the supply and reinforcement of the North Korean force continued. They were coming from Manchuria and Siberia. They were food, transporting supplies and ammunition at night, moving forward by train, by truck, and even by oxcart through the country roads. At this time all we were hearing behind the front line was another city had fallen to the North Korean forces and only the tip of the peninsula, Busan, had to be captured to claim total victory over the entire Korean Peninsula. They almost made it through.

It was a critical time for the Allied forces to make a decision whether to give up Korea or come up with a new winning strategy. We learned after the war that General MacArthur never intended to give up and ordered General Walker's forces to "stand or die," while waiting for General MacArthur's strategy to be put into action. General Walker's troops bravely slowed the enemy forces and by the end of the month had established a fairly stable line of defense. The Battle of Pusan Perimeter was a large-scale battle between United Nations and North Korean forces lasting from August 4 to September 18, 1950. It was one of the first major engagements of the Korean War. An army of 140,000 UN troops, having been pushed to the brink of defeat, were rallied to make a final stand against the invading North Korean army. UN forces, having been repeatedly defeated by the advancing North Koreans, were forced back to the "Pusan Perimeter", a 140-mile (230 km) defensive line around an area on the southeastern tip of the Korean Peninsula that included the port of Pusan. The UN troops, consisting mostly of forces from the ROK, United States and United Kingdom, mounted a last stand around the perimeter, fighting off repeated North Korean attacks for six weeks as they were engaged around the cities of Taegu, Masan, and P'ohang, and the Naktong River. The massive North Korean assaults were unsuccessful in forcing the United Nations troops back further from the perimeter, despite two major pushes in August and September.

What was General MacArthur's strategy? Surprisingly, the target General MacArthur selected was Inchon, 20 miles west of Seoul, and the target date, because of the tides at Inchon, was the middle of September. The amphibious operation had to be rapidly executed because of the tide. I learned that there was a possibility the Inchon landing would never have taken place if General MacArthur had not presented his winning strategy to his superiors and the entire Korean peninsula would now be under Kim Il-sung's three-generation dynasty, the only communist dynasty in the 20th–21st century with the worst human rights abuses in the world.

On July 23, MacArthur informed Washington of his plan and of course the plan was opposed. The joint chief of staff, General Omar Bradley, for various reasons, stated that such an amphibious operation was impractical. After a silence of three weeks, on August 23, General MacArthur called a strategic conference to debate the issue in Tokyo with General Collins, the Army Chief of Staff, Admiral Sherman (Chief of Naval Operations) and the Marines' chief, Lieutenant General Lemuel Shepherd Jr.(President Harry Truman appointed Shepherd as Commandant of the Marine Corps on January 1, 1952,). The Navy's objection was that there would not be enough time to complete the landing with the tides and unfavorable terrain at Inchon. Admiral Sherman said, "If every possible geographical and naval handicap were listed, Inchon has them all." Collins said Inchon was too far from the present battle area, which was Busan. In his autobiography General MacArthur revealed how he countered this question.

His presentation was as follows:

"The bulk of the Reds are committed around Walker's defense perimeter. I am convinced that they failed to prepare Inchon properly for defense. The very arguments

you have made as to the impracticality involved will
tend to ensure for me the element of surprise. Surprise is
the most vital element for success in war. Seizure of
Inchon and Seoul will cut the enemy's supply line and
seal off the entire southern peninsula. The vulnerability
of the enemy is his supply position. This will paralyze
the fighting power of the troops that now face Walker. If
my estimate is inaccurate and should I run into a defense
I will be there personally and will immediately withdraw
our forces. The only loss then will be my professional
reputation. But Inchon will not fail. Inchon will succeed.
And it will save 100,000 lives."

There was a complete silence. Then Sherman rose and said, "Thank you. A great voice in a great cause." On August 29, MacArthur received a telegram from the Joint Chiefs of Staff authorizing the mission.

When I read General MacArthur's own description of what he had to go through to have his Inchon landing strategy approved by his superiors, risking his own reputation, I admired his determination and commitment. He also repeatedly warned the US government about the danger of communism spreading in Asia, but Europe was the first priority of US government officials at that time. Even in Asian region, protecting Japan against Russia's territorial involvement was far more important than taking care of Korean issues. Koreans also bear some responsibility for the US government's reaching such a conclusion after observing the never-ending infighting between right- and left-wing politicians during the USAMGIK.

Many high-ranking US officers were surprised when President Truman announced his intention to defend the ROK against the North Korean invasion in 1950. If we hadn't had General MacArthur, there would be no ROK today, especially one with a successful democratic government and booming industry. All South Koreans would live in the Kim Il-sung dynasty under Kim Jong-un.

It is important that South Koreans, especially the younger generation appreciate the aftermath of WW2 and the Korean War through the experiences of those of us who lived it. Many families lost husbands, sons, and loved ones in the battle with North Korean and Mao's Red forces. The more we learn from eyewitness accounts from North Korean defectors of what's been going on in modern North Korea, the more we must credit Gen. MacArthur for preserving S. Korea from the domination of the Kim Il-sung dynasty. It may be that the U.S. could have avoided the Korean War entirely if they had sent the US military to Korea immediately after the Japanese surrender before Soviet Red Army came down to Korean peninsula from Manchuria. But their failure to do that was rectified when the U.S. organized 14 countries to form the coalition that did in fact successfully prosecute the Korean War.

Gen. MacArthur described his own experience on September 12, 1950, as follows:

"I stood at the bow of the Mount Kinley listening to the rush of the sea and watched the fiery sparklets of phosphorescence as the dark ship plowed toward the target, the armada of other craft converging on the same area, all now past the point of no return. Within 5 hours, 40,000 men would act boldly in the hope that 100,000 others manning the thin defense lines in South Korea would not die. I thought "I alone was responsible for tomorrow, and if I failed, the dreadful results would rest on judgment day against my soul." I saw the channel navigation lights in the harbor, so I knew they were taking the enemy by surprise. Then I went to my cabin to sleep. I woke up by a sudden thunder. The guns had opened up on Wolmi-do. This harbor island was now rocking under the bombardment of naval guns and aerial bombs. Immense explosions were erupting all along the shores. Then, the guns of Wolmi-do were silenced and the first assault waves were going in. If the Marines who were leading were beaten off or even pinned down for too long it would mean the enemy was in force. It would take only a few defenders to slaughter that first wave of invaders while the rest were held back by the enormous mud banks. At 8:00 AM, an orderly climbs up to the bridge and hands me a slip of paper. It says that first wave of marines have just landed and secured a beachhead without a single fatality. By the time the tide had gone out of Inchon's harbor only an hour later, leaving some of the landing craft squatting on the mud banks, Wolmi-do had been fully secured. This was a rare miracle and truly impressive military strategy by any measure considering all the disadvantages of Inchon harbor geography."

At home, strange and unexpected things kept happening. Everybody wanted to take advantage of my parents' kindness toward their fellow human beings. In the early morning after hearing the distant bombardment all night, someone knocked on our door. It was the 18-year-old North Korean soldier who belonged to the unit that used to occupy the dormitory behind our home and occasionally came to our home to pick fruit. He told us that all others in the same unit had been killed in Inchon and he was the only survivor. He wanted to know whether we could hide him in our home until he could find an opportunity to surrender to the UN forces when they arrived in Seoul. Apparently he never assumed that our parents were communists because we seemed to have been a well-to-do family living in a beautiful home before the war and that we were probably happy to see the allied forces recover Seoul. Our parents believed that he was telling the truth about his intention to surrender to the UN soldiers but it was out of the question to hide a North Korean soldier in the house. You never knew how it was going to be interpreted by the neighbors. So we told him we could not help him and asked him to leave via our vegetable garden to the dormitory until the UN soldiers came and then he could surrender himself.

About a week later, my father's nephew Young-gi, who never visited us during those three months under the communist occupation of Seoul, was passing by our home and, in a very loud voice across our vegetable garden asked my parents to look after his wife and his young daughter. He was with his bodyguard who was carrying a gun on his shoulder. It was clear he was escaping Seoul in a hurry before the allied forces arrived without even saying goodbye to his wife. As always, he thought our parents were bourgeois and thus we would be happy when the allied forces recaptured Seoul. His loud voice and open activity generated even more trouble for our parents in the neighborhood. My father's family did little to help my father but they did us harm many times, apparently without a second thought.

The noise of guns and explosions was getting closer and closer each day and we could see from the second floor of our home a deep red sky and black smoke rising from the center of the city. Seoul was burning. It was turning into a fireball from repeated Allied bombing. Again, our family had no choice but stay in the bunker to avoid the bombs and artillery shells.

During this time my mother's Japanese lady friend who was married to a Korean pharmacist came to visit my mother after a long absence and delivered shocking news. She was aware that some neighborhood people, mostly North Korean refugees who lived in the neighborhood, were organizing a group of people to accuse my parents as communists, and my parents might be killed by the mob during the lawless period. Our house would be confiscated and I might have to take care of all my younger siblings after our parents were killed. I was only thirteen years old at the time. She suggested that all of us leave the area until the South Korean government returned and law and order were restored. Mother was shocked at the news of a plot by our neighbors. I remembered that our neighbors, especially people living just across from our home, behaved as if they were communists or communist supporters during the communist occupation and they had even demanded distribution of rice from our family that was saved for my mother after her childbirth. Mother said we didn't do anything different than anyone else in the neighborhood during the communist occupation. This must have been a ploy to disguise their own behavior when the allied forces arrived because they behaved like communists. But it's no use to debate with people who are intentionally plotting your murder. There was no time to discuss or negotiate with anyone. The only thing we could do was to avoid the situation altogether.

Thus Mother asked Father to go to my aunt's house on the other side of Seoul to avoid the initial lawless period but she would stay at home with us. My mother was a frail, delicate, and emotional lady, but in emergencies she became very brave to protect the family. I was very proud of her risking her own life at that time. We owed many things to my mother since infancy, always taking care of us when we were sick, staying by our bedside many sleepless nights until we became well. But in this case it was her children who needed bravery and determination because it was dangerous for a frail woman who hadn't even recovered after delivering a baby only a month and half earlier to face a lawless mob who might kill her to cover up their own crimes. Even were my parents to be guilty of some kind of crime, it was still not up to them to judge. I admired my mother for trying to stand up to such people, but I was very worried about her safety.

It took several weeks for the Allied forces to recover Seoul after they landed at Inchon because North Korean soldiers in Seoul put up a vigorous defense. The US X Corps moved inland rapidly and one column headed for Seoul to cut communications to the South and to capture Gimpo Airfield. Another column moved on toward Suwon to capture the air base there. At the southern front line General Walker promptly crossed the Nakdong River in a ferocious assault. Signs of weakness on the enemy side began to show. The North Korean forces with their supplies and retreat cut off, gave way at an accelerated rate. Within a month the total number of captives rose to 130,000. The North Korean forces fought fiercely for Seoul, but by September 28 the city had been recaptured. General MacArthur moved at once to have the ROK government reestablished in Seoul.

It's interesting to learn that General MacArthur received a message from Washington at this time, saying, "Any plan for the restoration of Rhee's government must have the approval of higher authority." However, MacArthur objected to this order and reasoned that Rhee's government had to be reestablished. On September 29 he ordered the city of Seoul restored as the seat of formal government. From many other sources and records, I found that the US State Department had doubts about Syngman Rhee's ability to manage the country and the people but they had to identify an alternative (by this time, Koreans had already lost prominent leaders like Lyuh Woon-hyung and Kim Gu by assassination, and Kim Gyu-sik was kidnapped and taken to North Korea during the occupation). I suppose General MacArthur was eager to reestablish stability in South Korea as soon as possible.

One day a group of people invaded our home saying that a gun had been found in our vegetable garden and they wanted to search the house for a hidden North Korean soldier. Maybe someone saw that North Korean soldier coming into our house a few weeks ago. As I said before, our vegetable garden was located next to the street and had only a flimsy wire fence to prevent anyone coming in to steal vegetables from the garden. It was possible that some communist escaping Seoul threw his gun into our vegetable garden in open view. It could also have been that the same people who wanted to plot against our parents planted the gun there. In either case, we had no idea at all about the gun, even whether or not it was really there. My father never owned a gun and I had never seen a gun in our house. But it appeared that this was an excuse to arrest my parents. Since my father was not at home they wanted to arrest my mother and take her away. My mother was nursing the baby, Suk, who was only one and a half months old. She put the baby on her back and they placed the handcuffs on her and escorted her out. My mother looked very pale and frightened but composed. She was not crying and she asked me to follow her so I would know where they were taking her. I was only thirteen years old but I decided not to cry either because I realized that I now was the head of the household with five younger siblings - four brothers and a sister. I asked my brother John who was three years younger than I was, to look after the younger ones, and I followed my mother.

We passed the center of Seoul, where I saw for the first time in my life dead and burned bodies of North Korean soldiers with the smell of burning flesh on the street and many buildings destroyed by the aerial bombardment. It was like hell! Despite all the distractions of death and destruction I wanted to make sure I concentrated to remember the directions to get to the place they were taking Mother and how to get back home. If I didn't remember nobody would even care if Mother and my baby brother died of starvation. Human life was not worth any more than that of a fruit fly. We finally arrived at a building that looked like some kind of military police headquarters. I wrote down the address and directions for getting there from home so I could visit her and bring her meals because they would not supply any meals to the prisoners. This was for me a wakeup call in my early painful childhood experience - getting to know the existence of the ugly side of human nature. I had to figure out how to manage this crisis to save my parents as well as all my younger siblings.

Maybe because of this kind of appalling human behavior my father always emphasized Darwin's survival of the fittest theory saying that you must be fit to survive in this world. I have never forgotten this experience in all my life and this was my image of Korea and Koreans for a long time after I left Korea. This was also the reason why I never hesitated to give up my Korean citizenship. Because of my unforgettable childhood memories of the suffering of my innocent and gentle parents in the hands of these ugly people, I have always tried to help my parents who would have given up their lives to protect us, who taught us how to deal with unexpected human tragedy. I grew up very quickly and became mentally very strong. My other siblings were too young to remember, the last two not having been born.

For several weeks I cooked something edible with vegetables from the garden and brought meals to my mother every day. One day when I was gone to deliver a meal to my mother a group of people came with a truck and asked my ten-year-old brother John where our parents hid our valuables. My parents used to hide all our valuables in a closet under the stairway in the guest room which could not be opened unless the tatami on the floor of the guest room was removed. The tatami was blocking the entrance to the closet and it was not easily visible. Unfortunately my brother knew this closet existed and told those thieves so they ransacked all our valuables, including 24-karat gold nuggets, jewelry, fur, silks and South Korean currency which was not used during the communist occupation. When I came home and saw this closet door wide open and empty I sat down on the floor and cried, wondering what we were going to live on from then on. I screamed at my brother, "Stupid idiot, how could you be so dumb to tell them about this closet? We are now going to starve to death because of you." But he was too young and naïve and there was no point in yelling at him after the fact. Everything of worth was all gone. What kind of horrible human beings would do this to a family with six young children? These were the kind of people we were up against. Mother was right. This was the wrong neighborhood to raise children. The vegetable garden my father worked on diligently to feed his family created more trouble than it was worth. But I had to be courageous to make sure my young siblings didn't go hungry, to manage the household, and to bring meals to my mother. I could not even reach my father at my aunt's home because telephones were not working during the war.

A couple of weeks passed this way and one day when I was with my mother watching her eating her meal she said grace to God as always, and when the guard saw her praying he asked her whether she was a Christian. So she replied that she was a baptized Christian. Then he went out to talk to his superior about this and they discussed something and returned to the room and told her that there must have been some kind of mistake in arresting her and told her she could go home. It appeared that this was just a plot by our neighbors to steal from our family and to protect themselves from reprisal because they had cooperated with the communists during the occupation. This plot hurt our family badly, leaving bitter memories particularly for me and for my mother who never forgot until her last days. Mother was right again about those neighbors. They were really hideous people.

None of this would have happened to our family if my father had agreed with Mother to buy another home she liked in a different neighborhood with beautiful flower gardens and no schools nearby that might accommodate any North Korean military units. This experience was so frightening to my mother that she didn't want to stay at the house anymore so we packed whatever was left over including our family albums, and hired a wagon, locked up all the doors just in case, and moved out of the neighborhood. We went to my aunt's house where my father was staying. That house had only three bedrooms. Initially my aunt married a man whose family was a rich landlord in Yeo-nan in Hwanghae Province, but after the Korean War when they redrew the 38th parallel the western fertile land in Hwanghae Province ended up in North Korea and the ROK gained a little useless mountainous area on the east side. Before the war my uncle and aunt were wanted to buy a larger house but they didn't make it in time. So they remained in the three-bedroom home my uncle's parents bought for him when he was a student just behind Seoul National University (the old campus now). We were able to use one of those three rooms, cramped up all together.

When my father heard the story of what had happened he went to the authorities in the city who were handling such cases to explain the situation during the North Korean occupation. He cleared himself and got a piece of paper signed by the authority exonerating him of any wrongdoing. He didn't do anything except talk to Professor Sohn at the women's college to find out the school curriculum to find out whether English literature was on the list. He was only trying to figure out how to support his family. It would be a lie if anyone who was in Seoul during the Korean War said they knew the Allied forces would come back to recapture Seoul and recover South Korea. No one knew what was going to happen when the North Korean forces occupied almost the entire country. If General MacArthur hadn't risked his reputation to proceed with the amphibious assault on Inchon, there would be no ROK today. We would all be frightened, pitiful souls under Kim Il-sung's rogue regime. For this reason, I am eternally grateful to General MacArthur for saving my own future to live as a free citizen in a democratic society, pursuing my own career, without worrying about any human rights abuse.

Father thought that he was officially cleared of any crime committed during the communist occupation so there was no reason not to return to our own home. He asked me whether I could go to the neighborhood and find out whether our home was still empty or occupied by someone. But again mother was against the idea saying it was too early after what she had gone through and she didn't know how useful that clearance paper my father had would be since Seoul was still a lawless place run by military police and wild mobs. Not all government officials were back in Seoul attending to their official business. Father knew many people who could have helped him but he didn't know where they were having been scattered during the war. But Father loved that house too much to give up. I agreed with him on this issue because it was too difficult to live in our aunt's home with all our family members jammed up in one room while we had a very large beautiful home of our own.

Shortly after this conversation, I went to investigate what was happening in the neighborhood but this was a near-fatal mistake. As I neared the neighborhood, I saw one of our old neighbors who lived just in front of our home - the old maid who had a military-officer boyfriend. When she saw me on the street she asked me where my father was. I was trying to get away from her but she wouldn't let me. I was practically kidnapped by her. She escorted me to our old home and rang the bell. A woman in her late 20s answered the door and asked me to come in. I discovered that our home was occupied by a high-ranking military police officer but I didn't know much about the details of his reputation at the time.

This woman, the wife of this military police officer was interrogating me with a noticeable North Korean accent as if she herself were the military police and I was some kind of hard criminal even though I was only a child. She called her husband to discuss what to do with me. He probably was telling her to hold me there until his subordinates arrived to take me to my father. Then a couple of young fellows, military police, came in a jeep and asked me to get in and guide them to where my father was. I didn't know what to do; I felt helpless and guilty thinking of escorting them to where my father was. But what else could I do under the circumstances? I was lost for a while not knowing what to do. Then they were screaming at me to hurry up. They were also treating me like a criminal. I had never seen anybody like these people. When we lived in our old neighborhood all our parents' friends were well-educated, decent people. I didn't know what to do. What was happening to Korean society? Where did these ugly people come from, treating even a child like a criminal? But I had no choice and went along with them. Following their orders, I brought them to my aunt's home.

My father was surprised and showed them the legal clearance paper from the authority that exonerated him of all charges, but it didn't make any difference. The paper was useless as far as they were concerned; they didn't even look at it. Those young fellows were just following orders from their superior to arrest my father. They asked my father to come with them. My mother asked them where they were taking him but they wouldn't even bother answering mother. So my father was taken away but we didn't know where.

My mother began to contact everybody who might be able to help him. One of my father's former students from Dong-Kwang Middle School, the school my father built in Manchuria to educate Koreans children living there, Han Pil-tong, was a high-ranking military officer in the ROK Army. So my mother and I went to see him at his army barracks and asked him whether there was anything he could do. He said he knew the reputation of this man, Kim Chang-ryong, the military police officer. He came from North Korea, was extremely vicious and ruthless and was not afraid to eliminate anyone blocking his way. Han Pil-tong thought that this man wanted to get rid of my father to secure our property for his family. He suggested that time was very critical to find a politically powerful authority to deal with him.

At that time the Liberal Party in the National Assembly was the majority party and it was in fact Syngman Rhee's party. Its representatives carried lots of political power. Mother remembered the party representative, Hwang Sung-su, the man my parents actively campaigned for to get him elected from our district. He became even more powerful after he was elected by becoming a vice chair of the party at that time. Time was running out and Mother was trying to contact Mr. Hwang in a hurry. Finally, one day she got a chance to see him in his office and explained the situation. He asked someone to find out where my father was and told my mother that he was going to try to get my father out of there but advised her not to try to get the house back too soon since the situation during the war was very difficult to control by any civilian representative.

Almost two weeks had already passed since they took my father away from us and we didn't know what kind of condition he was in. Was he still alive? We had no idea! Shortly after mother talked to Mr. Hwang, we were told to pick up my father from military police headquarters. He was released. When we went to pick him up he was unrecognizably thin and pale. He looked so frail and he had no strength to walk. He told us that they didn't give him any meals and tortured him continuously to get a false confession that he was a member of Namno-dang, the South Korean communist party, but he refused to the end. If he finally agreed to the charge because he was unable to ride out the torture any longer that would have been the excuse for them just to shoot him on the spot. That's what they did to many civilians who were accused of being communists during this time. If Father did not make it I probably would not have been able to continue my life either because of my guilt of bringing Kim Chang-ryong's men to my father, leaving my poor mother to take care of five children all by herself.

During the politically chaotic period in Korea waterboarding, a practice presently highly controversial in the U.S., was used to torture innocent civilians by the military police and intelligence agents attempting to elicit confessions often to confiscate property, settle personal vendettas, or get stature by increasing their number of arrests. My father thought he was going to die in that cell. He didn't know why he was released suddenly but we knew why.

My father was at the brink of death. He was released in the nick of time. My mother said God had saved his life for the third time and this time I really believed it, although the credit goes to Mother who thought fast and contacted the right people to save him. She concentrated on helping my father recover from his poor health and dreadful experience. He was in a terribly weakened physical and mental state. If he was not such a healthy man to begin with he could have died during the torture without meals for two weeks. It's a miracle he survived, because anyone else would have died under the same situation. Kim Chang-ryong tried to let Father die of starvation and torture but at that time we didn't know the full story of what kind of evil Kim Chang-ryong was capable of. When I finally learned that so many civilian massacres had indeed been carried out at various locations during the Korean War by the retreating South Korean military police I wondered how God was able to spare my father's life in such an environment. It might have been God's will to save his life for my mother, who prayed for him every day.

Photo 7: The Capital building was completely destroyed by the allied bombing to recapture Seoul in September 1950. Korean women and children search the rubble of Seoul for anything that can be used as fuel. PD-US Gov-MilitaryArmy.

Chapter 16: Korean War, Phase II
(October, 1950–July, 1953)

My father's life may have been miraculously saved on the threshold of his death but the war was still very far from over. At this time our family was living in the empty home of my mother's cousin in Seoul because that family had all moved south to Busan. The husband of my mother's cousin was the captain of a commercial whaling vessel in Busan. The US government, not MacArthur, thought that unless the North Korean Army's capability was fully destroyed the South would be under indefinite threat of renewed communist aggression. Many among the western Allies, primarily the British, were opposed to sending UN forces into North Korea. Finally, MacArthur received the "Amplifying Instructions" as to further military action: "Your military objective is the destruction of the North Korean armed forces," he was told. General MacArthur was authorized to conduct military operations north of the 38th parallel but under the strict condition that his forces—ground, air, or sea— were not allowed cross the Manchurian border. The condition was that only Korean ground forces would be used in the northeast provinces bordering the Soviet Union or in the area along the Manchurian border.

MacArthur's tentative date for invasion of the North was no earlier than October 15, and no later than October 30. On September 30, the Joint Chiefs of Staff officially approved the plan. However, this decision immediately raised the question of Chinese (Mao's Red Army) intervention. The Chinese were reportedly moving north toward Manchuria. If China got involved, it would be a totally different war. MacArthur's local intelligence reported increasing concentrations of Chinese forces near the Amnok River (Yalu River), the border of Manchuria. Nevertheless, the CIA and the US State Department told General MacArthur that China had no intention of intervening in the Korean conflict. This was again another one of their very expensive miscalculations.

In October, we heard the radio broadcast reporting that the allied forces crossed the 38th parallel and were moving toward Pyongyang. At the same time, the US Navy landed at Wonsan. The Eighth Army moved rapidly forward toward Pyongyang, while the X Corps landed at Wonsan to use it as the new supply base. Despite all the suffering my father went through because of the war he was genuinely impressed by MacArthur's successful military campaign. It was his opinion that General MacArthur had not only saved the South from extinction by his brilliant and daring amphibian assault at Inchon, but he could also unite Korea at last - the task no one else had been able to achieve for five years - by reaching the capital of North Korea and the Manchurian and Siberian borders in a short time. The potential of Korean unification was good news to my father, despite all the agony he had to endure. He was longing for a peaceful and free country and a better life for all Koreans. He promised me we would visit Moran-bong, my birth place in Pyongyang.

At the end of October there was news that the US Army had taken Pyongyang. The fall of Pyongyang, the North Korean capital, symbolized the complete defeat of North Korea. To avoid a third world war General MacArthur's forces were strictly forbidden by Washington to attack across the Manchurian or USSR border of Korea even if there was a massive buildup of Chinese Red Army. Manchuria and Siberia were sanctuaries for all enemy forces no matter what assaults might come from there. This was a very serious problem for the Allied forces. On November 21, leading elements of the X Corps reached the Amnok River. But another problem arose. An estimated three fresh divisions of Chinese troops were building up at the Korean-Chinese border. The Chinese government claimed that they were merely individual volunteers who had gone to assist their Korean comrades. However, according to many other sources it was the Chinese government itself that organized this so-called volunteer army for full-scale war, knowing that the United States would not bomb their supply lines in Manchuria and Siberia. In point of fact, it was revealed that many Chinese military leaders did not like Kim Il-sung's arrogance while their own soldiers were losing their lives fighting to recover North Korea for Kim Il-sung, but they were forced by their government to pursue the goal of recovering North Korea.

On November 3, MacArthur furnished his superiors detailed information on the Chinese buildup: an aggregate of 868,000 men in all. Despite all kinds of restrictions placed on General MacArthur by Washington he felt that there was one weapon he could use -destroy the Amnok Bridge to cut the line of communication between North Korea and Manchuria over which large Chinese armies could cross. However, he was directed by Secretary Marshall to immediately postpone all bombings of targets within five miles of the Manchurian border. This policy basically killed all hope that General MacArthur could claim victory and send all US soldiers home before Christmas as he promised. This policy expanded the protection of the enemy protecting not only the bridge that was the only means the Chinese had for moving their men and supplies into Korea but also a five-mile-wide area on the Korean side of the Amnok River. MacArthur, who was more familiar with Asian history than anyone in the US State Department, felt that this was a far larger and more complex long-range problem than Washington seemed to comprehend. It turned out that General MacArthur's prediction was correct. China was involved later in Vietnam, Laos, and Cambodia.

At about this time the British Labor government suggested giving the communists a slice of North Korea to serve as a buffer zone and as evidence of the United Nations' good intentions. Slicing an already too small country to make a buffer zone? Was the British government willing to give a slice of its country to the Germans to end World War II instead of dragging in the United States to save the country? Many books written by various US military personnel who were involved in the Korean War have criticized MacArthur, but if he had been allowed to conduct the war according to his own strategy, he would have won the war and Korea would be united today. Just destroying the Amnok River Bridge to prevent the movement of their military supplies would have done the job. The Soviet Union at that time was not ready for World War III, and China had questionable abilities.

We heard the news that on November 27, the Chinese launched their forces across the Amnok River. My father was very disappointed that he might not see a united Korea in his lifetime and sadly apologized to me for not being able to take me to see Moran-bong, my birthplace. Thus, China entered into open war against the United States and its allies - an undeclared war. It's apparent from the beginning how important China felt it was to keep North Korea as a buffer zone and not allow US influence on their borders. The United States and its Allies began withdrawing. In January 1951, Chinese forces crossed the 38th parallel and quickly advanced to Seoul.

South Koreans fled Seoul again, leaving an almost deserted city behind. At night I could hear lonely dogs left by their owners emitting high-pitched sounds like wolves howling, making the city feel eerie. The cold and snowy weather slowly covering the empty streets devoid of human habitants made me feel as if we had landed somehow on a haunted planet. But of course if we also didn't hurry to leave, the Mao's Red Army would overtake us. This time, my parents wanted to make sure we left Seoul before it was too late no matter what. Needless to say again, our family didn't have much money, since we lost everything to Kim the Snake. My parents contacted Major Hahn Pil-tong in the ROK Army, my father's former student, who provided us an army truck with a driver and assistant to use for a limited number of hours. Where to go was another problem. We could not go far since the truck had to be returned to the army barracks within a short time. Father remembered that his former chauffeur had relatives living in the country in a place called Changan-mal near Pyungtak, 72 kilometers south of Seoul. Father contacted his former chauffeur and asked him whether there was any spare room in his relatives' house for our family to stay until the war was over. He said we could use their spare room so we left Seoul not knowing when we could return, if ever. Dark had fallen as we arrived at the farmhouse in the country. After unloading our few possessions, and us, the army truck immediately returned to its barracks. The truck and soldiers were needed in the retreat.

Our hosts were very kind people and showed much respect toward my father. They had a separate unit with one room and a little kitchen. The room was not large enough for all of us but we could lie down at various angles to fit in the room to sleep. After what we had already gone through we did not complain about the conditions. We were just relieved that this time we were able to get out of Seoul in time. We stayed there for a while but I don't remember exactly how long. My father and my brother, John, gathered firewood from the surrounding mountains and my little sister Oak picked edible plants in the wild so we could prepare a porridge-like food by mixing the forage with rice, barley, and lots of water. This was very simple country living. But even this kind of simple life did not last very long.

Chinese forces were moving closer so we had to move again but we didn't know where to go exactly. We had become typical refugees by then. We packed what we had. My father carried the heaviest load although he was not fully recovered. My mother carried the baby, Suk, on her back. My brother, sister, and I carried whatever we could handle. The rest of the small children also had to walk. We walked south following other refugees, avoiding the main road since that's where major military actions were taking place. We could hear thunderous explosions of American artillery, and we even saw some of those shells landing on nearby rice paddies while we were walking along the country road. We didn't see any Chinese soldiers ourselves but some other refugees had, so they were definitely nearby.

We walked southward all day long, aimlessly, without clear destination where we were going. Then we met a large group of American soldiers resting on the grass. They asked us whether we had seen Chinese soldiers. They had asked other refugees but those farmers did not understand English. My father explained to them that we had not seen any Chinese soldiers but some people had seen them and described an approximate distance north from there. One of the American soldiers threw some candies to my little sister Oak. Nice fellows, I thought. I was amazed at the relaxed behavior of those soldiers in a battle zone so near the front. Maybe this is how they could carry on in a battle. If they were worried about dying they could not fight.

It was getting dark. We found a little empty farmhouse by the road and decided to spend the night there in a small room. We had some food to eat and spread out the comforters my father was carrying on his back. All of us lay down at many different angles to fit ourselves in the small room and slept. We ended up staying there longer than we planned but I don't remember exactly how many days. Gunfire had died down and the country air was tranquil. It seemed that the Chinese forces had been pushed northward by the Americans so we walked a long way back to the farmhouse in Changan-mal to continue our simple lives there. Day-by-day, month-by-month we lived without learning anything new or accomplishing anything constructive. No schools were open. It was already February. We were running out of food so my father had to come up with some means of feeding his family. When he went to a barbershop in the nearby town, Seochung-ri, for his haircut, the owner of the barbershop suggested that my parents could use the space right in front of the barbershop to open a roadside retail counter. He could sell such things as dry squids, cigarettes, candies, cookies, candles, matches, and so on. My father, who was a professor and a school administrator, had never done any sales in his entire life. But what else could he do?

He discussed the proposition with Mother and they decided to try it. My mother, who was a teacher, was a good communicator and was willing to try anything to prevent our starving. My sister and I had to take care of the baby and younger children. When my parents opened this roadside business, I had to carry the baby on my back every day around noon to the marketplace so my mother could nurse him. They were working hard under the sun so my mother's fair skin was getting sunburned, becoming darker and peeling. Mother was beginning to look like a black market profiteer I used to see in the Southgate black market in Seoul. But they were doing a pretty good job running that business and were able to make enough money to feed the family and had enough money to rent a better place near the market, a separate unit of a large house. This way Mother could come home to nurse the baby during lunch break instead of my bringing the baby to the market every day.

Now it was March and the war was still going on around Seoul. By then, I had already missed a couple of semesters of school, so my father consulted with local VIPs and set up a temporary school. He found some teachers, including himself, to provide primary courses like Korean language, math, science and English. My father left the roadside stand to mother while he went to teach his classes and came back to run the shop after his class.

I thought that this kind of pathetic and unproductive life had to end somehow. We had no place to live even if we were able to return to Seoul since we had lost our home. At this time I met a daughter of a local VIP at the school my father set up and we became friends. Her father was in charge of the local train station. I found out that most trains passing by the local station belonged to the military but they did carry some passengers in some sections of those trains. I realized I could go down to Gwangju where our grandparents and two aunts' families lived by changing trains at Daejon. So I told my parents that I could get a train ticket through my friend's father and go to Gwangju and find out whether we could all move down there so we could resume our regular school program. Mother was extremely worried about a young girl by herself getting on a train full of military men during wartime but I was determined to follow through with my plan. I also told her that if they didn't hear from me within a couple of weeks, that might mean I had met some mishap and died on the way, but they should not feel sad because this was all my doing. I also pointed out to my mother that we no longer had our house in Seoul so there was no reason to go back to Seoul and we had to begin a new life elsewhere. Mother reluctantly agreed. I got the ticket, got on the train, and said goodbye to mother. Father didn't know I had decided to pursue this idea. He opposed the plan and I didn't tell him I was leaving.

It's very strange that I have a total mental block concerning what happened on the train but I do remember arriving at Gwangju station and seeing men wearing regular business suits with neckties, as opposed to the casual working clothes I saw near the front. I took a taxi to go to my grandparent's home because they didn't know the exact time of my arrival as the train schedule was unreliable in those days. As soon as I arrived I wrote a letter to my parents saying that Gwangju did not look like the war zone they were in. Grandmother had already registered me in the Gwangju girl's middle school to continue my education. All my aunts' families were doing fine economically, and therefore my parents should move down also to

Gwangju and start a new life there. Mother told me later that she was terribly worried about me. When they received my letter, she cried and thanked God for my safe trip.

They agreed with my recommendations, sold everything from the stand, packed whatever they needed, and came down to Gwangju. My grandparents and aunts were all surprised to see my mother's condition, saying that they would not have recognized her if they saw her on the street because of her darkened skin and rough appearance. It was an unexpected hardship for my mother but such was life in Korea in those days. Life had to go on no matter what. If we gave up we would have all died of malnutrition or starvation.

All our family temporarily stayed in the home of one of my aunts. Her husband, my uncle, was a Chinese medicine doctor doing quite well financially. My parents made sure my brother John and my sister Oak were registered at school immediately to continue their education. Then my father found a job as a professor at Joseon University, a private school, and began teaching English literature again. After my father got a job, my parents didn't want to impose too much on my aunt and uncle so they rented a large empty home and we moved out of my aunt's house. Since they brought some money they had saved from the roadside business we were fine financially, for a while, but the university was having a hard time paying salaries to the professors. Private universities do well during peacetime but not during war.

Months passed without my father receiving any salary. The prolonged mental stress coupled with malnutrition was beginning to cause severe health problems in our family. My mother contracted malaria and my father had temporary partial paralysis of one side of his face. My handsome young brother Soo developed a hernia in his left groin. He was limping around the house in pain but my parents didn't have enough money to take him to the hospital for surgery. One day, we saw my father, who had by then recovered from his partial paralysis, sharpening a knife, so Mother asked him why. He replied that he was going to perform the surgery on my brother at home with that knife. My mother was so frightened that she took my brother on her back and went to see a local doctor. She explained the situation, crying, and begged him to perform the surgery on credit. She promised that she would pay the fee as soon as my father received his back pay from the university. Dr. Koh, as I remember his name, was sympathetic and agreed to perform the surgery free of charge. Mother was very grateful to find a good and decent person in a world that could be so ugly.

There was another sad incident during this time. My mother found out one of her high school classmates had a large store selling men's clothes, so she went to see her and asked her whether she would be willing to sell one shirt for my father on credit so that he could go for an interview. But her classmate refused to do such a simple favor. My mother was so insulted that she never forgot this incident as long as she lived. My parents were decent people and always tried to help others in need, but when they needed help, there were not too many people who were willing to give it. Nevertheless, my father taught us to live our lives as compassionate people always maintaining a high moral standard. I feel privileged to have been brought up by such decent and intelligent parents in a chaotic society.

Around this time, April, 1951, there was a rumor that General MacArthur had been fired by President Truman, though the Korean War continued. What shocking news! General MacArthur was not just a military strategist but also had a very good knowledge of Asian history and he understood Asian people better than anybody in Washington. In his memorable address to Congress after his removal, MacArthur emphasized the importance of Asia and the Pacific to America's future:

"While Asia is commonly referred to as the gateway to Europe, it is no less true that Europe is the gateway to Asia, and the broad influence of the one cannot fail to have its impact upon the other. The peoples of Asia have thrown off the shackles of colonialism and now see the dawn of new opportunity. Asia has half the earth's population and 60 percent of its natural resources and with its progress the whole epicenter of world affairs rotates back toward the area whence it started. It becomes vital that America orient its policies in consonance with this basic evolutionary condition."

This is not to say that he never made any wrong decisions concerning Korean issues. He spent all his energy helping Japan recover after World War II and he did a very good job at this task, but he didn't pay much attention to protecting Korea from Soviet invasion right after World War II and did not send in American troops until Soviet troops had almost reached the 38th parallel. He agreed to withdraw all American troops from the South without fully equipping the South Korean military. Furthermore, he reinstated Syngman Rhee as president of the ROK against the advice of the State Department after his first successful reversal of the Korean War at the Inchon landing. Nevertheless, I still believe he could have won the Korean War by Christmas if he had only been allowed to destroy the Amnok bridge to cut the only enemy supply line from Manchuria and Siberia to the Korean Peninsula.

It was now 1951. Many more months had passed, but there was still no relief from the university. Mother began a new job search for Father, a job he would be paid for his work. She knew more folks in Gwangju than my father since her family and friends lived there. One of her distant uncles was the head of Department of Education in Jeolla Province. She visited him often to find out whether there was any opening anywhere suitable for my father's credentials. Many months passed by this way. Finally, one day he told her there was an opening in the country, in Chang-heung. The high school principal's position was vacant. Since father had successful administrative experience in the past he was more than qualified for the position if we were willing to move to the remote countryside. Considering our desperate financial situation he accepted the job. We moved again to Chang-heung and took up lodging in the school principal's house.

There we had a pleasant surprise. The school principal's house was a beautiful traditional Korean-style home, elevated from the large front yard. There were four bedrooms and a large central living room with shiny wood floors separating the first two bedroom units from the second. Ivy covered the very high stone wall in the backyard, protecting the house from the mountain immediately behind. It turned out Chang-heung was a pretty well off country town with many well-to-do farmers, doctors, and other professional people. The school itself was well subsidized. The house had a well where all the local people came to get their drinking water. For this reason the front door was permanently left open but that was not a problem because there were no incidents of house break-ins in the entire town. I remembered our old home during World War II where all of our neighbors came to get water. After so much hardship our parents finally found a place to relax and lead a normal life without worrying daily how to feed their children. I was glad that my parents never gave up on life, providing us with a good example of how to handle and overcome unexpected misfortunes and hardships. Life seems to have its own cycles of ups and downs, especially when there is war going on and civilians are trapped between two opposing groups of political or religious ideologies.

Since Father already had sufficient experience in running a school his spirits lifted right away and he got on the job immediately, searching for better-qualified teachers for math, physics, and English. But I didn't want to attend a country school so I packed a suitcase one night and the next morning I slipped out of the house to get on a bus to go to Gwangju. My grandparents' home was there so I could continue my education at the Gwangju girl's middle school. When my father found out I was missing next morning, he knew right away where I went and called the principal of Gwangju girl's middle school to send me back to Chang-heung. As soon as my grandmother took me to school I was called into the principal's room and was told to return to Chang-heung.

My father always insisted that he could not send his own children to another school while he was asking other parents to send their children to the school he was running, claiming that the school was as good as any other school in any city. So I had no choice but return to Chang-heung. I also had confidence that my father could accomplish his goal of improving the quality of faculty quickly based on his past accomplishments and I saw him already traveling long distances trying to recruit better-qualified teachers. Talented young teachers came from other cities to join the faculty even though Chang-heung was in the remote country. They not only respected my father's qualifications but were also impressed by my father's sincerity that made them feel respected. They all became good friends of my parents even after we left Chang-heung.

One of those faculty members, Cho Yong-churl, who was a graduate of Seoul National University with a degree in Engineering, considered my father like his own father and regularly visited him for guidance. When my father passed away Cho Yong-churl attended his funeral. Some years later Cho went to the University of Tokyo to continue his study in mechanical engineering and received a PhD. He became a professor of engineering. I must admit that I received one of the best high school educations at that school because of the excellent faculty my father assembled. I also tried hard to catch up the portion of my education I missed due to the war, living near the front line, and moving around frequently. I did this at home with my father's help. He helped me with math and English. Mother helped me with Korean language and history. Actually the most knowledgeable person in Korean history was my maternal grandmother, especially concerning the last years of the Joseon dynasty. She still had pretty good memory even in her old age. I already described how she documented her family history, including that of her male family members who fought as the local militia leaders during the Hideyoshi invasions in Jolla province, the area where she and her family lived and gave the whole document to my father.

My parents needed well-deserved peace and happiness to enjoy their married life after a long struggle. My mother gave birth to their seventh child, the fifth son, Hugh, a handsome and bright boy. The locals maintained that Chang-heung water produced many geniuses so we expected Hugh to be no less.

One of my father's most memorable accomplishments at that school was a well-organized school "Olympics"- an athletic event the school had never had before. Father recruited a young and talented physical education teacher who developed many kinds of sports games and trained the students to compete in the school Olympics.

One game was for track and field in which students would pick up a card in the middle of the run, find the person whose name was on the card, and continue running together to the end point with that person. One of the students picked a card which said the school principal and he approached my father who was sitting at the VIP table with local VIPs and faculty members under the tent. As soon as my father saw him coming toward him, he just jumped over the table and ran with the student so fast that they beat everybody. The audience went wild, applauding and laughing until they reached the goal. That's my father! That was a lot of fun indeed. Nobody expected the school principal to be so serious about winning and would run so fast.

Almost all of the students' parents came to this event, well prepared with all kinds of food as if they were coming to a big outdoor party. Everyone enjoyed the Olympics so enormously that the faculty and the local VIPs considered the event a huge success. My father also organized a beach party during the summer for the faculty and their families, which we couldn't have even dreamed of having during our time of difficulty. I still remember the scene of my little innocent brothers who suffered so much for so long, happily playing on the beach, listening to the sound of waves. That's how life is supposed to be for growing children - so they grow up to become peaceful, confident, and decent people helping others in need.

One day my father, who was forever a curious student, joined a team of faculty members who were going deer hunting and in the evening. They brought a deer they killed to our home, skinned the animal and processed the meat which my mother and I didn't want to watch. We gave the job to our live in maid to cook with lots of hot pepper paste, onions, scallions, tofu, and soybean sprouts. Then they had a drinking party at our home. They ate the cooked deer, rice, kimchi, fresh lettuce, and various vegetable dishes. They drank wine and enjoyed the evening, singing and laughing. I was happy to see my father enjoying life for change. He was a decent man who believed in making an honest living according to his principles by working hard, not by manipulating other people, not by bribing people in high places, and not by ingratiating himself to powerful people to advance himself. It's a mystery to me how he turned out to be such a good man without any hint of contamination after living through so much chaos and being the victim of so much betrayal. Who taught my father how to distinguish good from evil? Did he learn from reading so many books written by famous and righteous people?

We lived in Chang-heung for a couple of years but my parents always planned to return to Seoul for their children's education soon after the dust settled. At this time, the Korean War was still not over. On November 29, 1952, President-elect Dwight Eisenhower fulfilled a campaign promise by visiting Korea to find out what could be done to end the war. I remember Father reading a newspaper which had a photo of Eisenhower in army uniform and a cap at the 38th parallel examining the area in north with binocular. Father was impressed to see the president in the front line to make accurate assessment of the situation himself before making a serious decision. He was not used to seeing such behavior of Korean president Syngman Rhee who fled Seoul as soon as the war broke out. With the UN's acceptance of India's proposal for a Korean armistice, a cease-fire was established on July 27, 1953. I was sorry the war ended with no gain. The South lost some fertile farm land in Hwanghae Province in the west near the 38th parallel and gained a useless mountainous region in the east.

According to data from the U.S. Department of Defense, the United States suffered 33,686 battle deaths, along with 2,830 non-battle deaths, during the Korean War. South Korea reported some 373,599 civilian and 137,899 military deaths. Western sources estimate the Chinese Army suffered about 400,000 killed and 486,000 wounded, while the North Korean Army suffered 215,000 killed and 303,000 wounded.

Photo 8: Brigadier General *Courtney Whitney*, Far East Command; General *Douglas MacArthur*, Commander-in-Chief, United Nations Command, and Major General *Edward Almond* (at right, pointing), Commanding General, X Corps in Korea, observe the shelling of Incheon from the *USS Mount McKinley*.
NARA FILE #: 111-SC-348438, PD-USGov-Military-Army

Photo 9: The statue of General MacArthur in Jayu Park (Freedom Park) in Inchon Harbor built in honor of his successful amphibious landing in September 1950 during the Korean War. Photo by my brother Soo .

Chapter 17: Assassination of Kim Chang-ryong (January 30, 1956)

In January 30, 1956, there was startling big news all over the country and in every newspaper. Kim Chang-ryong was assassination. In the early morning of that day, Kim Chang-ryong was leaving home in a jeep accompanied by his driver. Another car suddenly blocked the road. As he shouted at the driver of the car to get off the road they shot him several times and sped away. Kim Chang-ryong, then aged 36, was taken to the hospital but it was too late. This evil man was finally removed from the human society. Korean news sources revealed that Syngman Rhee, the president of the nation, went into frenzy and ordered an all-out investigation into the assassination.

In less than a month CIC investigators arrested the assassins. The seven conspirators included four high ranking military officers in the Korean army and CIC. The driver was a sergeant and two shooters were civilian employees of the CIC (Colonel Huh Tae-young, the Seoul military region commander, Colonel Lee Jin-young , Major Ahn Jung-soo, the CID Unit 12 commander, Lieutenant Huh Byong-sik, military police and Colonel Huh's brother, Sergeant Lee Yu-hoe, Colonel Huh's driver, Song Yong-goh, a shooter, CIC civilian employee, and Sin Cho-sik, a shooter was a CIC civilian employee). All were former members of the CIC and had worked under Kim Chang-ryong. The two shooters were also members of the CIC. They were tried for the crime by a special military court. Colonel Huh claimed responsibility at the court-martial and received a death sentence whereupon his wife stepped forward and disclosed that her husband was ordered to commit the crime by his superiors: Lieutenant General Kang Moon-bong, commander of the Second Army, and Brigadier General Gong Guk-jin, former commander of the military police. Both generals denied any involvement, but they were arrested, tortured, and tried.

At the hearing Lieutenant General Kang stated that Kim Chang-ryong was a cancer in the army which was eating away morale by causing dissension among officers and men and indeed, he wanted to cut out this cancer. However he insisted that he did not instruct Colonel Huh to kill Kim Chang-ryong. Colonel Huh told the court that he had Kim Chang-ryong killed because Kim framed senior officers on false charges in order to earn Syngman Rhee's trust and to satisfy his insatiable lust for blood. Kim spied on senior officers of the army and dug up dirt on their private lives. After lengthy hearings, lasting for over 2,000 hours, the court found all accused guilty as charged. Lieutenant General Kang was sentenced to die. In the appeals court, Colonel Huh, Song Yong-goh and Sin Cho-sik received the death sentence and General Kang's death sentence was commuted to life in prison. Subsequently, Huh, Sin, and Song were executed. Five years later Lieutenant General Kang was released and reinstated after the May 16, 1961, military coup of General Park Chung-hee, who had been accused of being a communist before the Korean War.

If Syngman Rhee was not in such a frenzy to execute Huh, Sin, and Song it is likely they would all have been released after Park Chung-hee took power. The newspapers reported that the shooters sang the national anthem before they were executed, claiming that they did it for the country. Many people including my father thought they were being truthful but who would dare try to rescue them from being executed against the will of the nation's president who was in such a fringe?

Kim Chang-ryong, (1920–1956), was the man who almost killed my father in order to confiscate our property. Kim Chang-ryong (1920–1956) was the right-hand man of Syngman Rhee, the first president of the Republic of Korea. It was six years after he illegally confiscated our home, he was assassinated. Kim Chang-ryong was born to a poor peasant family in South Ham-gyong Province, during Japanese rule. He enrolled in the Japanese Army in Manchuria as an MP. He soon became a detective, whose work was to uncover moles and resistance activists in the Japanese intelligence service and went after Korean independence fighters. After the Japanese were defeated by the Allies in 1945 and Korea was liberated he came back to his hometown, Ham-heung, in the North, which was then under Soviet occupation.

As expected the communists wanted him as a Japanese collaborator so he kept a low profile. At the end of 1945 he allegedly visited his friend and former assistant Kim Yun-won in Chor-won who reported him to the communists. He was sentenced to death for "anti-Korean deeds." But as Kim was carried on a truck to the place of his execution he somehow managed to jump off the vehicle and escaped through the mountains in freezing weather to reach one of his relative's house three days later. As he recovered from his wounds he waited for the right moment to flee to the South. But again he was betrayed, captured and sentenced to death for the second time. Kim Chang-ryong managed to escape again by killing his Soviet guard with a chair. He then fled to the South accompanied solely by his wife. This must have been the same woman I met when I was kidnapped at our parent's old home. I recognized her very clear northern accent right away at the time.

Kim Chang-ryong arrived in Seoul in May, 1946, and joined several different corps of the ROK Army before eventually being assigned to G-2 (intelligence). He obtained President Rhee's trust by arresting Kim Sam-yong and Lee Joo-ha, two key members of the South Korean Labor Party (Namno-dang). Syngman Rhee, who knew that controlling the army was the only way to maintain his regime, saw Kim Chang-ryong as an efficient officer who could "clean up the mess in the army" and get rid of anyone threatening Rhee's position. So Kim Chang-ryong became Rhee's ideal right-hand man. Because of this favored connection Kim became reckless in investigations and inevitably made countless enemies among the army officers. Kim Chang-ryong, now a superior officer, formed the Korean CIC with the support of US Army officials and the US CIC. This was the unit responsible for arresting and interrogating thousands of assumed North Korean spies. General MacArthur and other American officers even nicknamed him "The Snake," because of his relentlessness, which was so great that by July 1949, about 5,000 soldiers as well as officers of the first ROK had allegedly been arrested and interrogated. The "purification" process saw many innocent lives ruined and countless barbaric acts committed by Kim Chang-ryong and his collaborators.

Nevertheless, he was promoted to Jun-jang (brigadier general) in 1953 and then to So-jang (Major General) in 1955, which further exacerbated the resentment that the other officers, including most probably Park Chung-hee who led the military coup of May 16, 1961, and became president of the ROK in 1963 and remained as president until 1979. We had no idea our family was up against such a powerful and malicious man - the security head for the nation's president, who also had no respect for human life. Kim Chang-ryong's enemies had already tried several times to assassinate him but all attempts had failed until his last day, January 30, 1956.

Although Kim was dead my father made no move to recover our home. The torture he received in Kim Chang-ryong's prison must have been excruciating. Besides, Syngman Rhee would protect his right-hand man's reputation even after his death. Thus it was not worth risking his life in trying to recover our home even if it was taken away from us without justification. This was such a time when killing a civilian was as easy as killing a fly. We were just thankful to God my father survived the ordeal. Many years later my brother Suk was trying to find out whether he could recover our parents home but the deed of the property had changed so many hands by then it was difficult to make claims. He told me someone built a big house on the land that once was my Father's favorite vegetable garden. Who said life is always fair? We just have to move on without looking back.

Chapter 18: Postwar Korea and the Rise of Sun Myung Moon (1954–1960)

Dust from the war had begun to settle by 1954, law and order returned and people's lives began to return to normal. One day I heard my parents discussing a new job opportunity for my father. He was contacted by Kim Du-hun, the president of Chunbuk University who was trying to recruit my father as his vice president and dean of the liberal arts college. Apparently he was familiar with my father's credentials and his reputation as a good administrator. My parents decided to take the job and move the family again, even though the job was not in Seoul.

The university was in Chonju, the capital of North Jolla Province. The position was better suited to my father's credentials than the high school post and the university provided housing which was a critical condition since we didn't have our own home anymore. They sent a big truck to move us to Chonju. The new home had a vegetable garden of about a quarter of an acre which pleased Father immensely since he always believed in growing organic vegetables for his family. All the children had to be transferred again to new schools. However, none of us had any problem with schoolwork because my parents always tried to fill the gap for time we missed due to the war and frequent moves from one place to another. Father helped me with English, logarithms, trigonometry and all the other math subjects I had completely missed. Other courses, such as literature or history, we were able to review ourselves to catch up. For my father his children's education was always his first priority so we all did pretty well at school. Most Asians have a high regard for education and we were no exception.

During this era in Korea bribery and corruption was business as usual in every aspect of life - to get a job, to enter a good college, or to get a permit to start a business. It was very difficult to find a job that paid a decent salary. But Father never accepted a bribe from anyone who wanted a faculty position at the university. Instead he went out of his way to recruit bright and qualified professors to increase the academic standing of the school. But it was still difficult to find well-qualified professors in the field of engineering or science such as chemistry and physics. Consequently Korea was still far behind in this area. Many intelligent young people came to join the university and they frequently visited our home to spend evenings with my father, or just to socialize with our parents who told stories of the old days at Kyung-sung University under the Japanese occupation or of our lives in Pyongyang or Manchuria. My father was a good storyteller and was very popular with young and very bright faculty members who sought his guidance. My mother enjoyed participating in those conversations and she was also popular with them. I usually served tea, going in and out of the room and listening to their conversations.

Around this time Father took a business trip to Seoul to take care of some school related matters with Department of Education. While he was there, his nephew Young-gi's wife came to see him to inform him that an old friend of Young-gi saw him in Paris, France. He believed that Young-gi defected from North Korea and was living in Paris with a French woman. Since he was a very good looking fellow, I suppose it was not too hard to find a French girl friend. His wife wanted to contact him but Young-gi didn't provide his contact number. The last time we saw Young-gi was when he was escaping from Seoul during General MacArthur's Inchon landing. During his college years he never paid any attention to his uncle's advice and enthusiastically advocated communist ideals and even became a member of Namno-dang, which got all his family members, parents and brother, executed during the Korean War. Not to mention the damaging consequences on our family. But he could not survive in the communist regime of North Korea for more than a few years so he defected. Since he was a French major North Korea probably sent him to France to take care of some business. After his defection he didn't even try to contact his poor wife. Perhaps he was afraid of being executed in South Korea if he came back. Probably he was also hiding from N. Korean agents.

Like any war the Korean War produced many widows. Women lost their husbands for various reasons. Some died in combat, some became the victims of the communists during their occupation, some were kidnapped to the North, some died in the battle, some became victims of personal vendettas. War became a convenient tool to vilify enemies, competitors or people who opposed their political views of being communists. It was also a perfect time for true religious leaders, as well as those not so true, to prosper by providing spiritual guidance and comfort to those who were deprived of love and emotional comfort.

One of the most famous of these religious leaders was none other than Reverend Sun Myung Moon, a man who remains very controversial to this day. Moon was a vehement anti-communist and vigorous advocate of Korean unification. He later spent five years in a N. Korean labor camp having been convicted of spying for S. Korea. He was released when UN troops overran the N. Korean prison. Later in life Reverend Moon created the Unification Church and recruited followers including many spiritually destitute people who sold all their personal and family properties to join the Unification Church and the communities Moon built. Rev. Moon received considerable criticism when he set up factories in his commune and producing merchandise such as underwear, shirts, and trousers, taking advantage of the labor of the dedicated followers who entered the church community. Critics often criticized these "communes" - a strange term to use for a man who was as anti-*commun*ist as any person on earth. They claimed he was the source of ill-gotten gain as he profited from the proceeds of church followers' labors. I cannot say from personal experience whether Rev. Moon was a dedicated man of God or a sex addicted monster as some critics claimed. However he did fulfill a need for a war weary and spiritually damaged country that badly needed the message he provided. Evaluating his sincerity would have to be left to those who personally experienced the Unification Church phenomenon.

A year passed again and it was time for me to prepare for college. I had to select my major. I was thinking about becoming a lawyer to defend innocent people who were unjustly accused like my father (a human rights attorney in modern terms) or a medical doctor to treat poor patients free of charge like Dr. Koh who performed surgery on my brother Soo when my parents were unable to pay. To my surprise, father advised me to select an area in science. He advised that "If you become a lawyer, you won't be able to practice freely because this is not a free country. You will probably be in jail all the time because you are too outspoken and this country does not tolerate criticism. As for the medical profession, it's not a pleasant occupation for a woman to spend every day with sick patients. It's also dangerous to treat patients with communicable diseases. Besides, it takes too long to go through an internship and residency before your medical practice. You must choose a field in science, a field in which you can become more prestigious as you become older, like a good French wine, by accumulating more and more knowledge as time passes."

Shortly after this discussion he went to a bookstore to search for some reference books and bought a general chemistry textbook, both volumes, written by two-time Nobel Laureate, Linus Pauling. He told me to read the introduction in which Pauling made a comment which attracted my father's attention: "If you become a chemist you will never have to worry about making a living because there will always be plenty of jobs available in the field." Then I realized that Father wanted us to be able to make a living in science or engineering without getting involved in politics and being constantly victimized during our lifetime. He understood Korean society at the time as well as the Joseon dynasty history of factional fighting which resulted in sacrifices by all male offspring of the party members that lost the fight. This was why my brother John and I decided to go into the field of engineering and science. It turned out it was wise advice since both of us never have had to worry about our jobs or making a living after completing our education in the United States. Like me, John does not have too many happy memories of Korea. Both of us decided to become US citizens and I would say without any hesitation that we have made significant contributions to America in our fields as well as to the US Treasury contributing high bracket taxes as naturalized citizens for a long time without any dependents.

I always valued my father's guidance as a child and teenager so I decided to concentrate in chemistry. Although chemistry was not my favorite subject in high school, I loved to use chemical symbols to describe chemical reactions because that's very neat and short. I began my college chemistry by memorizing the entire periodic table — H for hydrogen, N for nitrogen, O for oxygen, C for carbon, and so on. When I think of it now, it was a dumb idea spending valuable time in trying to memorize the entire periodic table, something you can always look up as needed. When I was young, I had a photographic memory for dates and years of historical events as well as certain mathematical equations, so memorizing was very easy for me then. (Now I have to enter my daily tasks into my cell phone to get through my day). I suspect that has something to do with the chemistry of the aging brain, which I'm working on, but progress is slow. I also tried to write down simple chemical reactions using symbols and balancing the number of molecules. All this effort was just to motivate myself into behaving like a real chemist having fun. Finally, I felt pretty comfortable about the thought of spending my life as a chemist even though it was not as exciting as politics or defending innocent people falsely accused of wrongdoing. Eventually, I branched out to other scientific fields such as hematology, cell biology and immunology and got involved in many pioneering projects for automation of blood analysis, having lots of fun working with many bright engineers and scientists.

The choice of a college was another question. My parents could not afford expenses such as room, board and college tuition if I chose a college in Seoul. My father always wanted to have his own children attend the same school where he was teaching to demonstrate that the school was good enough for his own children so it should be good enough for other children as well. Consequently I entered the Chunbuk National University and majored in chemistry, taking courses such as general chemistry, inorganic chemistry, organic chemistry, physical chemistry and laboratory courses.

Of all the courses I took I found organic chemistry the most interesting because the reaction of carbon compounds are more closely related to living things and human body functions. For many people organic chemistry is the most difficult of all. In ancient times, Romans who enjoyed getting drunk knew that when they drank sour wine it tasted like vinegar - acetic acid. I asked my organic chemistry professor whether there was a course primarily focused on body chemistry and the process of the reactions of chemicals in human body. He said that as a matter of fact there was a popular new field called biochemistry and courses were being added to some graduate programs at several universities in the United States at that time. I was delighted to hear this news. Biochemistry is the study of the chemical processes in living organisms. It deals with the structure and function of cellular components, such as proteins, carbohydrates, nucleic acids, lipids and other bio-molecules. It's the field to study cell metabolism and the endocrine system. Other areas of biochemistry developed in later years include the genetics (DNA, RNA), protein synthesis, cell membrane transport, and signal transduction. I finally found an area in chemistry in which I was really interested. In those days, my mind was always far away, dreaming of coming to the United States.

In Chonju my mother gave birth to another child - a daughter, "Mimi". Now my parents had eight children. I didn't know what happened to their resolution not to have any more children years earlier. Maybe they didn't understand birth control. How were they going to raise and educate eight children on a professor's salary in such an unstable society? I was concerned because my mother was always exhausted from taking care of so many growing children. I was also thinking that if every parent had as many children as my parents where were they all going to live? The earth is not going to expand but the world's population was increasing logarithmically, especially in a small country like Korea. I decided that I was not going to get married or have any children to make up the difference. In any case I didn't want to put my children through what I went through during the Korean War. I thought it's a pretty rough world in which to survive. However the reality was that my parents were going to need help from somebody and I could not think of anybody but myself. I made the decision to dedicate myself to my profession to be able to help my parents. This decision, right or wrong, shaped much of my later life. As it turned out I was overly concerned about things like population expansion. My brother Soo has informed me that recent surveys show that the South Korean population is shrinking because few couples are considering multiple children.

Although my father's dream of spending some years at Harvard University was completely erased because of the Korean War, I had the impression that he still kept his hope of going to the

United States. He finally got a chance to go to America and Europe in a cultural exchange program for professors and college administrators interested in learning how American and European universities are run. He was very excited at this opportunity. In summer of 1957, he traveled to the United States and to Western European countries for several weeks, returning home with mountains of photos. He was convinced that I should continue my study in America. During his trip he had met some Korean students on scholarships that subsidized their school expenses during their academic years. He was elated to hear such news and thought that I could do the same. I was very happy to get away from Korea after what our family went through. Living where humans actually had rights would be incredible.

Of course my father's thinking was different. He wanted me to obtain my PhD in the United States then return to Korea and become a college professor. But I had no intention of becoming a college professor. My observation was that professors never have enough money to make an acceptable living. In the 1950s college professors in South Korea were respected but never paid enough to provide decent lives for their families. Today in South Korea the living standard has improved significantly and college professors lead comfortable lives. Although I never had a desire to become a multi-millionaire I knew being poor meant a difficult, unhealthy life. My first priority was to do something innovative to build up a respectable career and lead a comfortable life without financial worries.

One day my father said the Department of Education in South Korea was holding nationwide examinations to select students to distribute scholarships, some partial and some full. The areas of those exams were English and Korean history. It seemed that they didn't want students to leave Korea without a good knowledge of Korean history. This is why I still have a pretty good knowledge in that area and the step-by-step process by which imperial Japan was finally able to annex Korea in 1910. So I prepared myself as best as I could not knowing exactly what kind of questions would be in the exam. The day came - I went to Seoul and took the exam not knowing whether I would get a scholarship since it would depend on how well other candidates did. Some of those scholarships were only partial and I knew my parents could not subsidize my expenses at all since they had seven other children to feed. Sometime later I learned that I received the best scholarship, a full scholarship, but it was only a one-year cultural exchange scholarship. But I thought I could resolve to get another scholarship to continue my study by doing well since I was willing to work hard to get good grades during my first year in the United States.

Now I had to prepare all the documents to leave the country so I was very busy for a while. Then my mother recalled an incident that took place in Pyongyang when I was only an infant. A passerby, maybe a shaman, said to mother after carefully examining me on the street, "This girl will grow up and go far away. She will be successful in her pursuits. She will do well financially. But she is missing one very important piece of luck: finding a rich husband." Mother was wondering how she knew I would be going abroad because girls were normally not permitted to leave Korea to study in those days. Then mother cautioned me not to go to any drive-in movies because she'd heard that's where girls lose their virginity. I told her not to worry because my head was filled with heavy thoughts about academic courses I had to manage to get through in the first year. This was the extent of my sex education from my mother. She never talked about the subject.

One day I asked her how women get pregnant expecting a detailed explanation from the former teacher, my mother. Instead, she was startled and said that modern young girls were not as naïve and pure as they were when she was growing up. But the only reason I asked the question was because our high school biology teacher said we had to develop more curiosity about everything if we wanted to become good scientists and therefore we should find out details on each subject to understand fully. I'm not sure this was what our class biology teacher expected but this was the result of my first scientific inquiry. I was simply very curious how babies were made and wanted to know the details. Many years later, I finally found the answer when I took embryology at the Medical school. It's the most mysterious and so precisely controlled process only God could have designed — from one tiny fertilized egg to a complete human being!

Photo 10: At the scholarship Award Ceremony at the Department of Education. 1: Minister of Education, 2: Vice-Minister of Education, 3: Author receiving the award from the minister and shaking hands with him. Many other applicants received partial scholarships to come to the United States to study. This was the golden era for the United States after the victory in WWII.

Chapter 19: To the Land of Freedom and the Fall of The First ROK (1959–1960)

It was early September in 1959. I said goodbye to friends and faculty members who came to the Chonju train station to see me off and wish me luck and success in my academic pursuits in America. All my family members were with me on the train to accompany me to Seoul so they could see me off at Gimpo Airport the following day. In those days going abroad for academic pursuits was a big goal, especially for a young girl and on a full scholarship! My mother was worried about sending me to a foreign country so many thousands of miles away where we had no relatives or friends, and without any money. She exchanged some Korean money she had saved for US dollars and gave me $150 for emergency use. The full scholarship I had received covered tuition, room, and board and $10 a week spending money. Not a lot, even then.

The next day we were at Gimpo Airport, where a large Northwest Airlines plane was waiting to board. My youngest sister, Mimi, was less than three years old and my youngest brother, Hugh, was six. Their little hands waved to me as I was walking toward the plane. Mother was very quiet, probably too worried to say anything. Father was trying to give me some advice and encouraging words but I wasn't really listening because my mind was empty. I didn't know whether I was extremely brave or incredibly dumb to leave the only home I had ever known in my life, no matter whether my memory of the place was sweet or bitter. Actually I had few regrets other than leaving my family because I always wanted to leave Korea, the country that mistreated my parents, decent and good-hearted people. I felt more comfortable than many might have because I had studied English diligently and had the benefit of a father who also spoke English. I got on an airplane for the first time in my life, settled into my seat, and listened to the roar of the engines as they lifted me into the sky and a whole new life.

It was a very long journey, a 15- or 16-hour flight from Seoul to Boston, and I could not sleep. The plane finally stopped in

Anchorage, Alaska, to clear passengers through US immigration. I looked outside from the airport and saw rocky and snow-capped mountains shooting starkly into the clear blue sky. I remembered reading in American history how America purchased Alaska from the Russian Empire in 1867 for $7.2 million at 2 cents per acre, or about $122 million in today's dollars. At the time Russia had lost the Crimean war and was desperate for money to finance their armies. They also feared that if they went to war with Great Britain for hegemony in the Pacific that Great Britain would simply seize the undefended Alaskan territory. It was a huge opportunity for the U.S., when the Russian Ambassador made the offer for the sale. Only Americans know how to expand their territory without a war—just pay for the land at a bargain price. I compared American expansion to the gradual shrinkage of the Korean Peninsula, as my father used to refer Korean history as Yongdu-Sami (Dragon Head to a Snake Tail).

The plane continued to the east and finally arrived at Boston Logan International Airport at 1:00 a.m. in the morning. The airport was very quiet and I could not see many people except some taxies. So I took a taxi and asked the driver to take me to Brandeis University in Waltham, Massachusetts which was about 17 miles from the Logan airport. I was relieved that my mother gave me some US currency so I could pay for the taxi. When we arrived on the campus we could not find anyone. I gave the driver the name of the dormitory, Shapiro B, where I was supposed to go. The taxi driver drove around the campus and found the dormitory and rang the bell many times. I was lucky to have such a kind taxi driver to do all that extra work for his customer without any complaint. The bell finally woke up the housemother who came out in her robe and escorted me to the empty room assigned to me for the semester with a roommate. It was 3:00 a.m. and I tried to get some sleep. When I woke up it was after 10:00 a.m. and the college cafeteria was already closed for breakfast so I missed my first meal in the United States. I was very tired and hungry but the campus was located in a rather rural area so I could not find a nearby coffee shop or restaurant within walking distance. I was thinking how much better it would have been if I had been able to come a couple of weeks before and stay with a friend or a relative to recuperate from the long trip and prepare for a new school but I didn't have that luxury. I had to kick start my new life on my own.

The next day I wrote dozens of letters to my parents, friends, and old school faculty members to let them know that I had arrived safely. I didn't complain about my hardship as a stranger in a foreign land. Brandeis University was a young and a relatively small, private research university with a liberal arts focus located in Waltham, Mass, nine miles west of Boston. The school was founded in 1948 as a non-sectarian coeducational institution on the site of the former Middlesex University. The university is named for the first Jewish justice of the United States Supreme Court, Louis Dembitz Brandeis (1856–1941). The Wien International Scholarship, which I had been awarded, is for international undergraduate students. The scholarship was established in 1958 by Lawrence A. and Mae Wien, so it turned out I was one of the first recipients. The Wien family had three objectives: to further international understanding, to provide international students an opportunity to study in the United States, and to enrich the intellectual and cultural life at Brandeis.

The campus was beautiful, the surrounding atmosphere was peaceful, and New England autumn leaves were turning into various colors, looking like a large field of embroidery. From the window of my dormitory room, I could see the wooded area and could hear many jet-black crows making loud and throaty calls, echoing back and forth. Koreans are very superstitious about crows. If you see crows or ravens around your house there will be a bad luck or a death in the family. On the other hand, if magpies visit your home or build their nest on your tree it will bring good luck to the household. Therefore it made me worry about my mother since she was not very healthy. I still don't like crows or ravens.

Other than that I could see that the university campus was strictly dedicated to academic pursuits and there were no eyes or ears watching every move of students or faculty members. Nobody was talking about politics, nobody seemed to be trying to build up a plot against anyone, and all I had to do was to concentrate on my studies. Universities are supposed to be ivory towers for higher education and they must be left for intellectual pursuits without any intervention from outside. By comparison, what was going on in Korea at the time was in direct contravention to the fundamentals of quality education.

The next day I went to meet with the foreign student advisor. I selected my courses, went to register, and met some other foreign students, mostly from Europe, who came on the same one-year cultural exchange scholarship program. It seemed to me that most of them were young and bright but they came just to spend a year in the United States, to enjoy the American experience, and then return to their homelands. Most of them were registering for light courses such as music, art, English, or psychology. My situation was very different. I had to accomplish a lot more than just spending one year enjoying my American experience. I had to find out quickly whether I was capable of continuing my study in the United States, entering a graduate school, and obtaining advanced degrees. I could not think about anything beyond that at the time. I registered for advanced courses in chemistry and was determined to do well and develop self-confidence. The school gave us a welcoming party and many foreign students gave good performances; they sang, danced, or played musical instruments. I had never had a chance to learn any musical skills to entertain audiences so I felt rather embarrassed.

There were a couple of other Korean students at the same school but not on the same scholarship program. One of them had a car and he offered to take me sightseeing with him. We went to see Harvard University, the school where my father was once planning to spend a couple of years in 1950 before the Korean War, a member of the Ivy League and the oldest institution of higher learning in The United States. There was also Massachusetts Institute of Technology, MIT, nearby, both in Cambridge. Many Korean engineering students dreamed about studying at MIT because it's known as one of the best engineering schools in the world. I was speechless when I saw the MIT campus extending over a mile along the northern bank of the Charles River basin. Then there was Boston harbor, where the historic Boston Tea Party took place in 1773. We also visited Boston Commons, 50 acres of land where numerous historical events took place, including hanging and witch burning.

I realized that America had not always been a rich and peaceful democratic country. I knew the colonists had to fight for their independence from the British. Then there was the American Civil War (1861–1865), the deadliest war in American history, resulting in the deaths of 620,000 soldiers and an undetermined number of civilians. Slavery was abolished, the Union was restored, and the role of the federal government strengthened. It also brought changes that helped make the country the large superpower it is today. I was thinking there was hope for Korea to become a peaceful and united democratic country someday. Signs of the wealth of the nation were seen everywhere; beautiful parks, extremely well-equipped research institutions and universities with huge libraries, abundance of food displayed in every grocery store, a variety of nice outfits mostly made in the USA displayed in department store windows, many different models of cars made by GM and Ford. I remember thinking, "This country is self-sufficient and they have everything they need and more. It doesn't need colonies for its survival as Japan did."

Most of all Americans seemed to be managing such a huge country and mixed population pretty well, advancing science and technology to boost its economy and become a world leader. This was my first impression of America in 1960 - very impressive! I feel almost nostalgic to think of my first impression of the grandeur of this country because the status of America has changed so much with so many problems in the world.

I went to my first class - organic chemistry. When I was trying to take notes the professor spoke so fast that I missed about nine lines out of every ten. He was writing down benzene structures in boat form and chair form, which I had never heard of until then. I only knew the structure of benzene, C_6H_6, as a six-carbon ring with three double bonds drawn flat in one dimension only. I knew then my chemistry education in Korea before 1960 was inadequate and I expected a hard time ahead of me. In a biology lab there was a quiz session. The lab had many benches and the instructor placed a microscope on each bench, each microscope set to examine a slide placed underneath. We were supposed to identify what was on the slide and move to the next microscope. I was doing fine until I got to a microscope and the question was whether the specimen on the slide 'mate' with other specimen, its name he wrote down on the exam paper. The problem was that I didn't understand the word 'Mate'. The word Mate never showed up in any of my English text books in Korea. I never heard of the word before, so I raised my hand and asked, "What does the word mate mean?" Some students giggled and the instructor hesitated to explain the meaning of the word. I couldn't catch what he was trying to say, so I just moved on to the next slide. Fortunately, I managed to get an A on the quiz without answering that question. But I didn't do as well in my organic chemistry course, in which I got a C. I had never received a C in any course until then, so this was a wakeup call to me. This is how one semester passed by and the winter vacation came.

My American roommate, Abby, asked me whether I would like to come down to New York during the winter vacation. Her parents were living in an apartment in New York City. I didn't want to infringe on their lives and declined the invitation. The university arranged for some of us foreign students on the cultural exchange program who did not have any other place to go to live in another house on the campus during the winter vacation. During this time, John F. Kennedy and his wife Jacquelyn were invited to attend a gathering on the university campus to meet with some of the faculty members and VIPs from outside. This was apparently a fund-raising event for the Kennedy/ Nixon campaign, and the VIPs were rich businessmen who were making large campaign contributions to JFK. We were allowed to get in and observe the event. We were all fascinated with this handsome and charismatic young man and his wife of elegant beauty. This was how a real democratic government chooses its president, not by assassinating all the rival candidates. I was fascinated. What a difference from the stubborn and grouchy old man, Syngman Rhee!

After the winter recess we began the spring semester and we were all looking forward to our spring vacation. The cultural exchange program director told us that we were scheduled to visit historical places like Jamestown which had been the capital of the American colonies for 83 years, from 1616 until 1698. It was regarded as the first permanent English settlement in what is now the United States of America. We were also going to Yorktown, where the Battle of Yorktown took place in 1781. It resulted in a decisive victory by a combined assault of American forces led by General George Washington and French forces led by General *Comte de*

Rochambeau defeating a British army commanded by General Lord Cornwallis. We toured through Jamestown and Yorktown, enjoying all the reenactments by local actors and actresses in old colonial customs. Then we went to look for restrooms. What a shock! Both men's and women's restrooms had signs for whites or colored. This was 1960 and the place was Virginia, not very far from the capital of the United States, Washington, DC, founded on July 16, 1790.

Washington, DC, is located on the north bank of the Potomac River and is bordered by the states of Virginia to the southwest and Maryland to the north and east. When we arrived in Washington, DC, all the students in the group got together and wrote a protest letter about the bathroom signs and sent it to the Washington Post, the largest and most influential newspaper in Washington D.C. area. The Washington Post was also considered as one of the most important newspapers in the United States due to its particular emphasis on national politics and international affairs. However, we never saw any article related to our protest letter published in the paper. Changing times and lives during the latter half of the 20th century have greatly improved understanding about humanity and fair treatment of fellow human beings, making America a more civilized place to live.

Since it was April the National Mall in Washington was spectacular with the blooming of the cherry blossoms. The National Cherry Blossom Festival is a spring celebration in Washington, D.C. commemorating the March 27, 1912, gift of Japanese cherry trees from Mayor Yukio Ozaki of Tokyo to the city of Washington. Ozaki donated the trees in an effort to enhance the growing friendship between the United States and Japan and to celebrate the continued close relationship between the two nations. This was only two years after the Japanese annexation of Korea. The Japanese were very clever in dealing with their international affairs. It's no wonder that Koreans could not get any help at all from the United States during and after the March 1st Korean Independence Movement, which was triggered by Woodrow Wilson's 14 Points declaration, when Japanese police slaughtered thousands of Koreans participating during the movement. Next we visited the Smithsonian Institution, which is a great educational foundation chartered by Congress in 1846 that maintains most of the nation's official museums and galleries in

Washington. The US government partially funds the Smithsonian, thus making its collections open to the public free of charge. But we didn't have much time to spend there either. It's a huge facility, which I visited years later.

When the bus was nearing our next destination, we could see the skyline of New York City, and there was a wild uproar of joy in the bus. I had never seen any city with so many tall buildings lined up neatly shooting into the sky. New York City is a leading global city, exerting a powerful influence over worldwide commerce, finance, culture, and entertainment. We visited the United Nations, an international organization whose aims are to facilitate the cooperation in international law, international security, economic development, social progress, human rights, and world peace. It was founded in 1945 after World War II to prevent future wars between countries and to provide a platform for dialogue.

There was a chapter in my high school English text on the United Nations so I knew a lot about the organization before I came to America. The UN served well during the Korean War to defend South Korea under the honorable white and blue UN flag. We didn't get a chance to go up the Empire State Building, the tallest building in New York City at the time since the World Trade Center had not been built in 1960. We saw The Statue of Liberty in Manhattan harbor which greeted millions of immigrants as they came to America in the late 19th and early 20th centuries. We stopped by Wall Street in Lower Manhattan which has been a dominant global financial center since World War II and is home to the New York Stock Exchange. I didn't know then how closely stock market activities are connected to both domestic and world affairs. And of course New York City has the haven of peace and quiet in Central Park.

Returning from the exciting trip I again concentrated on my study for the second semester which was easier since my English comprehension was significantly improved. The floor captain of my dormitory, Judy Levine, became a good friend of mine and I even spent a few days in her parent's home in New York City.

One day in April, Judy came into my room and said, "Have you heard what happened in Korea? How could the Korean people kill their own vice president and his family?" Since I didn't have any radio or TV in my room, I was not aware of the news. However, I knew that there was a problem in Korea because President Rhee refused to step down after his three terms and kept changing the constitution to continue his presidency. The 1960 election initiated his fourth term.

The April Revolution was a popular uprising in April 1960, led by student groups that overthrew the autocratic government of the first ROK under Syngman Rhee. The events were touched off by the discovery of a body in Masan Harbor - a student killed by a tear-gas shell in demonstrations against the elections in March. Rhee was determined to see his protégé Lee Gi-bung elected as the independent vice president, a separate office under Korean law at that time. But when Lee, who was running against Chang Myun, former ambassador to the United States during the Korean War, won the vote with an abnormally wide margin, it was apparent to the opposition that the election was rigged. That triggered a furious anger among segments of the Korean populace. When police shot demonstrators in Masan the student-led April 19 Movement forced Rhee to resign on April 26. The students didn't kill Lee Gi-bung but it was his son who killed all his family and shot himself when it became clear that the government was going to be overthrown. There is no way of knowing whether Lee Gi-bung asked his son to carry out this family suicide or it was totally his son's idea. Lee could have just resigned instead. This was a tragedy no matter how you looked at it.

On April 28, 1960, a DC-4 belonging to the United States CIA—operated by Civil Air Transport (a Chinese airline, later owned by the CIA, that supported US covert operations throughout East and Southeast Asia)—whisked Rhee out of South Korea as protestors converged on the Blue House. It was later revealed by Kim Yong-kap, the deputy minister of finance, that Rhee had embezzled more than $20 million in government funds. I am not surprised since he also embezzled funds from the PGRK which was running on a shoestring budget in Shanghai when he was the president of the PGRK. That was the reason for his expulsion from the PGRK by Kim Gu and others.

The former president, his Austrian-born wife, Franciscka Donner, and adopted son lived comfortably in exile in Honolulu, Hawaii. On July 19, 1965, Rhee died of a stroke. His body was returned to Seoul and buried in the National Cemetery on July 27 that same year. It's a misfortune that he was so unwilling to work harmoniously with other patriotic and intelligent Korean leaders of the time who fought for Korean independence. He should have followed the example of the first president of the United States, George Washington, who stepped aside when his second term was over setting a precedent for many generations to come.

After the fall of the first ROK, a new parliamentary election was held on July 29, 1960. The Democratic Party which had been the opposition during the first ROK easily gained power and the second ROK was established. The revised constitution dictated that the second ROK would take the form of a parliamentary cabinet system in which the president would play only a nominal role. This was the first and only instance in which South Korea turned to a cabinet system instead of a presidential system. Yun Bo-sun was elected as president on August 13, 1960. The prime minister and head of the government was Chang Myun. Father knew both men as decent and well-educated men who were interested in building a truly democratic Korea. Father and Chang Myun shared many similarities in their philosophy and goals regarding the future of Korea. Chang believed in educating the young generation of Koreans to create a generation able to contribute to building the new nation. Under Japanese rule Chang had worked as a teacher at Yongsan Youth Catholic Theology School from 1919 to 1921. He taught at Dongsung Commerce High School from 1931 to 1936, and as I mentioned in an earlier chapter, he was the principal of Heawha kindergarten of the Hehwa-dong Catholic Church when I was a student there during World War II. Chang's photo was in my lost graduation album.

Yun was born in South Chungcheong Province like my father. He graduated with an MA in economics from the University of Edinburgh in Scotland in 1930. He entered politics after the Japanese occupation ended in 1945 and was appointed by Syngman Rhee as mayor of Seoul. A year later, he was appointed as the minister of commerce and industry. Soon he started to disagree with Rhee's authoritarian policies and resigned. He then served as president of the Red Cross, before being elected to the National Assembly in 1954. A year later he and several others founded the opposition Democratic Party. Yun and my parents were members of the same church, Ahndong Presbyterian Church.

Chang Myun was a devout Roman Catholic who graduated from Manhattan College in the United States. He served as the first ROK's ambassador to the United States from 1949 to 1951, and became the second prime minister of the first ROK on November 23, 1950. In 1956, he was elected vice president. After Syngman Rhee's government was ousted by the student led pro-democracy uprising, he became prime minister of the second ROK in 1960. Knowing the decency of the two men, my father sounded very optimistic for the first time, thinking that this civilian government could work things out to finally establish a real democratic government. Likewise, the US government was also very optimistic about Chang Myun's leadership. They predicted that Chang was going to build a brand new chapter in Korean history, a truly democratic government of Korea.

During the second ROK, my father was contacted by the minister of the Communication Department in Seoul to return to the Chesin Communications School, the school he left after the fire incidence before the Korean War. He was asked to clean up the mess created by the student uprising. I suppose the lives of those students who belonged to the paramilitary youth organization were in trouble without the financial support they received before the collapse of Syngman Rhee's government. When my father returned to this school during the Second Republic he wrote the memoire describing what had really happened during his administration and who the real arsonists were who burned the school down. He didn't know any details when the arsonists struck in 1950 but I gather he was able to find out the details after the first ROK collapsed and the existence of the paramilitary youth organization was revealed.

During the second semester I busied myself filling out applications to local universities including Harvard asking for a scholarship in the department of biochemistry. Although Harvard undergraduates were almost exclusively white and predominantly male in the 60s, Harvard graduate school was accepting females and other minority groups and became more diverse in the post World War II period. When I received their application form I was surprised to see questions like "Was your father or grandfather an alumnus of Harvard?" I had heard that offspring of Harvard alumni had first priority to enter Harvard but I am sure that kind of unfair rules do not exist anymore. In any case, I received a research assistant scholarship from University of New Hampshire for the following semester.

I completed the second semester at Brandeis. Most of the other foreign students, returned to their homelands but I had to find a summer job in Boston. It was difficult since I had a student visa. My father said one of his former students had a relative living in Southern California and they had orchards. I was welcome to stay with them for the summer. So I planned to spend the summer in California. America is a large country and California is 3,000 miles away from Boston so how to get there was another question. My budget was very limited. One day I saw a note on the bulletin board in the student union asking for students who wanted a ride to San Francisco. One of the graduate students was returning home to San Francisco by car. I contacted him, Rudy, and he said it was perfect since he had already recruited two other students who wanted a ride. One was a German student, Ronny, who was on the same cultural exchange program as I was. Ronny wanted to travel cross-country by car to see more of America before returning to Germany. Another student was a female graduate student, Sandy, so I felt comfortable joining the group. We discussed how to split the expenses. I paid my portion to the driver in advance, and we set the date for departure.

At the end of May the second semester ended. I began the 3,000-mile cross-continental journey across the USA. The USA is truly a large country, the envy of many Europeans living so close to neighboring countries, not to mention Asian countries suffering for many centuries of war over territory. It's quite impressive! We had to reset our watches many times as we entered different time zones as we crossed the continent. Driving continuously, changing drivers between Rudy and Ronny, with only one night stop over, we arrived in San Francisco in one week by late evening and Rudy dropped me off at the home of the son of the people with whom I was planning to spend the summer. The next day my hosts wanted to show me around San Francisco. San Francisco has always been a popular international tourist destination famous for its landmarks including the Golden Gate Bridge, Alcatraz Island, the cable cars, Coit Tower, Chinatown, and its steep rolling hills. The city is also known for its diverse and cosmopolitan population, including large and established Asian American and LGBT communities. My first impression of the city was nothing but amazement. How could the air of this city feel so fresh! I was told that the fog that covers the city every evening sweeps away all the dust in the air to the Pacific Ocean. During World War II, San Francisco was the point of departure for many soldiers going to the Pacific Theater.

The next day I was driven down to the final destination, Fresno, which is located in the center of the expansive Central Valley approximately 200 miles north of Los Angeles and 190 miles south of San Francisco. I stayed with the Chung family for the summer. This elderly couple came to America via Hawaii during World War II as laborers and established themselves as middle-class farmers and eventually owning their own farmland and growing grapes, various melons and fruits. They were extremely kind and treated me well during my stay at their home. I worked packing peaches for three months and saved money for the coming semester.

The summer was gone and it was now September and I was preparing to return to school in New England. It takes about five hours to fly from San Francisco or Los Angeles to Boston directly but I decided to take a cross-country bus to save money. The bus trip would take a whole week and I had to sleep on the bus. This trip was very strenuous and no fun because there were no overnight stopovers and no friends to chat with. When the bus was approaching Boston we heard the news that Boston had been hit by a hurricane. Many trees were down and some rooftops were blown away. After a long journey from California I had to take another bus to go to Durham, New Hampshire, and finally reached the dormitory and I slept 16 hours. Fortunately, I have never again had to take such a long distance trip by bus but this was a good experience and I had a chance to see the Middle America, the Red States.

Chapter 20: The Winter of New Hampshire and The Fall of The Second ROK (May 16, 1961)

This was the beginning of the Fall Semester in September, 1960. The University of New Hampshire (UNH) campus was beautiful with New England's colorful autumn leaves. As I walked around the campus I saw a big inscription on the top of the library entrance which says "You will know the truth and the truth will set you Free". I thought, "Yes, this is why we must study hard to get to know the truth, so we won't be so confused not knowing what to believe or whom to believe. That was the main problem in Korea in the minds of so many young people." UNH was considered as a Public Ivy League School by higher education specialists. UNH was the only public institution in New England to rank in the top 10 of number of Fulbright fellowships awarded.

I met with my advisor, Dr. Teeri, who was also the chairman of the Biochemistry department. He was very kind and helped me to register my first semester in the graduate school. I registered twelve credits, Biochemistry, Qualitative Organic Chemistry and Nutrition. I was finally able to start learning about Biochemistry, my major academic interest at the time. Having spent a year in America made a big difference. It was much easier in taking notes in classes and I felt more comfortable communicating with faculty members and other students. My research project was evaluating nutritional values of various fish species, primarily protein quality.

Our graduate dormitory was coed - one side of the building was for boys and the other side was for girls - but we were using the same front door entrance and the lounge where we had coed parties. Winter was approaching and the New England winter is very cold and snowy. When I got up one morning and opened the window shade in my room the whole window was buried under the snow as if I were in an Igloo. My room was located next to the terrace where snowfalls accumulated all night. When I went down stairs to go to the cafeteria for breakfast other students were just standing there because they could not open the front door because the whole door was buried under the snow. They said that snow accumulation of the day was more than 13 FT. So we called for the snow plow truck and by afternoon we were able to get out of the dorm to go to the cafeteria. The cafeteria didn't have a normal menu that day so we had some Danish and coffee for late breakfast. I was busy studying and carrying out my research project analyzing all types of fish for their nutritional values and amino acid composition. One unexpected fact was that the mollusk family such as clams and oysters did not contain as much good quality proteins as regular fish which we eat although they are more popular as appetizers. This was how the first year passed by and I did quite well with all my courses. I began to realize that all my efforts were turning into positive results. It was very encouraging!

Back in Korea, my father was very enthusiastic about the prospect of Korea and reviving his own potential to help build a better future for the next generation. Although the country was still suffering with high inflation and unemployment, the second ROK was run by decent and well educated leaders who had the same ideals and goals as his own for building a new democratic nation. Right away, they were developing the five-year economic plans to lead the nation to recovery and into prosperity. Unfortunately, the second ROK did not get enough time to follow through their economic plan. Toward the end of my second semester at school I heard surprising news from Korea. A military coup had taken place on May 16, 1961. I went down to the lobby of the dormitory to watch the news on TV. General Chang Do-young, the army Chief of Staff in Korea was on TV with the obvious implication that he was leading the coup. But there were no details explaining how the coup took place, seemingly overnight, apparently without any resistance, and then walked into the TV station to appear in the morning to make the big announcement. It was really hard to believe!

Only later did we discover that the real junta chief was Major General Park Chung-hee and that the number of military who participated in the coup was relatively small - no more than 3,600 men. The rebels did not meet much resistance because President Yun Bo-sun, who had taken an oath to protect the constitution and the country, declined to deploy troops against the rebels. He even persuaded the U.S. Eighth Army and the commanders of various South Korean army units not to oppose the rebels. Thus it was a bloodless coup. Marshall Green, the senior American diplomat and *chargé d'affaires* in South Korea at the time of the 1961 coup d'état bringing Major-General Park Chung-hee to power, was appointed deputy chief of mission at the U.S. Embassy in Seoul. During this time Ambassador Green maintained the position that the United States continued to back the ousted, democratically elected Prime Minister Chang Myun. But the US military could not take unilateral action to suppress the coup without the approval of the president of the host country. As usual there have been many rumors that the CIA had something to do with the coup but declassified information suggests there was no involvement of the CIA.

Park Chung-hee was smart to use Chang Do-young as his front man to prevent any action by the US Eighth Army since Chang Do-young was trained in the United States and was known to the Eighth Army. Park's background on the other hand had unfavorable baggage. First of all, in 1940 he entered the military academy of Manchukuo, the puppet state of militarist Japan. Park was trained to become a member of the officer corps of the imperial Japanese army. In 1944 upon graduation from the military academy in Tokyo Park was assigned to the Kwantung army and dispatched to Manchuria as a second lieutenant. When Park was discharged from the defeated Kwantung army on September 2, 1945 he returned to his home village and spent a year of quiet desperation. In September 1946 he entered the S. Korean Military Academy and resumed the military career he had started earlier. Upon graduation in December of the same year he had earned the rank of Captain.

In 1948, Park was implicated in the Yursu Mutiny and was forced out of the army over charges that he had collaborated with communists. He was recalled when North Korea invaded the South in June of 1950, after which his career was marked by a steady rise through the ranks of the new army that rapidly expanded during the Korean War.

Chang Myun fought against the Rhee dictatorship for many years. He was a true believer in democracy. Moreover Chang's administration had successfully designed the first five-year economic development plan that would have proven beneficial for all Koreans. This five-year economic development plan was later "borrowed" by the Park Chung-hee administration. Park used virtually the same five-year economic development plan for his economic development after the May 16 military coup. In 1961 the Chang Myun administration attempted to resume talks on a treaty for future relations between Japan and the Republic of Korea and discussed eight of the proposed articles designed to normalize diplomatic ties. However the talks came to a halt because of the military coup d'état led by Park Chung-hee on May 16. On May 20, 1961, Chang was removed from the position of Prime Minister after less than one year in power.

My father was very upset and hugely disappointed in President Yun for not performing his presidential duty to protect the nation and its constitution and giving the country away to the military junta. Yun later explained that he wanted to prevent any bloodshed but he had large numbers of military personnel at his disposal to prevent the coup. Lieutenant General Lee Han-lim, who did not support the coup, commanded 20 divisions of the First Army which were in a state of readiness for the battle, and his intervention on behalf of the nation and it's people would have blocked the coup. As expected, both Lee Han-lim and Chang Do-young were ousted from their positions after the coup. When I visited Korea in 1970, I saw former president Yun at Ahndong Presbyterian Church which my parents attended every Sunday. He was a very quiet gentleman, looked frail and old, and didn't look like a man who could have made tough decisions to mount resistance against a military coup. In due course Park Chung-hee became the president of the third ROK. It was 1963.

This was how the modern history of ROK was evolving - a continuous struggle by the people to create a true democratic country, each time ending up with another dictator taking power. My father lost his second chance to rebuild his intended career because the third ROK government had infiltrated academia and reshuffled the heads of many colleges and universities. Park was very methodical in details to eliminate any authority who might raise a voice in protest of the military junta's usurpation of the government. More importantly he prevented them from influencing students who often form the vanguard of protest and revolutions. Ewha Women's University president Kim Hwal-lan and Yonsei University president Baek Nak-jun were ousted from their universities. My father also had to resign from his post.

Many years later, in January 2005, the government of the Republic of Korea released 1,200 pages of diplomatic documents related to negotiations on the Treaty on Basic Relations between Japan and the Republic of Korea in 1965 that had been kept secret for forty years. These documents revealed that the Japanese government proposed to the government of the Republic of Korea, headed by Park Chung-hee, to directly compensate individual victims of Japanese colonization of Korea. But the Park administration insisted it would handle individual compensation to the victims and appropriated the entire amount of the grant, $300 million. The Park administration negotiated for a total of $360 million in compensation for the 1.03 million Koreans conscripted into forced labor and military service during the colonial period but received only $300 million (approx.30 cents per victim). So the victims ultimately received little or no compensation because the Park administration used most of the grant for economic development, namely building social infrastructure, Pohang Iron and Steel Company, Gyeongbuk Expressway, Soyang Dam, etc. The fund may have been used to help the nation's economy but one suspect that was no consolation to the victims.

In New Hampshire I completed the first semester and it was now summer recess. I sent out many letters to find a summer job in Boston but they all politely replied that they could not employ anyone on student visa. So I went to Boston, scanned through the Help Wanted section in the Boston Globe everyday and visited the Human Resources department of each institution for an interview. One after another I was turned down because they didn't have a summer job position. I finally decided to look for a permanent job even if I still planned to return to the university to complete my master's degree, at least for the time being. I went to Harvard Medical Center and the

Clinical Chemistry Lab Director interviewed me. He was a young pathologist and I said I was interested in a laboratory technician's position and he asked me whether I was planning to go back to school in the fall, so I said "No, I am looking for a permanent job." Then, he asked me some clinical chemistry questions and hired me right way." I was relieved that he never asked me about my visa status and neither did the HR office. I found dormitory-like housing in Boston where about a dozen ladies lived. Everybody had a private room but used the community bathrooms and a large kitchen, which was fine with me just for the summer. So I had one-step improved summer job working in a related field, not in a packing house, earning a pretty good wage and learning something new. The lab supervisor was a Danish lady, very bright with very sunny attitude, always smiling. There, I saw for the first time a fully automated blood analyzer produced by the Big T, Technicon Corporation in Tarrytown, NY. I didn't know then I would later spend many years of my life developing more sophisticated automated blood analyzers at that company. Up to that time most chemical analysis in clinical laboratories were done manually using volumetric pipettes, flasks, burettes, test tubes, flame photometers and colorimeters - the equipment available before multi-wavelength spectrophotometers and flowcytometers became available.

During this summer I was invited to a picnic with a group of Korean students from MIT and Harvard and enjoyed a relaxing afternoon on the Boston Common. We had many more gatherings and social activities during this summer. Since this was a summer recess and we didn't have to worry about our schoolwork, everybody was relaxed and enjoyed the summer. Then September came and I had to resign my job at Harvard Medical Center to return to UNH where I completed all the requirements, my course work, research project, the theses and received my first Master's degree in biochemistry.

It was time for me to make plans for the immediate, the future and the distant future. For the immediate I felt that I needed more money than the small income provided by scholarships. I was even running out of decent clothes not to mention a car or nice apartment to live in. I remembered how exciting NYC was with all the cultural activities and the best facilities in the city. So I sent out many letters to find a job. I found a laboratory director, Dr. Solomon, who was wiling to sponsor my permanent visa after the interview under the condition that I manage his laboratory because he was too busy to oversee all the details of daily operations. He filled out the document, Immigration form for scientists and engineers on my behalf and submitted it to the Immigration and Naturalization Department of The United States. But I didn't expect this process to take seven long years.

In the meantime, I began to take some evening courses at Columbia University in Manhattan hoping to apply for a Ph.D. program but they would not accept any part-time student for the program. They suggested that I apply as a full-time student. But then I had to continue the same type of life I had been living without enough money to take care of all the necessary things in a normal life. Instead I thought I had an opportunity to catch up in the area of my education totally missing, the cultural education by taking an advantage of the most forefront cultural activities of the city of New York in music, ballet, arts, Broadway shows, museums and many more. This was the area of education I was far behind because of my family situation during the war as well as long after the war. It takes a long time for a family with many children to recover economically when an unexpected disaster strikes, losing all its possessions including the house. Unfortunately, that's what happened to many families in Korea.

Chapter 21: Homecoming Trip to the Third Republic (1970-1971)

It had been a long time since I had seen my parents and siblings due to the delay in getting my green card. I decided to visit Korea, leaving my brother John, who had come to the United States two years before and was attending the Brooklyn Institute of Technology. I wondered how much Korea had changed.

This was the Third Republic of Korea under Park Chung-hee who took over the Second Republic by coup d'état in May 16, 1961. He created the Korean Central Intelligence Agency (KCIA) on June 19, 1961, to prevent a counter-coup and to suppress all potential enemies, domestic and international. The KCIA extended its power to economic and foreign affairs under its first director, Colonel Kim Jong-pil, a relative of Park's and one of the original planners of the coup. Initially, President Yun remained in office to provide legitimacy to the regime but he resigned on March 22, 1962. Park Chung-hee was the real power as chairman of the Supreme Council for National Reconstruction with the rank of General. Following pressure from the Kennedy administration in the United States a civilian government was restored with Park narrowly winning the 1963 election as the candidate of the newly created Democratic Republican Party over Yun, the candidate of the Civil Rule Party. Of course Park had full control of the government and it was not very difficult for him to control the election and win in 1967, again defeating Yun by a narrow margin. It's ironic that Yun even bothered to run for president after allowing the military coup to take over when he was the president with all the power and 20 divisions of the First Army under his command.

It was twilight when my plane approached the Korean Peninsula. I looked down and saw many homes in the countryside with blue tiled roofs that had replaced the old grass roofs that had existed for many centuries. At Gimpo Airport, I was met by a KCIA agent who was scrutinizing all arrivals from foreign countries. I didn't know exactly what they were looking for but they were asking all sorts of questions, detaining me there longer than seemed necessary. I learned later that

KCIA had not only investigative power but also the power to arrest and detain anyone suspected of wrongdoing or harboring anti-junta sentiments.

Park had been running the Third Republic of South Korea for nine years by the time I arrived in Korea in 1970. He is generally credited for his pivotal role in the development of the South Korean economy by shifting its focus to export-oriented industrialization. In 1961, South Korea's per capita income was only USD $72. On the other hand North Korea had already recovered from the war and had become a great economic and military power. This was because the North was more industrialized than the South under the previous Japanese regime. North Korea also received huge amounts of economic, technical, and financial aid from the Soviet Union and other communist bloc countries such as East Germany and Soviet occupied Poland. Park's leadership produced a remarkable development of industries and rise in the standard of living of average South Korean citizens. However, his policy of normalization of diplomatic relations with Japan had been extremely unpopular and resulted in widespread unrest as memories from Japan's 35-year brutal colonization of Korea were still vivid.

It's believed that the Japanese economy recovered quickly from ruin after World War II because of the Korean War. The Japanese made a considerable amount of money selling supplies they manufactured to Korea as well as to US military personnel stationed in Japan during the Korean War. By normalizing relations with Japan, Park allowed the capital from Japan to flow into the country in addition to the fund for compensation. These aids and loans - although criticized by many Koreans to be too meager for the 35 years of occupation by imperial Japan - along with American aid, helped to restore the depleted capital of South Korea.

It must be noted that North Korea's economy at the time being bigger and more vibrant than that of South Korea Park did not have many options or much time to negotiate more satisfactory compensation and apologies from Japan. This issue still plagues the relationship between Japan and South Korea today. Park clamped down on personal freedom under the provisions of a state of emergency dating back to the

Korean War. Constitutional guarantees of freedom of speech and the press were often curtailed. The KCIA retained broad powers of arrest and detention. Under Park Chung-hee's regime political opponents were subject to arbitrary detention and torture. The electoral system was also rigged in favor of Park's Democratic Republican Party which routinely won large majorities in the National Assembly.

I heard an interesting anecdote from my mother concerning Park's Democratic Republican Party. They were trying to recruit college students into their party and the recruiters were roaming around college campuses encouraging the students to join. My brother Soo, who had just entered Seoul University Law School came home and told Father that he had just joined Park's party. My father never allowed any of us to join any political party because he was familiar with the Joseon dynasty's history and what had happened to all the male members, including children, of the families of the party that lost the political fights. So father was very angry with my brother and forced him to resign from the party the next day.

As usual opposition parties and leaders were subjected to varying degrees of official harassment. Park was narrowly reelected in 1967 against Yun. The Constitution of 1963 limited the president to two consecutive terms, and this was Park's second term. However, dictators never give up their power voluntarily and it would be interesting to see what he was going to do when his second term was over.

During his administration Park wanted to obtain weapons of mass destruction to protect South Korea from North Korea's increasing menace. He gained support owing to decreasing confidence in the United States' willingness to protect South Korea from a North Korean attack. This issue was not widely reported in the press. In late 1974, Park authorized a program to develop nuclear weapons technology. Park feared that the United States would abandon South Korea after the Vietnam War despite Korea's having sent troops to that conflict. North Korea's aggression seemed particularly fierce at the time. A commando raid on the Blue House in January 1968, followed three days later by the seizure of the USS Pueblo generated a frightening climate. N. Korean infiltration tunnels were discovered under the demilitarized zone in

1974–75. In 1974 a pro–North Korean assassin attempted to kill Park but the bullet missed and killed his wife instead. There could hardly be a more hostile environment.

South Korea's confidence in the United States declined still further after January 26, 1977, when incoming president Jimmy Carter ordered the withdrawal of nuclear weapons from Korea along with the Second Infantry Division. In January 1976, Park had to end continuing negotiations with France to obtain reprocessing technology and by December 1976 he had to suspend the nuclear weapons program altogether under immense pressure from the United States. Today N. Korea is threatening S. Korea with its vastly improved nuclear weapons. Koreans wonder why the United States continues to dictate what S. Korea should do to protect itself while withdrawing its military leaving S. Korea to protect itself. For S. Korea to acquire nuclear weapons to balance the nuclear weapons of N. Korea makes as much sense as the United States maintaining nuclear weapons to balance the nuclear weapons of Russia and justifying it with a theory called Mutually Assured Destruction (MAD). It's a theory that will probably result in the earth becoming a rather large asteroid, devoid of life, sometime in the not so distant future. Not that I believe it's a good idea for S. Korea to develop nuclear weapons.

I also ask why the United States has never challenged seriously Chinese or Russian tactics of acceptance of N. Korea's nuclear weapons program. Where is the balance of power on the Korean peninsula? China and Russia seem to rather enjoy watching the United States squirm while imposing one set of ineffective sanctions after another while North Korea just continues to enlarge it's nuclear and missile capabilities, threaten South Korea and indeed the United States itself. The second Korean War is enabled when N. Korea begins to understand that the United States is incapable of containing a nuclear armed N. Korea. Actually it would seem that is already the case having been Kim Jong-un's strategy all along. One test missile landing a few miles off Seattle and they're ready. While the US is spending endless attention on preventing a nuclear armed Iran, the far greater possibility of nuclear disaster is a second Korean War.

I was finally able to step outside the airport and feel free and happy again. I was met by a large group of people who came by chartered bus to greet me. I found out they were friends of my parents from Ahndong Presbyterian Church in Seoul. The majority of Koreans are Christians now, although some are still Buddhists. It was emotional to see my parents who had aged noticeably. My brothers and sisters had also grown up a lot since I had left Korea ten years before. My sister Oak had already graduated from Ewha University and was married to a businessman. My brother Soo was a student at Seoul University Law School and brother Churl was attending Korea University majoring in history. It was a highly emotional moment when I realized that my parents had so many friends who were willing to come to the airport to welcome their daughter – a young lady they had never met.

This trip was supposed to be just a short visit, but my mother was furious that I still wasn't married, so she insisted that I could not return to the United States unless I got married in Korea. They said I should meet some good candidates arranged by family friends. I told them that I had decided not to get married a long time ago because it was too serious a matter, especially an arranged marriage. But she wouldn't give up. I decided that at least I could avoid being rushed and hopefully avoid a big mistake. I decided to look for a job in Korea to buy time. I had several interviews and decided to take an offer from Dr. Kang Shin-ho, the president of Dong-A Pharmaceutical Company in Seoul. Dr. Kang received his PhD in Germany. At that time, the company had an agreement with Squibb Pharmaceutical Company in the United States to manufacture and distribute some of their drugs in addition to their own products. I met many young, friendly, and bright employees there, who had all majored in pharmacology at good universities in Seoul. Some of them were from the families of Korean War victims. One girl had lost her father who was kidnapped to North Korea during the war and another lost her father to a bomb. An employee who graduated from Seoul National University was from Jeju Island. None of these bright young people working at the company were from politically powerful and well-to-do military families. Besides manufacturing drugs under agreement with Squibb, the company also produced a new antibiotic, Kanamycin, under another contract with a Japanese pharmaceutical company.

They were also working on developing a vaccine on their own. They imported several monkeys to test the vaccine but one day a monkey escaped and ran all over the neighborhood. We had a very difficult time catching him even with help from the police. Since it was a cold winter day I am sure that monkey did not enjoy his romp. The company's employees were all very hardworking and dedicated and all the managers were down to earth and on very good terms with their employees. There seemed to be no behind-the-scenes politicking going on within the company. I was glad I had this opportunity to get to know good and intelligent Koreans not associated with political or military power. My negative image of Koreans might have been the particular class of people who acquired power during the politically chaotic and lawless wartime. Or perhaps our family just had the misfortune to be thrown into bad company.

Photo 11: Dong-A Pharmaceutical R&D staff and (1) Dr. Kang Shin-ho (2) R&D Director (3) Author in1970.

I noticed that economic conditions in Korea were markedly improved compared to when I left the country ten years before. But I still didn't like the political situation under the dictatorship and was not planning to stay in Korea more than a year. One thing that made me feel very happy staying at home was that I was able to spend time with my parents and also help them financially by contributing my entire salary to meet the financial demands made by my younger brothers and sisters who were attending expensive universities and high schools. The youngest, Mimi, was still in a grammar school. As I noted before Father had moved to Seoul during the Second Republic under Yun and Chang Myun because he was asked to clean up the mess created by the students during Syngman Rhee's government. My father became the head administrator of Chesin Communications Institute again but when Park's coup d'état abolished the second government he had to resign as did other educational administrators like Ewha University president Kim Hwal-lan and Yonsei University president Baek Nak-jun. He was such an unlucky man during his life. As soon as he was making progress in his career, political scheming would destroy his efforts. That was why my mother never had an easy time handling family finances. So it was always my pleasure to help my parents financially after what they had gone through without ever giving up educating their children through college. A year in Korea helping the family was the least I could do. Even after I returned to the U.S., I always attempted to send financial support whenever possible.

But my mother was still adamant about my getting married while I was in Korea. Otherwise she would not let me return to America. Believe it or not I decided to acquiesce and began meeting people who could be candidates for a future husband arranged either by my parents or by family friends. We knew that matchmaking was old fashioned and it's difficult to match a couple successfully especially in a short time. I was going through this process just to please my mother, who was so desperate to marry me off before I left Korea. I did place one condition - it had to be a man who did not mind living in the United States. I don't know exactly why but I had already decided America would be my home. It was where I wanted to live and enjoy the freedom to pursue my career. It seemed like democracy and the rights of individuals were a long way from Korea's future no less enough reconstruction to establish beautiful universities I had seen in America. I wanted to be free to do anything I wanted to do. There was also much more opportunity in

America than in Korea for a female scientist. Maybe the awful memories of my childhood in Korea were still deeply implanted in my memory. Also I hadn't quite finished my educational goals in America. So I had to go back to America to continue my progress toward the ultimate goal.

Finally I met a professor at the same university where my father was teaching. He was planning to go on a cultural exchange program to the University of Wisconsin for a year and the fund was renewable for another year if he wanted to stay longer. I thought that was a good start. We were allowed to date for one month which was very superficial dating by American standards but I thought he sounded intelligent, decent and fairly good looking. What pleased my mother most was that he belonged to a Yangban family. I never really gave importance to an aristocratic upbringing because that's not something you earn by hard work but inherit from your family bloodline. But according to my mother people from Yangban families are taught traditionally good manners from early childhood, they learn to respect elders and they know good social behavior. And they are usually well educated at good schools. So we decided to get engaged and went to a large department store to buy an engagement ring.

I submitted my resignation to Dong-A Pharmaceutical Company. Dr. Kang was very gracious even though I had worked for the company only one year and he had extended many special privileges to me. He even came to my wedding. Many of the pharmacologists who worked with me also came. My parents gave me a huge wedding inviting over 500 guests since my father knew lots of people and my mother was very popular at church. Many of my parents' church friends also came. After the wedding we retreated to spend the first night at a remote hotel in Uidong where they also had a famous culinary institute. We were scheduled to depart Korea the next morning to travel to Boulder, Colorado where my husband would spend the summer and begin his summer program. As we were ready to go to bed we had several visitors – his colleagues at the university. They came with many bottles of wine and hard liquor and said that they came to see him before we left for Colorado next day. They drank and chatted until very late. I never found out how they knew where we were or why they thought they would be welcome to intrude on our wedding night. But they did. And my new husband did not invite them to leave. This was how we spent our first wedding night, not a particularly auspicious beginning for a sustainable marriage!

Photo 12: The above photo was taken at my father's birthday on my visit to Korea in 1970 -1971. This is the only picture ever taken together because our family members lived many thousand miles apart. Missing are my brothers John and Suk – John having gone to the US for his education and Suk being in the Korean military at the time. The family members on mother side who were living in Seoul at the time joined us for this occasion. (1) Father, (2) Mother holding her grandson Kenny, (3) Author, (4) Sister Oak, (5) Sister Mimi, (6) Brother Soo, (7) Brother Hugh, (8) Brother Churl, (9) Brother-in-law Changrim, (10) Aunt Myngnam and her husband (12), (11) Aunt Inam and her husband (13) and (14) Aunt Myungnam's son-in-law.

Chapter 22: Back to America and Life in Wisconsin (1971 – 1972)

Fall of 1971. In the morning after our wedding day, many people including members of his and my family came to Gimpo airport to see us off. I said farewell to my mother for the second time and got on the plane and we flew twelve hours to Denver, CO. Looking down from the plane, my husband, Hyo, kept saying "what a blessed country, what a big piece of land, beautiful mountains, creeks and vast farmland!" Anyone coming from another country, regardless whether they are from Europe, Asia, Africa or Australia, and seeing this country from the air for the first time could not help feeling the same way. America is really a blessed country in many aspects; its location, geography and abundance of natural resources although not every American may realize how lucky he or she is to live here. Our destination was Boulder which is the home of the University of Colorado at Boulder situated 25 miles northwest of Denver at an elevation of 5,430 feet. When we arrived at Denver airport we took a shuttle bus to go to Boulder. Boulder Valley is where the Rocky Mountains meet the Great Plains. Boulder was a breathtakingly beautiful place, the university accommodations for the exchange professors were very comfortable and the cafeteria had plenty of food even for lunch - meat dishes, fresh fruits and vegetables. After a good meal people usually take a siesta in early afternoons. No classes were given during siesta time, so whole place went to sleep. Although I was not aware at the time, I learned about this school later that six Nobel Laureates, seven MacArthur Fellows, and 17 astronauts have been affiliated with CU Boulder as students, researchers, or faculty members.

It was very relaxing and enjoyable to spend a summer in Boulder taking siestas in sleepy afternoons, not much pressure for Hyo since he was just taking summer orientation courses. He even seemed to enjoy his very first American experience there. One day, a friendly American man from another state who was taking summer courses at the university, asked us to join him for a scenic drive up to the Rocky mountain national park so we agreed. What a majestic mountain!. Between North Park and South Park was Middle Park, a wide flat valley tucked in between the Front Range and the large ranges that fill up the heart of the high country. These high valleys called parks for their open expanses of treeless ground are the heart of Colorado's Ranching country, the southern Rocky's most distinctive feature. Hyo who specialized in agricultural economics was amazed and speechless when he saw many thousands of milk and beef cows roaming around the flat valley without anyone watching, an indication how grand the scale of American ranching business was as compared to that in Korea where the land is very limited. What I was really surprised was that there were many more flat valleys and villages as we drove up the mountain. They may look like a layer cake made of ranches from space. We drove all day and I still remember watching the sunset over the jagged skyline of these quiet, grassy valleys as one of the finest experiences Colorado offered to us during the trip.

We had comfortable lodging all paid for by the program and I could have spent the whole summer in Boulder enjoying the weather, spending my leisure time reading interesting books in the University library such as biographies of people whose contributions helped improve people's lives. But of course I couldn't do that because I had developed a restless personality over the years, always feeling I had to do something constructive, work harder, and make more progress toward my eventual goal whatever that was. Consequently I could not usually take more than a ten day vacation. So I was looking for a summer job on the campus but none was available. I was concerned about our finances as well since Hyo's monthly allowance from the program was probably enough to live in the university dormitory, but not enough to rent a more comfortable apartment.

After one month in Boulder I flew to New York leaving Hyo in Boulder to complete his summer orientation program. At the time, my brother John was living in a Stevenson Institute dorm - a WWII military ship moored on the Hudson River on the other side of New York City. He picked me up at Kennedy airport and gave me a ride to the apartment of one of my girlfriends who lived in the city. I stayed there for two months. My former boss, Dr. Solomon, offered me a summer job in the same laboratory I had previously managed as a temporary summer replacement because many employees were on summer vacation. As fall approached Hyo came to New York to join me. John again gave us a ride all the way to Madison, Wisconsin, so we were able to bring all my stuff I left with him when I went to Korea. This way we could begin our married life with some comforts while Hyo went through his exchange program at University of Wisconsin.

We arrived on the university campus where many volunteers were helping new arrivals to find places to live. After searching through all the available apartments near the campus we found a nice new apartment with daily bus transportation to the university nearby. Hyo met with his advisor, the department chairman, and took care of his registration and I looked for a job and immediately found one at the Wisconsin State Lab as a chemist for the Department of Health. I was part of the state-wide screening program to monitor blood chemistry of the Wisconsin state population. The State lab seemed to be very well funded, was situated in a very large 3-story building and had many different departments. This is where I met Mary, a nuclear physicist, who became a good friend of mine for many years, even well after I left Wisconsin. The lab had a budget to purchase an ultra modern and rapid multi-channel blood chemistry analyzer in order to accommodate the many blood samples coming in from all over the state. The Lab Director decided to send me to Technicon Corp in Tarrytown, NY, the manufacturer, for training class on the SMA12/60 blood analyzer. I noticed that this instrument was manufactured by the same company that manufactured the very first automated single channel blood chemistry analyzers I saw at Harvard Medical Center when I was working there during the summer of 1961. The SMA 12/60 class room at Technicon was full and they seemed to have a shortage of instructors. Evidently their newly released instrument was very popular and selling so many units that they could not keep up with the demand. I said to myself, "Oh my God, doesn't every company wish they have such a problem?"

Technicon was built on a simple idea - a bubble technology Dr. Leonard T. Skeggs discovered by accident as many inventions are. The instruments based on this simple technology became extraordinarily successful the moment they put them on the market.

Now they had a multi-channel blood analyzer based on the same bubble technology they used on their single channel analyzers. In brief they injected air bubbles in a continuous flow of samples to avoid contamination from one sample to next. Here I saw the power of invention in successfully scaling up an existing technology no matter how simple the idea was, to much greater productivity. Advancement in science and technology has been a key factor in the American success story. Invading other countries for territorial acquisition as England, Spain, France, Russia and Japan did during the first one half of the 20th century could now be seen as obsolete and more than a little barbaric.

I found the Wisconsin winter harsh. The icy sidewalks never melted throughout the winter so walking was a bit hazardous and needless to say so was driving. I was very busy with my job because of the heavy workload and I, like everyone else, was also learning new computer languages - the binary numeral system, Linc-8, and many other new computer programming concepts were beginning the computer age and laboratories were trying to keep up with the trend by computerizing all data processing. On balance I liked most of the people I met at the Wisconsin Dept. of Health including the director of the lab, Dr. Ron Lassieg and especially the Head of the Department of Health, Dr. Price, who was an Austrian with deep blue eyes and very kind mannerisms. When I resigned my job one year later, Dr. Price gave me a big party at his home. A majority of the employees in the State Lab were University of Wisconsin graduates who had never lived outside of Wisconsin. Unlike California there were few Asians in Wisconsin and they were unfamiliar with Asian names. Thus, if any mail was addressed to a strange name they would bring it to me.

But there was a fly in the ointment. Hyo was not very happy at school or with American life and often complained about many trivial things. At the end of 1971, I was invited to a New Years' Eve party sponsored by the State, and Hyo and I went to the party together. It was a very cold and snowy night but almost everybody came. They drank, chatted, joked and enjoyed themselves. Unlike New York City there were not too many things to do after work for entertainment in Madison, Wisconsin, and therefore people are not going miss a party or a football game. One lady who probably had a bit too much to drink approached us and joked to my husband saying "How come your wife speaks good English but you don't?" I quickly explained to her that I lived in the States many years but he just came. Then I didn't think anything of her joke and forgot about it. However when we came home after the party Hyo was furious about her comment and would not stop his rage all evening. I reminded him that she was drunk so she didn't really know what she was saying. Besides, I told him, instead of being so angry he should be proud because she actually complemented his wife. Then his rage turned ugly and he became violent. He threw a scissor at me but fortunately I was able to avoid getting hit.

Until that night I had not seriously analyzed our marriage. I guess preoccupation with my work and resettling and making new friends had been a consuming diversion. Whether I was happy, he was happy or the marriage was working was not in my thoughts. Since we were already married I planned to make it work. But this changed my thinking and then all the other negatives began surfacing; he was trying to control me too much, he did not seem to respect my rights as an individual, he expected me to follow orders like a subservient wife even if I was working, he didn't allow me to accumulate laundry until weekend to do laundry only once a week, he did not want me to use the hair dryer when he was still sleeping although I was getting ready to go to work, and so on. I may have actually made the decision subconsciously much earlier but it was then I decided that I could not stay married to him. And the thoughts flooded back…After all I chose him under duress – were it not for my mother the marriage would not have happened. He had after all agreed to come to the US with me. I had not agreed to live in Korea with him. And then there was the issue of children. What then!. But I didn't say anything to him at the time. The year passed quickly and his first year of academic work ended and he wanted to return to Korea to his teaching job at the University. But I refused to go with him. I could not erase the scene of his violence that night in my mind. For me once is enough, I had to get out of the marriage as soon as possible. I don't believe in the alimony system and I didn't want anything from him, except my freedom.

Chapter 23: Beginning of My Corporate Career (1972)

Shortly after I sent out letters of job inquiry to New York area, I received responses from two places; Technicon Corporation in Tarrytown, New York, and Mt. Sinai Medical center in New York City. Technicon also sent me a round-trip airline ticket to come for an interview in New York. Technicon was a company that pioneered development of automated blood analyzers. The R&D Director, Dr. Hochstrauss, and three other project managers and HR person interviewed me and then offered me a job with a significant salary increase. The next day I went to Mt. Sinai Medical Center. The laboratory director asked me some technical questions related to the job's responsibilities and then offered me a job as the manager of their clinical laboratory. I decided to take the Technicon offer and the company paid all moving expenses from Wisconsin. So in 1972 I began my corporate life, living in Westchester County, New York.

I loved my job, getting involved in many pioneering projects and working with many bright engineers and technical consultants. The man to whom I owe my career in America was well known in the area of medical science as an extremely bright and generous genius, Dr. Leonard Ornstein, who was a consultant on our project and a full professor of pathology at Mt. Sinai Medical School in New York City. The company was so successful that the employees didn't have to make any contributions for medical and dental insurance or to a 401(k). The company paid for both. Those were the good days for all employees. I ended up working there over 20 years. Unfortunately working conditions gradually deteriorated over the years as the company went through numerous acquisitions and layoffs after the first owner sold the company. I lost many colleagues during my stay at the company. But Wall Street attorneys who were handling the corporate mergers and acquisitions made fortunes for themselves each time the company changed hands. This was probably the beginning of the shift in the status of wealth redistribution from the middle class to the upper one percent in America what we ended up with today.

Back home in South Korea, Park Chung-hee declared martial law in 1972 and recast the constitution into a highly authoritarian document ushering in the Fourth Republic of South Korea. After surviving several assassination attempts he still had no desire to step down. He intended to continue his presidency by any means by suppressing any opposition candidates like Kim Dae-jung. My father as an intellectual who highly valued individual freedom was very frustrated and unhappy about the situation. Since he had no power to change things he joined Mother in dedicating themselves to church affairs and helping people in need instead. He wanted to find some peace of mind. I thought I should invite them to change their environment and asked them to come and spend some time with me and my brother John who was working and living in Connecticut at the time. But Father thought that Mother needed a vacation far more than he did and he was also pretty busy taking care of church affairs. So finally, Mother came alone in 1974. My brother John and I took vacations from work and showed her around the landmarks in New York City, Connecticut, and New Jersey. I think she really enjoyed the different environment and the royal treatment.

There was an unexpected event that took place at a shopping center that amused her so much that she could not stop laughing. Streaking was a popular activity at this time. A group of young guys streaked by us very fast wearing only transparent rain coats. Since it was so unexpected and so sudden that we couldn't really see much detail – which was a good thing. Everybody at the shopping center who witnessed this incident was smiling and even the two cops who arrived at the shopping center in a police vehicle, probably in response to someone's phone call, didn't seem to be all that anxious to catch them. In fact they seemed to enjoy the show. Mother also seemed to have enjoyed much witnessing this unusual event and even commented, "Those fellows have really good-looking bodies." "What was that, Mother? Were you really looking so close?" I asked her jokingly. I was happy to see her laughing and enjoying herself for a change. Life should be enjoyable! But our vacation time passed by quickly.

I had to go back to work and winter was approaching. I was at work one day and people were rushing around and leaving early because of the weather report of a heavy snowstorm approaching. At least once or twice every year we had snowstorms in New England and New York. But I thought it was too early in the beginning of the winter and being a workaholic I wanted to finish my experiment. So I called mother and explained that I might be late if there was a heavy snowfall. It turned out this was a really stupid mistake. Around 3:00 pm. snow was beginning to fall heavily and now everybody was leaving so I also got into my car and began driving. But the traffic was already bumper-to-bumper and the road was covered with heavy snow. This did not allow the cars to move so I was just sitting in the car even though the distance from the company to my home was only about five miles. In those days we didn't have cell phone technology available so I could not call Mother to inform her of the situation. There was not enough time for snowplows to clear the road before so many cars blocked the roads. It took almost three hours for me to get home. Mother's face was as white as snow and her hand was as icy cold because she was so worried that I might have been involved in an auto accident and died. As always she blamed herself for causing bad luck to happen because she had come to stay with me. I don't know why she always blamed herself whenever there was any mishap in the family but I presume it was from the Christian belief that we are all sinners until God forgives us or something like that.

One of my coworkers, Hazel, who left home early before the snow fall, called my home while mother was waiting for me so anxiously but Mother could not understand English well enough to figure out what she was calling about. So the phone call made her even more worried thinking I was in an accident and died. One thing that relieved Mother a little was that Hazel giggled before she hung up because Mother didn't understand her when she tried to ask her whether I got home alright. Mother assumed that Hazel wouldn't be giggling like that if she were reporting bad news. The language barrier was the major issue for Mother to live in America. When I was at work she had nobody to talk to, no one nearby to call, and could not drive anywhere.

When Mother returned to Korea my parents informed me that my brother Hugh was graduating from high school soon. Also he was under rogue influences from his circle of friends - skipping school to go mountain climbing or engage in other activities during school hours. They didn't know what to do and they didn't have enough energy to handle the problem. I remembered how bright a kid Hugh was when he was very young. When he was about four years old he was playing with neighborhood children who were a few years older than he was, in fact already in grammar school. It was a cold winter day. I was soaking up warm sunlight coming through the picture window, watching Hugh playing with children in the front yard right outside the window. The children were showing each other how to write certain letters and numbers writing them on the ground with chalk. To my surprise Hugh also knew how to write letters and how to count the numbers. I was stunned because nobody had ever tried to teach him these things since we thought he was too young to learn. May be he picked up his knowledge from his playmates. After that I tested him, showing him letters, numbers, and English alphabets. He had no problem remembering what I showed him once. He was able to identify them in newspapers or magazines. I remember telling Mother that we had a young genius in the family and he probably inherited his genius from his father's brain. My mother didn't say "so what's wrong with my brain" but maybe that's what she was thinking. OK so maybe I should have said "he inherited it from such a bright and intelligent family" but I never took diplomacy in school.

When I left Korea Hugh was still a preschool boy. I didn't know exactly what happened to him after I left Korea but I was pretty certain he lost interest in school because of the family environment. My parents were getting old and his brothers and sisters never seemed to be happy because their demands were not met. In addition Mother was always physically exhausted because of her age and the fact it was getting increasingly difficult to find a domestic helper since there were better paying jobs available. After I analyzed the situation I told my parents to send Hugh to me because I was confident that he still had the same brain as when he was young and I could help him to get back on the right track. I had managed all types of people at work as a project manager and coordinated with some very manipulative sales and marketing folks, so it should be much easier for me to manage my own brother. My plan was to leave him no other choice but study and concentrate on schoolwork to complete at least his undergraduate college work in a completely different environment. I was sure he could pick it up from there and take care of his own life.

Hugh was willing to come and join me, which was already a good sign. He was interested in continuing his education and that was another good sign. But he had to complete his military duty before leaving the country according to the South Korean regulations. After his high school graduation Hugh joined the navy. Since Hugh was a charming, handsome, and personable fellow, he served his military duty in the Korean Navy mostly as the captain's personal assistant, eating fresh abalone and making friends with people who worked in the ship's kitchen. Since he had only a high school diploma his military service was longer than my other brothers who all graduated from college and served as officers for only two years. Hugh served three. He finally arrived in the U.S. in 1977 and I registered him right away in the Westchester County Community College despite his protest that he should spend a year just learning English.

I didn't know then that he had experienced a very frightening incident during his military service that he would probably never forget. When he came to live with me in Hartsdale, NY, I had a large fish tank in the living room with many colorful tropical fish in the tank, decorating the room with their beautiful colors. One day I found two dead fish floating on the surface of the water so I asked him to fish them out as I was going out for some errands. When I returned home after a couple of hours, the two dead fish were still floating in the tank. I asked him why he hadn't taken them out. He said he did not want to touch those dead fish because they reminded him of the dead North Korean sailors on the deck of the navy ship he was on. Evidently, his ship encountered a hostile North Korean ship near the 38th parallel. There was quite a battle although my brother's ship won. After the battle was over they pulled the bodies of North Korean sailors from the sea, leaving their bodies on the deck overnight until they reached-port, which was at the southern tip of the peninsula. I didn't know that affected his emotions so powerfully.

It seems that none of my brothers are tough guys. My mother used to say that I was the toughest among all my siblings. She thought that had something to do with mirth place, Pyongyang, which became the capital of North Korea after 1948. Interestingly, my mother's observation was not unique because one of my former bosses also liked to tease me saying, "You must be a North Korean Spy because you are much too tough to be a South Korean". Well, I had to be very tough sometimes in dealings with dishonest and manipulative people who tried to climb up the corporate ladder without proper knowledge and qualification in the corporate rat race, hurting well qualified and decent employees. I could write a whole book about the corporate rat race. Remember, Darwin's Survival of the Fittest theory!

Nonetheless, Hugh has done very well in America - he not only completed his undergraduate college work but also received a graduate degree in computer science related to business and became CFO of an investment company in NY City. He is still a very nice fellow even if he is running a tough financial business in New York.

Chapter 24: The Second Military Coup and The Gwangju Massacre (1979–1993)

On October 26, 1979, I was at home leisurely watching the evening news on TV. All of a sudden, there was an interruption for Breaking News but I could not believe my ears. President Park Chung-hee of the third ROK was shot by the KCIA director, Kim Jae-gyu. Park was a very meticulous man with tough military training and had always been careful about his safety. He made sure he was very well protected by KCIA bodyguards. It was a paradox that he was killed by the KCIA director who was supposedly a longtime friend of his. But there were no details. I thought to myself – if impossible things can happen, it will happen in Korea. The details appeared later, little by little, day by day.

Apparently it was true that Kim Jae-gyu was the lifelong friend and confidant of Park. They were born in the same town and were in the same class at the Military Academy. Kim rose to the high rank of lieutenant general after having been chief of the army's security command and the deputy director of the KCIA. Meanwhile his friend Park Chung-hee had become President of the Republic. Then the existing KCIA director, Kim Hyung-wook defected in Washington, D.C. during a scandal called Koreagate, Kim Jae-gyu was appointed shortly thereafter as the head of the KCIA, an extremely powerful position under the authoritarian Park regime.

Koreagate was a political scandal involving South Korean political figures seeking to influence 10 Democratic members of Congress. It involved the KCIA allegedly funneling bribes and favors through Korean businessman Tongsun Park in an attempt to gain favor and influence for South Korean objectives. The reasons behind the scandal involved political, social, and financial issues. Korean leaders, including Tongsun Park and President Park, were very concerned about Nixon's decision to withdraw American soldiers from South Korea and felt it was urgent to build support for preserving the United States military still remaining in South Korea. The Park government was also attempting to gain approval of a substantial package of assistance for South Korea's military modernization programs.

After Koreagate was publicized, political relations between the United States and South Korea became shaky at best. South Korean officials believed the story had been exaggerated, spun, or concocted entirely by American journalists. Political experts on both sides also suspected that the scandal was being cast in this manner to aid Gerald Ford's election strategy. According to this interpretation, the Ford administration without doubt intended to neutralize the Democratic Party's exploitation of Watergate and Ford's pardon of Richard Nixon as issues by linking key Democratic congressmen to Koreagate.

Ironically, Park's assassination took place at a private dinner party hosted by Kim Jae-gyu for President Park. Kim opened fire killing Park and his chief security officer Cha Ji-chul. He was arrested soon after the shooting by General Chung Sung-hwa, who later was himself implicated in the assassination by Chun Doo-hwan. At first it was assumed that the shooting had been the result of an emotional outburst but an investigation later showed that it was indeed a carefully planned assassination. At his trial Kim asserted that he had killed his friend to avert the bloodbath Park had been planning for his opponents, mostly student demonstrators, and that the only way to restore real democracy in South Korea was by killing Park. The government investigation led by General Chun Doo-hwan contended that Kim shot Park solely to preserve his own power and sentenced him to death. Kim and four KCIA aides were hanged.

Since Kim Jae-gyu and all his conspirators were executed we will never know the real truth about Park's assassination as has happened many times before in Korea. But one thing is clear; Park did not have any intention of stepping down from his presidency in his lifetime and was willing to suppress student demonstrators by any means. It seemed that a fierce argument erupted at the party between Kim Jae-gyu and Cha Ji-chul. Kim, a relative moderate, made a last-minute plea to Park to ease his harsh treatment of unruly dissidents and Cha criticized Kim for his softness. Father, who never approved of the military coup that ended the second ROK, a truly civilian government, said this was nothing but a power struggle among power-hungry factions of the KCIA and the military. He was so disgusted with the whole affair by then that he didn't even care to know the truth behind Park's assassination.

During his first two terms as President, Park was responsible for economic reform and he is generally credited with playing a pivotal role in the development of the South Korean economy by shifting its focus to export-oriented industrialization. Park's leadership saw a remarkable development of industry and a rise in the standard of living for average South Korean citizens. However Park clamped down on personal freedom under the pretense of a state of emergency dating to the Korean War when constitutional guarantees of freedom of speech and of the press were often restricted. The KCIA retained the broad powers of arrest and detention and opponents were frequently tortured. The electoral system was also heavily rigged in favor of Park's party, Democratic Republican Party, which routinely won large majorities in the National Assembly. Opposition parties and leaders were subjected to varying degrees of official harassment.

Park was narrowly reelected in 1967 against Yun Bo Sun. The Constitution of 1963 limited the president to two consecutive terms. Nevertheless with the assistance of the KCIA Park's allies in the legislature succeeded in amending the constitution to allow the current president - Park - to run for three consecutive terms. In 1971 Park won another close election, this time over Kim Dae-jung. Just after being sworn in for his third term, Park declared a state of emergency "based on the dangerous realities of the international situation." In October 1972, he dissolved Parliament and suspended the constitution. In December a new constitution, the Yushin Constitution, was approved in a rigged plebiscite. The new document dramatically increased Park's power. It transferred the election of the president to an electoral college, the National Conference for Unification. The presidential term was increased to seven years, with no limits on reelection. In effect, the constitution converted Park's presidency into a legal dictatorship. Park was reelected in 1972 and 1978 with no opposition. That was exactly the reason why students were demonstrating to correct the situation. They wanted to restore real democracy in the nation. No doubt, Park Chung-hee had no intention of ever stepping down. So what Kim Jae-gyu said about his reason for assassinating Park and Cha Ji-chul, Park's hard-line advisor, to prevent their plan of using harsh penalties on demonstrating students, could likely have been true.

Chun Doo-hwan, the General who presided over the conviction and execution of Park's assassins, was a graduate of the 11th class of the Korean Military Academy in 1955. He was also a member of Hanahoe, a powerful private group of military officers that supported his actions. As head of the Defense Security Command, Chun was in charge of the investigation into the assassination of President Park Chung-hee. On December 12, 1979, in what became known as the Incident of December 12th, Chun ordered the arrest of General Chung Sung-hwa, the ROK Army Chief of Staff, who arrested Kim Jae-gyu shortly after Park's assassination, needing to further investigate his involvement in the crime. Chung Sung-hwa resisted which led to a bloody shootout at army headquarters and the Ministry of Defense. By the next morning, Chun and his fellow 11th-class military academy graduates including Major General Roh Tae-woo, commanding general of the Ninth Infantry Division, and Major General Chung Ho-yong, were in charge of the Korean military.

General Chung Sung-hwa was an innocent victim of the plot by Hanahoe members including Chun Doo-hwan and Roh Tae-woo, who engineered the takeover the government after Park's assassination. Chung Sung-hwa was then the most powerful man in South Korea after the assassination of Park Chung-hee. During the Korean War (1950–1953), Chung helped defend Daegu against the North Korean assault. In 1961 he was made a brigadier general and he built a good reputation for honesty and incorruptibility. He became the army's Chief of Staff in February 1979. Chung tried to eliminate the influence of the Hanahoe military group in the South Korean political arena. Immediately after Park's assassination, he didn't try to take over the government but instead he supported the prime minister, Choi Kyu-ha, to take over the presidential position. Of course the Hanahoe members had to eliminate Chung, who was blocking their goal of taking over the government.

In April 1980, due to increasing pressure from Chun and other politicians, Choi Kyu-ha had to appoint Chun as head of the Korean Central Intelligence Agency. On May 17, 1980, Chun declared martial law and dropped all pretense of civilian government, becoming the de facto ruler of the country. Many politicians were arrested including opposition left-wing liberal politician Kim Dae-jung, who was later sentenced to death despite protests from the United States. Later Chun commuted Kim's sentence to life in return for the US support but protests across the nation were further suppressed. Around this time, I frequently saw the scenes of demonstrations and the specially equipped police force in Korea in evening news. Those police men were wearing special helmets and carrying special tools to protect themselves against the demonstrators. Residents of Gwangju resisted Chun's sentencing Kim Dae-jung to death and later commuting to life imprisonment. They armed themselves with stolen guns and military jeeps. Chun made no effort to negotiate with the student leaders in Gwangju. Instead, he dispatched South Korean Army units to crush the protest. Although there is a difference of opinion as to the accuracy of the actual death tolls, it has been claimed that the actual death toll was 1,000 to 2,000, based on reports by foreign press sources and critics of the Chun Doo-hwan administration. My aunt and uncle who were the teachers of many of those students believe the figure was well over 1,000. They told me it was a real tragedy to see so many young people losing their lives at the hands of the South Korean Army.

The 1980s marked a surge in anti-Americanism in Korea widely traced to the events of May 1980. A new generation of Gwangju residents believes that the United States did not support their democratic movement and, more importantly, the United States did authorize Chun to send in the 20th Division of the ROK Army to put down the Gwangju uprising. The result was naturally an anti-American movement that threatened to bring down the whole structure of American support for the ROK. These matters remain controversial. But it is clear that the United States authorized the ROK Army's 20th Division to retake Gwangju—as acknowledged in a 1982 letter to the *New York Times* by then ambassador William H. Gleysteen. The United States has always denied foreknowledge of this deployment, most definitively in a June 19, 1989, white paper; which additionally downplays Gleysteen's and others' characterizations of US actions. Whatever the case it's a fact that the Korean Army killed Gwangju's pro-democratic demonstrators on orders from a military junta that manipulated the situation to illegally take over the government. The United States could have done a better job by advising Chun to send in a team of negotiators first to decrease the tension among the students before sending in the military unit to kill the demonstrators, who were mostly students. This is another case of ill-fated US involvement in Korean affairs which triggered anti-American sentiment in Korea.

During Chun Doo-hwan's reign the Gwangyu Uprising was represented as a rebellion inspired by communist sympathizers - a tired and transparent excuse for murdering people in Korea. This dirty tactic was used in South Korea for a long time in an attempt to fool the US government and grab power by oppressing innocent civilians who were fighting for true democratic civilian government. Gwangju was my mother's hometown. Mother's sisters and brother witnessed this bloody event which took place on May 18, 1980. I met many of them at Mother's funeral many years later and they still remembered the incident with tears in their eyes as an unforgettable tragedy where many naïve young people lost their lives - a continuation of the tragedy and suffering of ordinary Korean people because Korea lost capable and benevolent leaders like Lyuh Woon-hyung or Kim Gu who really cared about the country and the well-being of the Korean people.

As expected, the puppet president, Choi Kyu-ha, who was prime minister under Park and took over the presidential position after Park's assassination resigned in August 1980 under pressure from Hanahoe members. Chun was elected as his successor by the National Conference for Unification, the puppet "electoral college" Park set up to continue his presidency for life. In February 1981, Chun was elected president under a revised constitution as the Democratic Justice Party (the renamed Democratic Republican Party) candidate after resigned from the army after promoting himself to a four-star general. Chun seemed to have learned well from Park Chung-hee how to wriggle himself systematically into the position of President – Indeed a Shakespearian drama ending with a tragedy. This was what the South Korean people were going through. Korea was still far from reaching the goal of building a democratic civilian government. It was still a very long, bloody, and perilous journey. My family, especially my aunts and uncle whose students were killed during the Kwang-ju uprising, thought that Chun was worse than Park Chung-hee who had a bloodless military coup because President Yun just allowed them to succeed without fighting. On the other hand, Chun Doo-hwan had already killed more civilians than Park during his long tenure.

When I visited my parents during Chun Doo-hwan's rule, there was a very funny and extremely popular comedian who looked exactly like Chun Doo-hwan with bald head and similar facial features. He was on TV almost every evening imitating Chun at his press conferences talking tough to intimidate his opponents. He was hilarious and people loved watching him and having lots of fun. But of course, he didn't last too long. He simply disappeared and his TV show was cancelled. Dictators don't tolerate comedians making fund of them. Watch out Saturday Night actors in America!

My father was extremely upset about the situation in Kwang-ju because there seemed to be no end to this military dictatorship. More importantly, he was frustrated that there was no democratic process to overturn the power of the criminal government. Once dictators grasp power, there are very little civilians can do as demonstrated in Russia, China and in North Korea, the three generations of communist dynasty with the worst human rights abuse has lasted more than a half century and it's still going strong with WMD threatening South Korea and even the US.

I suggested the Holy Land for a pilgrimage to take their mind off all the problems at home and enjoy their lives while they were still alive and have enough energy to travel and fulfill their unrealized dreams.

Chapter 25: The Holy Land Pilgrimage and California Dream (1983–1992)

In 1983 I invited my parents to come to New York to spend some time with me and my brothers Hugh and John. I also took some vacation time from Technicon to accompany my parents to Israel. When we arrived at Ben Gurion International Airport, we were detained quite a while for some reason never explained to us. After finally being released we took a taxi to our hotel. As we drove along Highway 1 we could see the panorama of the Temple Mount and the famous Dome of the Rock. The weather was very hot and dry and the bright white sunlight blinded me. I was thinking, "Is this the place so many different religious groups want to take over?" It didn't look like a hospitable place to live. Not surprisingly, Jerusalem, by virtue of the number and diversity of people who claim it as central to their religion, is considered the most holy city in the world. The Jewish temple in Jerusalem was the place the young Jesus was found at the age of 12 preaching to the masses. When we were in Jerusalem we had a Jewish tour guide who could explain all the historical events that took place at each site. Surprisingly my father knew most of the events that took place in Jerusalem - knowledge he acquired from the Bible study classes taught by American missionaries when he was a college student. We spent two days visiting the Old City, the Garden of Gethsemane, the Mount of Olives, and the Dome of the Rock - the church supposedly built on the same spot where Jesus had his last supper with his 12 disciples. My mother, who was physically very weak, never complained as if she was spiritually connected to God and talking to him in silence. We went to see the Wailing Wall and Mother wrote something on a slip of paper and left it in a crack. I would give a deep thought to know what secret message she wrote on that piece of paper.

The next day our charter bus drove along the shores of the Dead Sea without any mechanical problems to Masada, an ancient fortress in Southern Israel. After the First Jewish-Roman War a siege of the fortress by troops of the Roman Empire led to the suicide of 965 Jewish rebels and their families who preferred death to surrender.

We had to ascend by cable car to the top but we decided that Mother should remain below in the air-conditioned bus because it was much too hot up there for her condition. She didn't seem to be too happy about our suggestion although she didn't insist on joining us. So Father and I took the cable car and toured the ancient fortress where the Zealots made their last stand against the Romans before their mass suicide in AD 73. When we returned from the cable car ride we found that mother had been crying because she could not go up there with us. Even though she was physically weak her mind was always young until her last days.

Our next trip was to the Dead Sea which was one of the world's first health resorts. The mineral content of the waters, the very low content of pollens and other allergens in the atmosphere, the reduced ultraviolet component of solar radiation, and the higher atmospheric pressure at this elevation have specific health effects. We thought my mother could benefit from the Dead Sea so we all went to float on the Dead Sea for a while but it was so salty that I could not stay in the water too long. I had to take a very long shower to avoid becoming a human sardine.

The Sea of Galilee in Nazareth was our next stop. This was my favorite of all the places we visited during our pilgrimage. As soon as we arrived at the Sea of Galilee I could feel the fresh air and warm wind coming from the wide-open water caressing my face. Much of the ministry of Jesus occurred on the shores of Lake Galilee. The gospels of Mark, Mathew, and Luke describe how Jesus recruited four of his apostles from the shores of Lake Galilee including the fishermen Simon and his brother Andrew, and the brothers John and James. One of Jesus' famous teachings, the Sermon on the Mount, was given on a hill overlooking the lake. Many of his miracles were also reported to have occurred here including walking on water, calming a storm, and feeding five thousand people. I could imagine the beautiful and peaceful site where Jesus's disciples sat, feeling this warm wind, breathing fresh air, and listening to Jesus's sermon. He was a truly great teacher to imperfect humankind. Whatever one's particular opinion of Jesus' divinity, it is difficult to argue with Jesus' vision of what the world could, and should, be. Particularly when compared with the likes of Koreas' dictators of both North and South, past and present, and the sadness and sorrow their vision has brought. People would do well to live by Christian principles whether they believe in the Christian religion or not. The after life will be what it will be. Our only choices can be made while incarnate to use a biblical term. Nazareth is the capital and largest city in the North District of Israel and also serves as an Arab capital for Israel's Arab citizens who make up the vast majority of the people in Israel.

Haifa was our next stop where we boarded a Greek cruise ship of the Epirotiki Line to visit the pilgrimage sites. Haifa has a history dating back to biblical times. It has been conquered and ruled by the Byzantine Greeks, Arabs, Ottomans, Egyptians, and the British. Haifa has a Mediterranean climate. My father enjoyed swimming in the sea while my mother and I watched him from the window of our hotel room. The next day, we boarded the Epirotiki Line ship to visit the pilgrimage sites in Patmos and Ephesus. The facilities of this luxury ship were superb and my father was excited to notice that the ship was actually moving although we could not feel any motion. He was in and out of our cabin to inform us that the ship was actually moving. Because of the mild and sleepy Mediterranean climate my mother, who suffered from insomnia on land was able to sleep in the cabin and my father teased her calling her "the lady who can only sleep on a luxury ship in the Mediterranean Sea." We watched the gorgeous Mediterranean sunset on the deck and took many photos of it. I was happy to see my parents enjoying life, and realizing that God does not require suffering as a condition of existence.

Patmos is mentioned in the book of Revelation and it's an important destination for a Christian pilgrimage. We visited the cave where John was said to have received his revelation (the Cave of the Apocalypse), and several monasteries on the island dedicated to Saint John. I could not imagine writing even a line of any document in that cave because it was very dim even with the electric lights they installed for tourists. There wasn't enough fresh air coming in to breathe comfortably. I don't know how St. John was able to write the whole book of Revelation in the cave.

Our next stop was Ephesus, an ancient city of Anatolia. This is one of those places you never forget even after a short visit. As soon as I stepped on the ground of Ephesus I felt I was in a time tunnel taking me back to the early first century AD, walking down the marble pavement among marble statues on both sides. There were Roman Celsus Library remains, the Gates of Augustus, the Temple of Hadrian, and the Ephesus Theater. Our tour guide told us that Ephesus contained the largest collection of Roman ruins but only an estimated 15% had been excavated. The ruins that were visible gave us some idea of the city's original splendor and the names associated with the ruins were highly suggestive of its former life. The marble tiles of the pavement had many imprints of arrows pointing in one direction guiding people to some important place. What could that place be? Those arrows were pointing to the famous brothel that existed in Ephesus. So it appears to be true that prostitution is indeed one of the oldest professions in the world.

The Library of Celsus was built in AD 125 by Gaius Julius Aquila in memory of his father and once held nearly 12,000 scrolls. Ephesus is also the site of a large gladiator graveyard. The Emperor Constantine I, best known as the first Christian Roman emperor, rebuilt much of the city. There had been many battles and occupations by different powers in Ephesus and it was eventually abandoned in the 15th century and lost its former glory. After hearing the history of Ephesus, I could just imagine the lives of ordinary people when the region was so frequently occupied by different religious powers. Paul the Apostle used Ephesus as a base and spent more than two years there on his third missionary journey.

Kuşadası, a resort town on Turkey's Aegean coast, was our next stop. It was a very busy market - I bought a beautiful greenish-blue turquoise ring and a matching pendant. The Roman Empire took possession of the coast in the second century BC and in the early years of Christianity, Mary (mother of Jesus) and Saint John the Evangelist both came to live in the area. Learning about the history where the Virgin Mary lived I am even more convinced that Jesus Christ really existed. In 1086 the area came under Turkish control and the Aegean ports became the final destination of caravan routes to the

Orient. However Turkish control was overthrown by the Crusades and the coast again came under Byzantine domination until 1280. What a complicated history! Kuşadası was brought into the Ottoman Empire in 1413. The Ottomans built the city walls and the caravanserai (a roadside inn where travelers could rest and recover from the day's journey) that still stand today. During the Turkish Independence War, Kuşadası was occupied from 1919 to 1922, first by Italians, then by Greek troops. It was eventually recaptured on September 7, 1922 by Turks.

Athens was our final stop before returning to the United States. The history of Athens is one of the longest of any city in Europe. It became the leading city of Ancient Greece in the first millennium BC; its cultural achievements during the fifth century BC laid the foundations of western civilization. My father admired the teachings of ancient Greek philosophers who seemed have influenced his thought process and he often quoted them to guide us. Socrates was an Athenian philosopher who believed that a person should always try to do the right thing no matter what happens. Plato was one of the most influential philosophers in Western thought whose early dialogues dealt mainly with methods of acquiring knowledge, and most of the last ones with justice and practical ethics. My father also loved Aesop's fables, a collection of stories credited to Aesop (620–560 BC), a slave and storyteller who lived in Ancient Greece; Father often told us Aesop's Fables to persuade us to go through our lives practicing his wisdom. I still remember Aesop's fables such as "The Tortoise and the Hare," "The Boy Who Cried Wolf," and "The North Wind and the Sun."

As we approached Athens, the first thing we could see from our ship was the Acropolis standing high on a hill, the best-known acropolis in the world. Although there are many other acropolises in Greece, the significance of the Acropolis of Athens is such that it is commonly known as "The Acropolis." Archaeological remains occupied the entrance to the Acropolis, a monumental gateway called the Propylaea. All these temples were there to worship various Greek gods and there were many. After our Acropolis visit we returned to our hotel and my mother was so tired that she fell asleep, this time on land but still within the Mediterranean weather. I stayed with her while my father went out to see more of Athens by walking for the rest of that afternoon. He was a perpetual student despite his age, always curious about everything and eager to learn more, a trait I seem to have inherited. The next day we flew back to New York so they could spend the rest of their vacation with me. This was probably the best thing I ever did for my parents while they were still with us and had enough energy left to travel. After the long trip they returned to Korea, a country still under dictatorship.

One day in September 1991, I received a very long phone message when I came home from work. The caller introduced himself as Vern Chupp, a project manager and an optical engineer working on an exciting new system - a fully automated flow cytometer (a laser based biophysical technology employed in cell counting, cell sorting, biomarker detection by suspending cells in a stream of fluid and passing them by an electronic detection apparatus. The system allows simultaneous multi-parametric analysis of the physical and chemical characteristics of up to thousands of particles per second) combined with hematology and immuno-phenotyping (a technique used to study the protein expressed by cells. This technique is commonly used in basic science research and laboratory diagnostic purpose. This can be done on tissue section or cell suspension) in one system. He was looking for someone capable of handling the science portion of the project. He found my name after reviewing some technical patents related to the subject matter. He said that the company representatives didn't mind coming to New York to discuss the matter with me if I was too busy to travel to California for an interview. This call was from Sequoia Turner in Silicon Valley.

The time was just about right for me to change my job because I had just completed my PhD in cell biology and anatomy from New York Medical College the year before. I worked on my PhD for many years because I was also working full time at Bayer Corporation as a project manager. Although I had a pretty secure job even without a PhD, I still wanted to achieve my original academic goal, which I had been unable to complete because I needed to help my parents, buy a car and a home. Understandably no universities wanted to accept a part-time PhD student and it had been many years since I received my MS degree in biochemistry. Therefore I had to repeat all the courses I had already taken before for my MS in biochemistry but it helped me to update my knowledge in the field since biochemistry field became much more complicated in molecular level. And I had to take new courses such as hematology, histology, embryology, immunology anatomy plus the corresponding laboratories. Then I had to negotiate the acceptance into the New York Medical College PhD program.

Since I had already made significant contributions for the company by developing new products and obtaining many technical patents to protect the products the company developed for twenty years before their arrival, Bayer Corporation agreed to submit a letter to the chairman of the department of New York Medical College. The letter clearly stated that the company would allow me to attend seminars and take some of the courses during the day if they were not given in the evenings, as long as I took the majority of the courses required for the degree (72 credits) after work hours and they would allow using the company-owned flow cytometer to collect data for my PhD dissertation. I also had to submit three recommendations from university professors in related fields - one from outside and two from inside their school. Fortunately Bayer still retained the same tuition refund program that began with Technicon Corporation in its glory days. To meet the requirement to collect the tuition refund I had to maintain a grade point average above B+. Ultimately my cumulative score was 3.85 out of 4.0. I was exhausted during this period, and my immune system was weakened so much that I was catching the flu every winter. I also became unusually emotional from lack of sleep and overwork. I found myself crying one day listening to music on the radio. After I completed my doctoral program I made efforts to find out what song made me cry. I found out it was Lionel Richie's song, "Say You, Say Me." I bought the CD to listen to it again and again but I didn't cry anymore. It is a beautiful song; I love all his songs.

I was intrigued with this exciting project in California Vern Chupp described on the phone but I was reluctant to leave the place where I had spent the bulk of my professional life and had built my career in the field. On the other hand I was not happy with the situation. The company had already changed ownership three or four times. Each time the former owner milked the company and the new owner blamed the employees for not making the company profitable. That was really nonsense since we routinely worked hard and had in fact launched one of the most successful hematology systems such as H*1 that sold three times more than the marketing forecast at that time. There was a predictable pattern each time when a new owner took over the company. They start with a big layoff of hardworking employees. The reason I was never in danger of being laid off was because I was always on the key project the company was developing. There is a saying: "If you want to protect your corporate career in the United States make sure that they need you, never mind whether they love you or not." All that matters is profit.

Consequently I began to research a company called Sequoia Turner in Silicon Valley. The rumor was that Abbott Laboratory was in the process of purchasing this company. So I searched Abbott Lab. and found that Abbott was the number one diagnostics company in the world at that time. Then I wanted to find out about Bayer where the company stands in the field. My search revealed that Bayer was the second-best diagnostic company in the world. I thought it was an improvement to move from the second best to the best. Why not consider changing? I agreed to drop by the company for an interview after I attended the American Society of Hematology conference in Denver, Colorado, in December of that year.

After the ASH conference, I flew to San Francisco. The Sequoia Turner medical director, Wieland von Behrens, MD, who also attended the ASH conference recognized me on the plane and invited me to stay in his home overnight so he could drive me down to the company next morning. He was a very friendly Australian. His wife was also a physician working in San Francisco. I preferred to stay in a hotel for my own comfort. The next morning, he picked me up from the hotel and drove me to the company office via Hwy. 280, a scenic state highway passing Crystal Lake and grassy mountains after the winter rainfall. When we arrived in Mountain View I saw palm trees slowly waving in the wind from the Pacific Ocean. I remember thinking, "What am I doing in New York?" I had flown out of LaGuardia Airport in a blinding snow storm a few days earlier. This was my first impression of the Bay area and I already wanted to live there for the rest of my life. The company's project manager, Vern Chupp, was a very nice and unpretentious man with deep blue eyes - someone I thought I could trust and enjoy working with. The interview went pretty well. As expected, Abbott Lab acquired the company in January 1992, and I received a written job offer from them. They offered to pay for all my moving expenses and temporary lodging until I found a permanent place to live.

Now I had to make the difficult decision to quit a job I had for 20 years and move 3,000 miles to California. As expected, there was another rumor of a big layoff at Bayer so I decided to volunteer to be laid off so I could collect a large severance package to buy a home in California. I made an appointment with the top officer who came from Bayer headquarters in Germany. Since he sounded so angry each time he gave a speech in the auditorium all the employees were afraid to even breathe in front of him, not to dare asking him any questions after his speech. His name was Dr. Hiller, but employees joked that the letter *T* was missing from his last name. The previous owners, Revlon and Cooper, milked the company so much that Bayer found out the company asset was not worth what they paid for it and that's why they were so angry. They were planning to lay off a very high percentage of the employees to balance the budget. But again, that was not the employees' fault. Rumor has it that Bayer bought Technicon, which was under Revlon by this time, to establish Bayer Diagnostic Division headquarters in Tarrytown, New York, and repurchase the rights for Bayer Aspirin from Sterling Company, to which Bayer had sold its rights after World War II when Germany became so unpopular in America. Germans are by nature very thorough and meticulous people. They went as far as taking out the big "T" symbol, representing Technicon Corporation, embedded into the front wall of the building because they wanted to change the company name altogether to Bayer Corporation. So that was the end of the Technicon Corporation and that was enough for me.

For some reason I never had any fear of expressing myself to powerful top executives. I went ahead and made an appointment with Dr. Hiller to volunteer to be laid off. As soon as I walked into his office I had a pleasant surprise. He was very charming, offered me coffee, cream or sugar? He brought me the coffee and praised me for drinking black coffee. I didn't know why he was so nice to me. I told him I had heard the rumor about a big layoff and I would like to volunteer to be laid off. To my surprise he said he already checked the history of my performances at the company and found that I had made many valuable contributions to the company so he refused to lay me off. I was very disappointed at his reaction because I could have collected over $100,000 severance pay since I had worked for the company for so many years. I could have made a down payment to buy a new home in California where real estate prices were, and still are, among the highest in the nation. Therefore I had no choice but submit my resignation giving one month's notice. I put my home on the market and moved to California for my new adventure.

Photo 13. At my graduation from NTMC. (1) Author (2) brother John (3) brother Hugh and (4) my nephew (son of my sister Oak.

Chapter 26: The Sixth ROK and Sunshine Policy (1993–2003)

Meanwhile back in South Korea, Presidency Chun Doo-hwan continued to promote strong centralized government, and the rapid economic growth of the Park era continued. The revised constitution in 1981 was less authoritarian than its 1972 predecessor, the Yushin Constitution, but still granted very broad powers to the president. But a primary provision restricted the president to one seven-year term. Strangely Chun did not attempt to amend the document so he could run for reelection in 1987. It appears that he and Roh Tae-woo, his accomplice to take over the government after Park's assassination, had previous arrangement to inherit the presidency after Chun's term is over. They also figured out they could accumulate enough fortune during their one seven year term and retire. During Chun's visit to Rangoon, Burma (Myanmar), in October, 1983, a bomb exploded at a mausoleum he was about to visit, killing 21 people, including South Korean cabinet members. Chun himself narrowly escaped death as he arrived at the scene two minutes late. North Korean involvement was widely suspected.

While Chun was president he accumulated a multimillion-dollar fortune from various sources including bribery. By 1986, despite the Korean economy enjoying rapid growth combined with modest inflation, there was much opposition to Chun's regime among the people led by activist students. In June 1987, Chun named Roh Tae-woo as the ruling party's candidate in the 1987 elections. As expected, discontent boiled over leading to nationwide protests. In the same month, US president Ronald Reagan sent a letter to Chun in support of the establishment of "democratic institutions." Following these events, on June 29, Roh announced a program of reform, including direct presidential elections, restoration of the banned politicians including Kim Dae-jung, and other liberalizing measures. This enabled Roh to differentiate himself from Chun and helped his position by dividing opposition between Kim Yong-sam and Kim Dae-jung. Roh was elected as the next president of South Korea.

Like Chun, Roh Tae-woo was also a member of the army beginning in 1955. Roh rose steadily through the ranks and was promoted to major general in 1979. A member of the Hanahoe, a secret military group, he gave critical support to a coup d'état later that year in which Chun became the de facto ruler of South Korea. Roh was a military general when he helped Chun lead troops to the Gwangju Democratization Movement in 1980. In June 1987, Chun named Roh as the presidential candidate of the ruling Democratic Justice Party. This was widely perceived as handing Roh the presidency and in 1987 and it triggered large pro-democracy rallies in Seoul and other cities. In response, Roh made a speech on June 29 promising a wide range of reforms. Chief among them were a new, more democratic constitution and popular election of the president. In the election the two leading opposition figures, Kim Young-sam and Kim Dae-jung, were unable to overcome their differences and so they split the vote. This enabled Roh to win by a narrow margin and become the country's first democratically elected president.

I noticed that both New World Encyclopedia and Wikipedia list Roh Tae-woo's government as the Sixth Republic of Korea but the true civilian government is his successor Kim Young-sam's government in 1992.

Roh's rule was notable for hosting the Seoul Olympics in 1988 and for his foreign policy of Nordpolitik, which represented a major break from previous administrations. Nordpolitik was the signature foreign policy of reaching out to the traditional allies of North Korea, the People's Republic of China and Soviet Union, with the ultimate goal of normalizing relations to improve South Korea's economy. This policy left North Korea so isolated that it would have no choice but to open up and reduce military tensions. The policy was named after the West German policy of Ostpolitik ("Eastern Policy") toward then communist East Germany, although Ostpolitik was aimed directly at normalization of the relationship between two German states. The successor of Nordpolitik is the Sunshine Policy, which actually bears many similarities to the German Ostpolitik. True to his word, Rho remained committed to democratic reforms. Roh was much smarter than Chun in handling his presidency.

Despite the belief by some Koreans that the United States supported military governments, the US has never supported military coups in South Korea. But the US military could not take unilateral action to suppress the coup without approval from the president of the host country. However once a coup became successful the United States always tried to negotiate with the military governments, in this case both Park's and Chun's, to return to civilian government. The US has always wanted to build a democratic noncommunist civilian government in South Korea as a symbol of their success in Asia. The military governments might well have lasted much longer in South Korea without the US pressure for a democratic civilian government.

Without American government pressure there would have been no President Kim Dae-jung, since he was kidnapped by Park's KCIA agents in August 1973 in Tokyo in response to his criticism of President Park's Yushin Constitution. The KCIA's plan was to kill Kim Dae-jung and dump his body into the sea on the way to Korea. If US helicopters had not been circling above that ship, that might have happened. In 1980, Kim Dae-jung was arrested and sentenced to death on charges of sedition and conspiracy in the wake of another coup by Chun Doo-hwan and a popular uprising in Gwangju, Kim's political stronghold. With the intervention of the United States the sentence was commuted to 20 years in prison and later he was given exile to the United States. Kim temporarily settled in Boston and taught at Harvard University as a visiting professor to the Center for International Affairs until he chose to return home in 1985.

It's been more than a half century since the Korean liberation but a stable democratic government still has not been established in South Korea. Many innocent civilian lives have been lost fighting for a democratic government. Yet the Korean people never gave up and continued risking their lives to see the end of the military government. During Park Chung-hee's reign, Kim Young-sam, a member of the National Assembly, called on the United States to stop supporting Park's dictatorship in an interview with the *New York Times*, and for that Park wanted to have Kim Young-sam imprisoned. The Carter administration, concerned over increasing violations of human rights, issued a strong warning not to persecute members of the opposition party. When Kim was expelled from the National Assembly in October 1979, the United States recalled its ambassador back to Washington, and all 66 lawmakers of the New Democratic Party resigned from the National Assembly.

When it became known that South Korea was planning to accept the resignations selectively, uprisings broke out in Kim's hometown, Busan, during which 30 police stations were burned. It was the biggest demonstration since the Syngman Rhee presidency and spread to nearby Masan and other cities with students and citizens calling for an end to the dictatorship. This type of crisis was one of the causes of the assassination of Park Chung-hee in October 26, 1979, by KCIA director Kim Jae-kyu, to whom Park had said that he himself would give an order to fire upon demonstrators if the situation got worse.

In 1992, Kim Young-sam became the first democratically elected civilian President in over 30 years in South Korea. He was inaugurated on February 25, 1993, as the 7th president of South Korea. I called my parents to congratulate them for finally living in a country under civilian government. I told them I would take them to Jeju Island for a vacation to celebrate. My parents didn't know much about the new president, Kim Yong-sam, and whether he was capable of overseeing a massive anti-corruption campaign on behalf of Chun Doo-hwan and Rho Tae-woo, which was about to come.

I took a vacation during the summer and went to Korea to take my parents to Jeju Island, a beautiful place with a dormant volcano, Mt. Halla, in the center. It's so sad the islanders had suffered so many tragedies for so long. At the time, I hadn't realized so many victims of the Jeju massacre during the First Republic were still buried in a cave on Mt. Halla because it had been a big secret for a long time after the tragic incident. It had been illegal to talk about it and anyone who brought up the issue was prosecuted. Thus, these bones of victims, men, women, and children had been lying there silently in this secret grave for a long time without justice or even acknowledgment of their existence. In 1992, this beautiful island was booming with tourism and luxury hotels, entertainment centers, and restaurants. There were flowers all over the island. But the graves on Mt. Halla loomed over the merry-makers.

Kim Yong-sam served a single five-year term presiding over a massive anti-corruption campaign culminating in the arrest of his two Predecessors, Chun Doo-hwan and Roh Tae-woo. On November 16, 1995, Kim Young-sam announced retroactive legislation - "A Special Law on May 18 Democratization Movement". As soon as the Constitutional Court declared that Chun Doo-hwan's actions as unconstitutional, the prosecutors began a reinvestigation. On the 3rd day of December, 1995, Chun and 16 others were arrested on charges of conspiracy and insurrection. At the same time, an investigation into the corruption of their presidencies was begun. In March 1996, their public trial began. On August 26, the Seoul District Court issued a death sentence to Chun Doo-hwan but his sentence was commuted to life in prison on December 16, 1996. The Seoul High Court issued a sentence of life imprisonment and a fine in the amount of 220 billion won (Approx. 189,000,000 USD). On April 17, 1997, the judgment was finalized in the Supreme Court. Chun was officially convicted of leading an insurrection, conspiracy to commit insurrection, taking part in an insurrection, issuing illegal troop movement orders, dereliction of duty during martial law, of attempted murder of superior officers, of murder of subordinate troops, of leading a rebellion, of conspiracy to commit rebellion, of taking part in a rebellion, and of murder for the purpose of rebellion, as well as assorted crimes relating to bribery.

After his sentence was finalized, Chun began serving his prison sentence. On December 22, 1997, President Kim Young-sam, commuted Chun's life imprisonment sentence on the advice of incoming President Kim Dae-jung who wanted to avoid further chaos in the nation and concentrate on building a successful democratic civilian government. Chun was still required to pay his massive fine but at that point he had only paid 53.3 billion won, not quite a fourth of the total fine amount. Chun famously said, "I have only 290,000 won to my name." The remaining 167.2 billion won could not be collected at the time. According to the "Special Law on May 18 Democratization Movement", all medals awarded for the military intervention during the Movement were revoked and ordered to be returned to the government. There are still nine medals that have not been returned.

In July 2013, a team of 90 prosecutors, tax collectors, and other investigators raided multiple locations simultaneously including Chun's residence and his family members' homes and offices because of Chun's 167.2 billion won unpaid fines. Among the properties searched were two warehouses owned by publisher Chun Jae-kook, Chun's eldest son, which contained more than 350 pieces of art by famous Korean artists, some estimated to be worth 1 billion won. The National Assembly passed a bill called the Chun Doo-hwan Act, extending the statute of limitations on confiscating assets from public officials who have failed to pay fines. Under the old law, prosecutors had only until October 2013 but the new law extended the statute of limitations on Chun's case until 2020, and allows prosecutors to collect from his family members as well if it's proven that any of their properties originated from Mr. Chun's illegal funds.

In 1998, Kim Dae-jung became the eighth president of South Korea. Kim Dae-jung's administration formulated his well known Sunshine Policy and implemented it. The term originates in "The North Wind and the Sun," one of Aesop's fables. The national security policy had three basic principles: (1) no armed provocation by the North will be tolerated (2) the South will not attempt to absorb the North in any way (3) the South actively seeks cooperation.

North-South cooperative business developments resumed including a railroad and the Keumgangsan Tourist Region where several thousand South Korean citizens traveled every year. In 2000 Kim Dae-jung and Kim Jong-il held a summit meeting - the first between heads of state of the two nations. My father never trusted dictators and thought that Kim Dae-jung was naïve to trust Kim Jong-il to carry through unification of the Korean Peninsula. I wondered whether Kim Dae-jung was familiar with the history of how Kim Il-sung treated one of the most respected elder Korean statesmen, Kim Gu, during the North and South Joint Conference held in Pyongyang in 1948. Kim Il-sung showed absolutely no respect toward Kim Gu and made false promises concerning the supply of electricity to the

South and the release of Cho Man-shik from prison. The single objective of the Kim Il-sung dynasty has always been to retain their power forever, not unification.

On Sept.15 of 2000, I watched on TV as North and South Korean athletes marched together into the opening ceremony of the Sydney Olympics. They were holding a placard that simply read "Korea". One hundred eighty athletes and officials from North Korea and South Korea marched together in the Olympic stadium with the same uniforms and to the tune of a national folk song. Behind the placard, the unification flag, a single blue-on-white flag depicting a map of the Korean Peninsula, proudly waved over smiling joint marchers. They drew thunderous applause from the audience. Warmly welcoming the joint Korean marchers with a standing ovation, the crowd gave them a longer applause than all others. The band played an emotional Korean folk song, "Arirang." IOC president Antonio Samaranch and other officials stood up, clapping their hands and waving to the Koreans. I found myself becoming very emotional, with tears in my eyes while I was watching the scene because they all seemed so happy. I was thinking, "Why should ordinary Koreans have to suffer so long because of the power-hungry few at the top who will never yield the country to whom it rightfully belongs - the people of Korea?"

In his 2000 Nobel Peace Prize speech, Kim Dae-jung said, "The KCIA agents took me to their boat at anchor along the seashore. They tied me up, blindfolded me, and stuffed my mouth. Just when they were about to throw me overboard, Jesus Christ appeared before me with amazing clarity. I clung to him and begged him to save me. At that very moment an airplane came down from the sky to rescue me from certain death." The airplane was a US helicopter trying to save Kim Dae-jung's life. Koreans who still have strong animosity toward Americans must also realize that it was the US government that has constantly pressured military dictators to turn the country over to Democratic processes. There is one unique and outstanding feature of American government as the world power is Protecting Human Rights. They try to spread this concept all over the world. Neither China nor Russia has ever pressured the Kim Il-sung dynasty to step down in favor of real democracy. They don't care about the Korean people as long as North Korea remains their communist ally.

In 2000, after the summit, talks between the two nations stalled. Criticism of the Sunshine Policy intensified and South Korea's unification minister, Lim Dong-won, lost a no-confidence vote on September 3, 2001. After the terrorist attacks of September 11, 2001, the US president George W. Bush proclaimed North Korea a third leg of the Axis of Evil, along with Iraq and Iran. North Korea responded by cutting off talks with South Korea. In 2002, a naval skirmish over disputed fishing territory killed four South Korean sailors further chilling relations. Credible allegations later came to light that Kim's administration had arranged the 2000 summit meeting only after payments worth several hundred million dollars to North Korea. President Roh Moo-hyun, who succeeded Kim Dae-jung, continued the policy in 2002 and 2003. In 2003, the issue of North Korea's possession of nuclear weapons resurfaced with North Korea accusing the United States of breaching the agreed-upon framework. Roh remained committed to the policy and continued to supply North Korea with humanitarian aid. The two governments continued cooperation on the projects that had begun under Kim Dae-jung and also started the Kaesong Industrial Park with South Korea spending the equivalent of just over $324 million on aid to North Korea in 2005. A pro–North Korean trend in public attitudes surfaced in South Korea, although there were significant differences between generations, political groups, and regions.

Many observers saw a weakening of the US-ROK alliance as a result of the Sunshine Policy. South Korea had favored North Korea's interests over those of its ally the United States. At this time, South Korean politicians ignored the sacrifices of its own soldiers so as to avoid upsetting North Korea as well as the ill effects to South Korea's national interest as well as its alliance with the United States that have been caused by North Korea. Internationally and at home the South Korean government was criticized for repeatedly abstaining from UN votes condemning North Korea's human rights record. The Roh's government defended the abstentions by citing the special character of inter-Korean relations.

On October 9, 2006, following North Korean nuclear and missile tests, South Korea suspended aid shipments to North Korea and put its military on high alert. Even supporters of the Sunshine Policy expressed concern about how South Korea could maintain a cooperative policy toward North Korea when such provocative acts continued. Finally, the newly elected president of South Korea, Lee Myung-bak, and his party took a harsher stance toward North Korea beginning in March 2008. The South Korean government stated that any expansion of economic cooperation in the Kaesong Industrial Region would only happen if North Korea resolved the international standoff over its nuclear weapons. Relations again chilled with North Korea making threatening moves such as a series of short-range ship-to-ship missile tests. After North Korea's nuclear test in 2009, the relationship between Seoul and Pyongyang was again strained. South Korea's response to the nuclear test included signing the Non-Proliferation Security Initiative to prevent the shipment of nuclear materials to North Korea. In November 2010, South Korea's Unification Ministry officially declared the Sunshine Policy a failure thus bringing the attempt to an end.

Unification therefore seems to be left to the eventuality of North Korea invading South Korea with their nuclear arsenals when North Korea's economy totally collapses. Unification of the Korean Peninsula under the present North Korean regime would be almost like committing suicide for South Korea. It took a long time for South Korea to reach its present status in the world as a developed country with Seoul as the design capital of the world. Some of my American friends wonder why North Korean citizens do not rise up against their own brutal regime as South Korean citizens have done. That's a very sensible question. Consider that North Korean citizens are not given a chance to think critically from infancy or to observe and learn of the realities of the world. Thus there is scant chance that leaders like Gorbachev or the former Chinese premier Zhao Ziyang can ever develop in North Korea. I greatly admire those two past world leaders because they had enough intelligence to figure out that the policies of their own governments were problematic even though they were born in those countries and grew up being taught communism from their infancy.

Why don't Russian and Chinese leaders do more to change the North Korean regime? Those two countries were responsible for planting and helping Kim Il-sung to consolidate his power in North Korea, and therefore they are the logical parties to take responsibility for dissolving the North Korean regime. China certainly has the power to change the North Korean regime if it really wants to. The Kim Il-sung dynasty has nothing to do with communist ideals but is only interested in prolonging its power and its dynasty forever. China no longer has to worry about having South Korea's democratic government at their border, since South Korea is not interested in changing the Chinese political system. Many of its own citizens have already traveled outside of China and have seen the lives of people in the free world. It would better for China to have the South Korean government at its border than the North Korean government, since there will be no refugees coming to China from South Korea. We all know that China does not want the country at its border with its US military presence. But its leaders should seriously reconsider the scenario: if Korea were united, there would be no need for the US military to remain in the Korean Peninsula. A united Korea could follow the model common to the Nordic countries: a combination of free-market capitalism with a comprehensive welfare state and collective bargaining at the national level. Neither the United States nor Russia has any problem dealing with any of the Nordic countries. As long as North Korea continues threatening South Korea with its nuclear arsenals South Korea needs the US military to protect itself. In the end a unified Korea would be a win-win situation for China and its leaders should rethink their policy toward North Korea.

Chapter 27: Last Days of My Aging Parents
(1995–2002)

My parents were never ostentatious people but they became even more reserved as they grew older. They seemed to be content with their achievement in putting eight children through college – a truly admirable accomplishment especially given the circumstances in which they had to live. My brothers John and Soo went to national universities so their tuition was not very high but all the other children went to private universities with expensive tuitions. My two sisters, Oak and Mimi, went to Ewha Women's University. Brother Churl went to Korea University, brother Suk was fortunate to go to the same university where my father was teaching so he received tuition-free education.

The younger children grew up in a much different social environment than John and I since South Korean culture was transforming into a more materialistic society departing from the old Korean tradition of respecting elders and supporting old parents. However I also understand the negatives of carrying "respect" for parents to extremes when I learned about what Father went through with his family demands. In some cultures the elders can sometimes ask for more authority than they are entitled to under the guise of "respect" so I understand the desire of youth to establish some lines of demarcation between their life as children subject to their parents and their lives as adults with all the privileges and responsibilities that pertain.

When I spent a year in Korea at my parent's home working for Dong-A Pharmaceutical Company in 1970, I witnessed that my younger siblings were continually putting financial demands on my parents without showing much concern about the financial situation. They were only doing what their peers were doing in a society oriented toward the Western culture of individualism, wealth, and enjoying life, rather than worrying about their parents' health or financial conditions. Although the South Korean economy was improving a great deal that did not help older folks like my parents.

They had passed their prime earning years during which they could have taken advantage of the economic progress of the country. Yet, they had raised eight children under the most difficult circumstances and that alone should earn them profound respect from all of us.

After Hugh left Korea in 1977 my mother's remaining task was to take care of my sister, Mimi, the youngest child, and help her through Ewha Women's University. Years later, after Mimi married a medical doctor mother was finally able to have some time for herself. What did she do then with her free time? She entered a seminary - Presbyterian University and Theological Seminary in Seoul to study theology (though not necessarily to join the clergy) from which she graduated. When I visited her during this period I saw her trying to memorize the names of the biblical figures of Abraham's family tree listed in the Old Testament. I was surprised to see that her memory was still acute well into her later years. After her graduation, her Ahndong Church invited her to give sermons on various occasions. I was very proud of her not giving up her dream - she kept going with the same energy she used to protect and raise her children. I still do remember how upset she was when I joked with her saying, "Mother, you believe everything written in the Bible and you are trying to live according to the Ten Commandments. You will be sorry if you find out there is no heaven after you die." She was very mad at me because I had attacked one of the few things in life she truly believed in. I sincerely apologized and promised her that I would read the Bible to educate myself. I kept my promise and read the Bible from cover to cover although I still cannot believe everything I read. I do believe Jesus Christ really lived and that he was a great philosopher/teacher, especially after our pilgrimage to the Holy Land. But I also believe Christianity is the best religion because it's based on love and forgiveness, not revenge.

In the spring of 1995 when I was living in Silicon Valley, I received a phone call in the middle of the night from my fourth brother Suk in Korea. Father had a stroke and was hospitalized in critical condition. I hurriedly made an airline reservation with Korean Air and left a telephone message for my boss Vern Chupp. I called my brother John in Boston to inform him of the incident and left San

Francisco next morning. Korea is 5,613 miles away from California – a 10 hour flight. I couldn't sleep as my mind kept reliving my life with my father. I felt like he was born in the wrong time and the wrong place and was unable to fully explore his enormous potential. He suffered a great deal and almost lost his life because Korea was in such a mess during most of the prime of his life. But he had never complained about his life's hardship and he never gave up life. He managed to raise his eight children through it all and all of his eight children at least completed undergraduate educations, while half of them completed graduate degrees. With his wisdom and knowledge of Korean history he was able to guide us, preventing us from becoming victims of propaganda and keeping us from being battered by the mob mentality of the moment as many young Koreans were. I am forever grateful for his guidance.

The plane arrived at Gimpo International Airport (this was before the new Inchon International Airport was completed). I could already feel the change in the atmosphere at the airport. There were no visible KCIA agents watching every arrival like predatory birds and stopping people to ask intimidating questions. This was during the first real civilian government in South Korea when Kim Young-sam was president. My brothers Soo and Suk met me at the airport and informed me of what had happened to father. As always, he was diligently cleaning up the small wild garden under the tall ginkgo trees in the front yard when suddenly he collapsed. He was found unconscious and was transported by an ambulance to Korean University Medical Center.

The car was very quiet on the way home as my brothers were deep in their own thoughts. I was also seeing images of those ginkgo trees which had special meaning to my parents; they seemed to generate fresh air you could almost feel. I also felt something special when I stood under those trees. The two trees, male and female, were brought from a Buddhist temple by Father's distant niece who became a female Buddhist monk after losing her brother and husband during the Korean War. She planted those trees herself, so my parents could breathe fresh air and prolong their lives.

On the way to my parents' home from Gimpo Airport I was surprised to see very heavy traffic on the road. I hadn't been in Korea for many years so I didn't realize how much it had changed. Almost every family in Seoul seemed to have one or two cars. When I left Korea in 1960 it was unusual for an ordinary family to own even one car, and even in my visit in 1970, there were far fewer cars on the road. I was glad to see so many people could afford a car, a sign of an economic boom in the country. But I didn't know why everyone wanted to drive in Seoul. Using public transportation would be much faster than driving in heavy traffic. When I visited Kobe, Japan to attend a hematology conference the only cars I saw on the road were taxis. Apparently it was customary for Japanese to take public transportation.

Finally we arrived at my parent's home. Mother was patiently waiting for me. She looked much older and frailer than the last time I had seen her, which was already 12 years since I had taken Parents for the pilgrimage to the holy land. She was crying and I tried to comfort her without much success. Even though I was very tired I decided to go to see my father at the medical center right away so all of us got in the car and went to the hospital.

Father was in the emergency room, oxygen mask covering his face. His heartbeat was being monitored by an EKG machine. I stood by his bedside watching him carefully and I could see that he was only semi-conscious. Seeing him in that condition, connected to all kinds of machines was disheartening. I was thinking, "Does this what happen to people when they become old? Isn't there any pleasant and peaceful way God could take good people into eternity by his side?" I squeezed one of his hands on my side of the bed and he responded by squeezing my hand back. His eyes were slightly open but he still could not talk. I was happy that he knew I had come all the way from California to be with him. I don't remember how long I was there but it was a long time. We were unable to communicate because he was fading in and out of consciousness. Unlike US hospitals we had to hire a private nurse's aid to take care of his personal needs because the nurses in the hospital only take care of medical needs.

The next day, my brother John arrived from Boston and we went to see father again. John was speechless, deep in his own thoughts. Maybe he felt guilty about not doing much for his father while he was still conscious, even though father never complained about that. My father was like a Buddha, a man of few words. He never complained about anything. He lived his life as if he accepted everything saying, "Happiness is in contentment." When John held his hand Father again squeezed John's hand, confirming that he recognized his first son. John looked emotional but they could not communicate much more than that.

Many members of Ahndong Church came to see him every day and prayed for his recovery but he never really recovered his consciousness. Two weeks passed and the hospital intensive care bill was staggering and accumulating every day. The government of South Korea didn't have any Medicare program at that time so his children, or those who were willing or able to help, mostly my four brothers, John, Soo, Suk, Hugh, and I chipped in to pay the hospital bills. We fully intended to keep up with it as long as necessary, but ultimately there would be a limit to how long we would be financially able to do so. We could not transfer him to a hospice since that's a place for people who are really dirt poor and expected to die soon. We could not bring him home because my mother was too frail to take care of him by herself and my two brothers who had family living in Korea were unable to take him in because of family circumstances.

The third generation was even more different from the second generation in their thinking process. Sacrificing themselves to take care of aging parents or gravely ill grandparents may have seemed unthinkable to them. This was how much Korean culture had changed in only 35 years since I left Korea in 1960. My youngest sister, Mimi, who was married to a medical doctor at the time, whose family owned a diabetic medical center, insisted that we had to bring father home because that's what all respected families do. Other than that, she neither volunteered to take Father to her home nor offered to pay the bills for the nurse if we could find a nurse who was willing to make daily visits to take care of him at home. She is a product of a new generation with a different culture.

My mother was crying saying that she had raised her eight children and devoted herself to taking care of us when we were sick but now none of us wanted to take care of their own father in his sick bed. She was absolutely right; that was the situation. I felt very guilty and told her that I would be willing to take Father into my home if I was living in Korea but unfortunately my job was in America and I had to return if I was to continue supporting his medical expenses.

I had also begun to receive e-mails from my co-workers in America asking when I planned to return to take care of the project and resolve problems they were facing, so I felt that I could not stay in Korea indefinitely. At the time I was responsible for managing a large project and it was a critical time to complete final details and prepare for a market launch of a new system. John and I discussed what to do since he was a research and development director working for another company at the time and he also had to return to his job in the U.S. We both felt guilty for leaving the situation to our mother even though we had other siblings in Korea because John and I are the eldest children. Finally my mother and my two brothers in Korea told us that we should return to the United States and they would notify us if the situation changed. So we left our father at the hospital intensive care and John and I returned to the United States. I wired a large sum of money to pay the hospital bills. We are fortunate in the United States where elderly have Medicare to take care of this kind of situation. South Korea now also has a similar program to help elderly sick people.

Sometime later they brought my father home. My frail poor mother was taking care of him with help from a nurse who came to provide home care. The summer weather in Korea was hot and humid - not an ideal condition for a sick body in bed all the time. My father continued his life in this condition for many more months. On July 15, 1995, we received the news that Father had passed away. Their church friends and the minister played a key role in his funeral and burial at the site we bought many years ago as our family burial site on a beautiful mountain located some distance south of Seoul. My brothers told me that they had to have his funeral right away because of his condition and the unfavorable weather to preserve the body. For this reason, John and I were unable to get there in time to attend his funeral. I always feel ashamed for not attending Father's funeral and promised myself to get there in time when Mother's condition became critical. Mother was seven years younger than her husband, and even though she was often in poor health in her old age, Father used to tell her jokingly that she would live seven more years after he passed away, and he was exactly right: she lived another seven years after Father's passing.

After Father passed away we had to move my mother to a more convenient place to live. Their home was an old-style single-family home that needed a lot of maintenance. As she got older, it was preferable that she move near one of her son's families, either Soo's or Suk's. She didn't want to come to live with me in the United States because she was very attached to her church and her church friends. She also did not speak English very well and didn't have any friends nearby to chat with on the phone daily as she enjoyed doing. In that sense I am very different from mother because my phone calls are always very short, right to the point, no chatting. She asked me to come to live with her in Korea but that was not an easy decision for me because I saw how difficult a time my parents were having in their old age because of their financial situation. I wanted to be financially independent after my retirement and I had no children whom I could rely on, no that I necessarily think children to take care of their aging parents these days.

The only way to achieve my goal was to essentially complete my career before retirement. I had the goal of having a mortgage-free home in an area with nice weather, accumulate enough of an annuity payment, Social Security, 401(k), guaranteed medical care, and return on good solid investments to live after retirement without significant degradation of my lifestyle – which was modest and not given to excess. I had already spent the most productive years of my life in America making my contributions, including high-bracket tax payments without any dependents to claim since helping my parents did not qualify for any tax deduction in this country. I often brought home less than 50% of my salary after taxes. I could not abandon something I had been building for decades to move to Korea, especially with no expectation of employment when I go there. I felt very guilty for saying no to my mother, but in all fairness there were three siblings living in Korea who could take of Mother with little sacrifice.

I discussed with my two brothers Soo and Suk who were living in Korea where to move Mother. Soo thought Mother should be moved near his family and Suk thought Mother should be near his. I appreciated their kindness, thinking they were still better than we who were living in America. My sister Oak in San Francisco and I went to Korea to sell our parents' home. We searched and bought Mother a new condominium near Suk's family in Suwon and moved her in. Suk promised us that he would take mother to Ahndong Church in Seoul every Sunday. That was the most important activity to mother - attending her church services. After my father was gone God was her only constant companion day and night, giving her emotional comfort to go on with her life.

I invited mother to spend some time with me in California on my 60th birthday. The 60th birthday in Korea used to be a very big occasion to celebrate because 60 years was once considered a long life. Today that's not the case so I didn't think anything of it, but four of my brothers came to celebrate my birthday anyway, my brothers Soo and Suk with Mother from Korea, John from Boston and Hugh from New York. So, many of our family members were able to spend some time together enjoying the beautiful weather of the Bay area. Even my mother, who suffered from insomnia, was able to sleep. We tried to show her all the famous landmarks such as the Golden Gate Bridge, Alcatraz Island, the cable cars, Chinatown, and the steep rolling hills of San Francisco. My nother really liked the Bay area weather but she could not stay long because my brother Suk who owns his own company in Korea, a successful businessman, had to go back to take care of his business and he had to accompany her. When she was leaving, she told me she wanted to visit me again, but she never made it back, although she never gave up the plan until the last days of her life.

In 1999, I had to go to Kobe, Japan, to make a presentation at International Society of Laboratory Hematology conference. I took advantage of this occasion to extend my trip to Korea to spend some time with Mother and at the same time provide some assistance to the company employees at the branch office in Korea. Since they had been sending me many e-mail questions on the new system we were marketing in Korea, it was an ideal opportunity to extend my travel. I stayed in a hotel near the company branch office which was quite a distance from Mother's home. When I called her on the phone to inform her of my arrival and told her that I planned to be at her home as soon as I finished my business, she said she could come to see me at my hotel right away. I discouraged her because she was already 85 years old and frail and it might take more than one connection to get to the hotel by train. But she insisted on coming to see me and she hung up. I didn't know what to do, so I stayed in the hotel room just in case she was really coming.

I don't remember how long it had been when I heard someone knocking on the door. There she was, a frail old lady, still delicate and pretty, standing right outside of my hotel room. We hugged each other and I suggested going out to a nice restaurant for dinner but she was not very interested in dinner. She just wanted to talk, talk and talk. It seemed that she really missed having someone to talk to. Why didn't we, any of her eight children, take better care of our aging mother? I felt guilty. This kind of situation would not have happened in the old Korea since she would be living with her eldest son's family. I called for a room service and asked her to stay with me overnight since the hotel room had two separate beds. But she declined saying she didn't want to interfere with my business the next morning and she left alone in the dark. I could not go home with her because I had a meeting with the company people early the next morning. I was very worried about her safe arrival at home. Although she was old, her mind was still young and clear and she was quite a sport. Late that night, she called me to inform me of her safe arrival home. What a relief!

The next day, after taking care of my official business, I went to her condo and spent a week with her, listening to more stories about relationships among family members who lived in Korea. She had lots of grievances and said that she was beginning to feel some pain in her back. She blamed the long-distance car ride to church from Suwon to Seoul every Sunday. I suggested that she go see a doctor for an accurate diagnosis and I left Korea feeling guilty as always.

In 2000, I was determined to spend more time with Mother while she was still with us. I took my three-week vacation around Christmastime because I could add another week of company holiday recess between Christmas and New Year stretching it to a four-week vacation. I went to Korea and spent the whole month of December with her, going to church together, taking her out to restaurants, strolling with her after dinner in the park behind her building and taking her to the hospital for a checkup. She complained that the pain on the left side of her back was not going away but her doctor was unable to pinpoint what was causing the pain. I told her to ask her doctor to take an MRI of the region which would provide detailed images of the internal organs of the body.

Then my four weeks ended and I was scheduled to return to the United States to get back to work on January 2, 2001, but there was a heavy snow in Korea and all airlines canceled their flights. I spent the night at the airport, fortunately in the VIP room, because they could always resume their flight any time when flight conditions improved. But I didn't call mother because she might want to come to spend the night with me at the airport.

When I arrived home in the United States, I called her to tell her the whole story. There were a couple of things I promised her during my stay with her. I would read the Holy Bible from the first page to the last. I would publish her diary that she had been writing every day which she handed over to me. I would make sure our family members stayed together. Reading the Bible and writing her diary were her therapy, writing down all the pains and worries in her life to keep her mind at peace within the arms of the heavenly father. I didn't know then that this would be the last time I would spend with Mother while her mind was still clear, without the effects of drugs on her brain. One of the reasons I decided to write this book is to include at least some of the pains she described in her diary, because my brothers rejected the idea of publishing her diary.

In 2001, I think it was around October, I received a phone call from my sister-in-law, Suk's wife. She said that Mother's MRI revealed a growth between her left lung and her back, and her doctor diagnosed it as a form of adenocarcinoma. Her doctor did not tell Mother because she didn't want to upset her after hearing her strong desire to live. Worse yet, there was no promising treatment to cure her because the position of the growth made it very difficult to perform surgery. The doctors thought that she was too frail to go through chemotherapy either. What doctors were willing to do was to give her pain pills and morphine to deal with her increasing pain, predicting that she might last a year. All bad news! I was surprised at the news because nobody in our family had cancer. Her parents lived very long, and her five sisters and one brother were still alive. What caused her cancer? Was it air pollution, her emotional state, or something else? I told my sister-in-law that I planned to be there in December to spend a whole month with her as I had done many previous years and asked her to hire a full-time domestic nursemaid who was trained to take care of such patients. But I could not tell Mother she had cancer because she seemed to be afraid of dying.

In any case I was there in December and saw the process of her mental deterioration because of increasing doses of morphine to counter her increasing pain. She did not recognize me when I walked into her hospital room. She thought I was my cousin. But shortly after that she returned to her senses and said that she had been waiting for me all that time. Then she lost it again; she was hallucinating, seeing things that were not there. She was remembering incidents happened a long ago when she was a high school girl—the Gwangju students' revolt against Japanese occupation. She kept saying that the Japanese police were coming to arrest her classmates. This memory had been stored in some part of her brain for over 77 years but she had never mentioned it before. And she was seeing not only memories but also some of her unfilled dreams; she said she was a photojournalist reporting international events. But I didn't know how her morphine treatment accessed this long-forgotten memory from a hidden corner of her brain. It was frightening to watch her coming in and out of her senses. Maybe we should have put her through the dangerous surgery instead. Anything might have been better than watching her lose her mind completely.

It was not possible to communicate with her normally, even though I had flown over 5,600 miles to comfort her. I didn't think there was any reason to keep her in the hospital because all they were doing was giving her morphine so we brought her home. My sister-in-law had hired a full-time, experienced nursemaid to take care of her at home. When we arrived home nothing changed; one moment she was her self and the next moment she was someone else. She was very intensely looking at the patterns of flowers and leaves on the curtain next to her bed but she seemed to be seeing something else—eyes and faces in those patterns. What's worse, her digestive system was not working properly, making it very difficult to prepare meals for her. Her church friends came to visit her often, sang her favorite hymns, and prayed for her, but she didn't always recognize them either. I wanted to ask God why he let her go through this kind of horrifying process. If her time had come why not just take her quickly in peace without putting her through this kind of pain? All her life she had lived according to the Ten Commandments. Please, God, take her to the Garden of Eden, so she can enjoy peace and tranquility with no more pain and suffering! I prayed to God to take her quickly. I spent the whole month like this and again it was time for me to return to America for my job. When I was saying goodbye to my mother she was standing at the door, waving at me, saying she wanted to recover soon and come to visit me. I knew that was her dream and felt very sad, but I knew Mrs. Song, the nursemaid, could take good care of her. I can still see mother's image at the door waving at me saying she was going to visit me soon.

When I returned to the United States I called my brother John and suggested that he take a couple of weeks of vacation from work and go to Korea to spend some time with Mother because that would be his last chance to make up for lost time. He agreed and went to spend a couple of weeks with Mother. Although Mother's mental state was no longer normal due to morphine treatment, they spent some valuable last time together. When John returned I asked my sister Oak to spend time with her so she would not regret not seeing her after mother was gone. When Oak returned she told me that mother was terribly afraid of dying and thus she couldn't be a real Christian because good Christians would be happy to go to heaven to be with their Lord. Oak is a Christian who literally believes every word in the Bible just like Mother. I don't know why Mother was so afraid of dying but I don't think many people are content with dying no matter whether they believe in God or not.

Mother used to think that it was her fault if anything went wrong in our family. She always blamed herself if any of us got hurt in an accident or got sick or had a misfortune. Once she realized she had cancer, even if we didn't tell her in so many words, she might have thought God was punishing her for something she did. Maybe this was why she was afraid to die. I should have told her that she was an angel and did not commit any sin in her life to the best of my knowledge. In my opinion, the idea of telling Christians they are all sinners until God forgives them is not a very healthy doctrine for people who do their best to have faith.

On Saturday, September 21, 2002, I received a phone call from my sister-in-law, who informed me that mother was critically ill. I wanted to make sure to get there before she was gone so I tried to arrange a seat on Korean Air but I could not fly until the next day. I arrived and my brother Suk drove me directly to the hospital but it was too late to communicate. They told me she was waiting for me until about 45 minutes before but she was now unconscious. I tried to wake her up, saying, "Mother, I am here, mother, can you hear me?" There was no answer. I just stood there watching. She was breathing but her hands were cold. I remembered her request to read the Holy Bible last year when I stayed with her and I wanted to tell her that I had read it, but I could not wake her up. About an hour later, my brother John arrived from Boston and he tried to talk to her as well, without any success. So he also missed the chance to say goodbye to Mother. I asked her doctor whether there was any way he could wake her up even for a few minutes by injecting a stimulus, but he said no. My brothers and I just sat there—I don't remember for how long—but there was no change in her status. Actually, she was breathing heavier as time passed. I remembered many stories of how clinically dead people saw everything that's going on in the room and told their stories when they miraculously came back to life. I was wondering whether she could see us beside her bed trying to talk to her even though she could not talk to us or if God would decide to return her to life even briefly, so we could tell her we loved her. She looked very peaceful and all the wrinkles on her face disappeared. She was no longer in pain.

John and Suk suddenly broke my thoughts, suggesting that I go to Mother's home to get some sleep and they would keep her company in the meantime and would call me if there was any change. So I went to her home to get some sleep. Sometime later, I received a call from them that mother was gone and the hospital wanted to transfer her body to the morgue in the basement. I said she did not like cold, particularly freezing temperature. Why couldn't they leave her in the same room until the morning when her body cools down? But the hospital did not want to leave the body to deteriorate at room temperature. The next morning Suk notified all our family, friends, and relatives and planned her funeral. Many bouquets of flowers began to arrive from my parents' friends, her fellow church members, and friends and acquaintances of both of my brothers Soo and Suk. Mother's photo was displayed among pretty flowers and I was thinking she would be very happy about that. This display was for everybody who came to show respect to her by bowing to her picture before sitting down and having some drinks and food. We family members took turns standing there to greet the visitors. Most of mother's sisters and their children also came. Since I had not seen them for so long, I felt like a stranger who had spent decades in space; like Charlton Heston in the movie *Planet of the Apes*.

As is a Korean custom almost everybody who came to pay farewell to mother brought an envelope containing money as a contribution to be used for funeral expenses. The funeral process was taken over by her church minister, beginning from her favorite hymns and prayers, and my brother John had to deliver an unprepared and awkward eulogy, since nobody told him about it in advance (we thought Soo was going to deliver the eulogy but Soo wanted to show respect to his elder brother John). I had an urge to stand up and deliver a eulogy myself, telling everybody what mother had done to save our family during the Korean War and how all her children owed their lives to her. But it's not Korean custom for a female offspring to do so. Finally her coffin decorated with pretty flowers was brought up from the basement and transferred to the hearse to take her to her final resting place for burial. We all went in many different cars heading to Bong-hang Mountain, located in Chun-An, South Chungcheong Province, where our family plot was located.

Almost ten years before mother had called me and expressed her desire to buy the family plot on that mountain overlooking a beautiful valley. Four of us (John, Soo, Suk and myself) chipped in to buy the family plot containing six burial sites for parents and their five sons and their wives there. Since each couple is supposed to be buried together even if they don't die at the same time, six plots are enough for all of them. But I don't believe my two brothers who live in America plan to be buried there. My father was buried there seven years prior to my mother's passing. The whole Bong-hang Mountain was developed by a real estate development firm to be used for burial sites for many families after consulting a fortune-teller specializing in selecting burial sites for prosperity of their future generations and my mother also believed that theory although she was a devout Christian.

When we went there I saw a very nice statue at the entrance of the mountain that was built as a monument for the people who died in the Korean Air 801 crash in Guam on August 6, 1997. The funeral ceremony was conducted by the church minister and friends. As mother's coffin was lowered I felt peace in a very strange way because she no longer had to suffer, and I knew she went to heaven to be with her Lord whom she worshipped all her life, and our father who got there seven years earlier. I hope she is happy there enjoying the peace and tranquility of all she believed in. She was a woman of uncommon bravery, a woman who literally lived through hell to protect her husband and her children from war, the ultimate criminal act of the human being.

Epilogue

Writing this book has been one of the most important projects in my life. I feel honored to have had intelligent and decent parents who guided their children wisely so that none of us succumbed to a criminal society that dragged its people through unimaginable horrors; a society that so often murdered its own young people because they wouldn't accept criminals as leaders. Regrettably, I never had a chance to express my gratitude directly to my father while he was still alive. My original intention in writing this book was to expose the well-hidden secrets that have been exposed in these pages. I also hoped to recount the experiences of a family living in a war zone, experiences so many civilians living in the war zones in Syria and Iraq are going through today. I am relieved to have been able to complete this difficult memoire that blends the view of bloody eyewitness history of a divided nation trapped between two world powers after WWII. This is a contribution to my parents, to the beloved Korean leaders killed by hired assassins, and to thousands of innocent civilians who were murdered by criminal authorities without a single trial.

This book has gone through an unplanned metamorphosis as more and more secret government information, previously buried for many decades, became available during the past 60 years as the country made a transition from a colony to a liberated country through violence, assassinations, war, and civil disputes. Needless to say, the division of the nation determined by the involvement of two world powers with contradicting political ideologies is the primary reason Korea entered into the dark, violent era after the liberation. But what shocked me most was the inhumanity of some Korean people toward fellow Koreans, particularly the atrocities committed by Korean army personnel against their own people including women and children regardless of who gave them the order to kill those innocent people.

Koreans I knew when I was growing up before we moved to the last neighborhood before the war were all very kind, honest and righteous people. All our parents' friends and their church members were compassionate and caring people. So where did all these vicious people come from; people like Kim Chang-ryong, Yum Ung-taek, the jurists who created the Bodo League, and our last neighborhood people? The statistics show an interesting commonality. Most served in the Japanese police, military, intelligence, or legal system during the Japanese occupation during which they went after the Korean independence fighters. After the liberation they fled to the South to avoid brutal execution by Kim Il-sung. When they came to the South, they joined security organizations such as the military police, the secret murder squad like Yum's paramilitary organizations and acquired power from above, and went after civilians to arrest, torture, or murder under the pretense of national security. It's shameful that the first republic's President Syngman Rhee's government hired those national traitors to serve in the system with police power which they used against so many innocent civilians. They are the kind of people the majority of good Koreans despise but unfortunately they ruled the liberated Korea post WWII gaining a foothold under Syngman Rhee. I also believe the US military cannot escape responsibility for turning a blind eye to civilian massacres that took place.

Kim Il-sung's ambitious war to place the entire peninsula under his dynasty further accelerated civilian massacres in the South. Immediately after the Korean War Kim Il-sung executed all members of the South Korean Communist Party who moved to the North before the war to avoid persecution in the South, including Park Hon-yong who had become vice premier and foreign minister of North Korea. Kim Il-sung blamed them for losing the war. Sadly, Koreans who naïvely believed in communism as their savior lost their lives everywhere, in the South as well as in the North. All in all, 20% of the Korean population perished because of the Korean War initiated by Kim Il-sung with help from Russia. Any closed political system that does not protect human rights of its own citizens and their individual freedom is not a good regime regardless of its political ideology and rhetoric. The national economy, the protection of human rights, the provision of equal opportunity and individual freedom must be the focus for governments and that's what people must fight for.

Korea War referred to as a forgotten war was probably one of the bloodiest war of the twentieth century. According to the data from the U.S. Department of Defense, the United States suffered 33,686 battle deaths, along with 2,830 non-battle deaths, during the Korean War. South Korea reported some 373,599 civilian death and 137,899 military deaths. Western sources estimate that the Red Chinese Army suffered about 400,000 killed and 486,000 wounded, while the North Korean Army suffered 215,000 killed and 303,000 wounded. It was a true tragedy that left the fundamental problem of Korean unification unresolved while Kim Il-sung himself had lived to his ripe old age leaving the three generations of dynasty with WMD.

After countless obstacles - dictatorships, bloody war, many civilian massacres, and two military coups - the persistent and unyielding people of South Korea finally won their freedom and a truly democratic civilian government in 1993. South Korea's robust economy soared at an annual average of 10% for over 30 years in a period called the Miracle on the Han River, rapidly transforming it by 1995 into an advanced developed country with Asia's highest income equality and the world's 11th largest economy. A long-desired open communication, transparency and the focus on innovation finally contributed to its success. South Korea was named the world's most innovative country in the Bloomberg Innovation Index, ranking first in business R&D intensity. I admire the resilience of the Korean people to fight for freedom. Although I have adopted the U.S. as my home I wish nothing but peace and prosperity to the hardworking and intelligent people of Korea. We went through hell! Young people in South Korea who are not always happy with their government must realize how much worse it was when we were growing up and appreciate all the progress the country has made and try to preserve it. There is no guarantee of the permanence of the present society. North Korea can invade South at any time with their nuclear arsenals.

It's also critical to know the facts about what's really going on in North Korea, the only communist dynasty in the 21st century with labor camps, frequent purges and summary executions. The citizens of North Korea still suffer from human rights abuses, starvation, lack of individual freedom, fear of imprisonment in labor camps, and unjust executions. As reported by the UN Commission of Inquiry it is a well-known fact that North Korea is the worst communist regime remaining to this day and age. Kim Jong-un's threats combined with the existence of a nuclear arsenal must be dealt with seriously and very soon. This situation does not improve with time. His own father, Kim Jong-il, told his closest advisor Mr. Pak, who defected to South Korea some years ago, that he was willing to use their nuclear arsenal as a last resort if another war breaks out. He would prefer to die in a nuclear disaster than be defeated by the combined forces of South Korea and the United States. If Kim Jong-un has the same mentality as his father, he prefers nuclear disaster to defeat and the loss of his kingdom. Can we be certain he even realizes the devastation that a nuclear disaster would wreak?

It was the former Soviet Union that installed Kim Il-sung to bring the Korean Peninsula under their influence and ideology. And it was Mao's China who helped Kim Il-sung regain the North during the Korean War. Most analysts agree that North Korea cannot maintain its government without the Chinese government's economic aid and political protection against change. It is in the Chinese government's self interest to eliminate the nuclear threat from N. Korea. No matter what the circumstance of any future war the possession and use of nuclear weapons by any combatant could conceivably spill into significant portions of the Chinese homeland. N. Korea is loose nuclear cannon. That fact notwithstanding do the Chinese think the U.S. will stand by while N. Korea develops missiles capable of reaching the U.S. mainland? And would it not seem that it is likely only a short time remains until they develop that capability? Is that what China wants on its borders?

If Korea becomes united under the current democratic civilian government of South Korea, there will be no more refugees escaping to China for food; China would not have to send economic aid to Korea, and they could continue friendly trade with Korea. And most of all, their main concern—US forces remaining in Korea—would no longer be of concern. That would be a win-win scenario for China. Why not act on it before it's too late?

There is a saying among Koreans: "The blood of all Koreans who died during the Korean War can stain Han River blood red." God forbid there should be more blood spilled in the Korean Peninsula!.

Photo 14: Seoul at night in 2016. There is no sign of complete destruction of the city during the Korean War. It's now a thriving city of innovation.

List of Photographs

Front Cover Art by Mike Bertelsen, modified for the Book Cover.

45753373R00150

Made in the USA
San Bernardino, CA
16 February 2017